Novels of Testimony and Resistance
from Central America

Novels of Testimony and Resistance
from Central America

Linda J. Craft

University Press of Florida
Gainesville / Tallahassee / Tampa / Boca Raton
Pensacola / Orlando / Miami / Jacksonville

02 01 00 99 98 97 6 5 4 3 2 1

Library of Congress Cataloging-in-Publication Data
Craft, Linda J., 1948–
Novels of testimony and resistance from Central America / Linda J. Craft.
p. cm.
Includes bibliographical references and index.
ISBN 0–8130–1508–1 (c: alk. paper)
1. Central American fiction—20th century—History and criticism.
2. Historical fiction, Central American—History and criticism.
3. Reportage literature, Central American—History and criticism.
4. Alegría, Claribel—Criticism and interpretation. 5. Argueta,
Manlio, 1936– —Criticism and interpretation. 6. Arias, Arturo, 1950– —Criticism and
interpretation. 7. Belli, Gioconda, 1948– —Criticism and interpretation. I. Title.
PQ7472.N7C7 1997 96–45381
863—dc21

The University Press of Florida is the scholarly publishing agency for the
State University System of Florida, comprised of Florida A & M Univer-
sity, Florida Atlantic University, Florida International University, Florida
State University, University of Central Florida, University of Florida,
University of North Florida, University of South Florida, and University
of West Florida.

University Press of Florida
15 Northwest 15th Street
Gainesville, FL 32611

To my family
Richard, Teresa, and Marc

Contents

Preface

The inspiration for this book grew out of personal experience occurring over fifteen years ago. The adoption of my two children from El Salvador—the first in 1979 (we left the country ten days before General Carlos Humberto Romero did, when a coup ended his presidency) and the second in 1981, during the height of the turmoil—riveted my attention on Central America. Since then it has never waned. Literature has been for me a point of entry to understanding the circumstances surrounding the upheavals of our neighbors to the south during the 1970s and 1980s. This academic project has deepened my interest in growing North American multiculturalism just as has my family, who have certainly contributed to this trend toward diversity. My discovery, I hope, will also be that of my children and their compatriots who have been resettled in the United States as they someday seek out their roots and their heritage.

My intended readers include fellow academics, graduate and undergraduate students of Latin American literature, history, anthropology, and other disciplines, as well as any other enthusiasts of contemporary Latin American culture.

My thanks and appreciation go to many people—I can literally say from A to Z, Achugar to Zimmerman—who have helped me complete this book. At Northwestern University Hugo Achugar directed the initial project, much of which had to be done *a larga distancia,* while Humberto Robles, Susana Jákfalvi-Leiva, and Lois Baer Barr gave generously of their time and their invaluable comments. I appreciate the enthusiastic support of colleagues and friends Sandy Anderson, Paloma Calvo, Mary Coffey, Felicia Cruz, Penny

Fahey, Inman Fox, Sonia García, Susan Herman, and Tasha Seago-Ramaly.

Elzbieta Sklodowska and Marc Zimmerman have given me special encouragement as well as further resources and ideas to challenge my thinking. Amelia Mondragón, Dolores Aponte-Ramos, Dante Liano, Julio Rodríguez-Luis, Mario Roberto Morales, Mary Addis, Janet Gold, Ed Hood, Judith Maxwell, Margaret Crosby, and Maureen Shea have provided me with readings, copies of papers and manuscripts, background information, and suggestions that have proved immensely useful. I wish to thank authors Claribel Alegría, Manlio Argueta, Arturo Arias, and Gioconda Belli for the interviews they graciously granted me and for the books, newspaper clippings, and computer disks they sent as I needed them.

It has been a pleasure to work with the staff of the University Press of Florida; they have guided this project patiently and cheerfully.

Special thanks must go to my mother, retired English teacher Rose S. Barth, for her meticulous proofreading of final drafts.

I am particularly grateful for the patience, encouragement, and love of my husband, Richard, and my children, Terri and Marc.

Introduction

When Rigoberta Menchú won the Nobel Peace Prize in 1992, the world turned its attention appropriately to the plight of indigenous peoples in Guatemala and throughout the Americas. What better moment to rethink the consequences of Conquest than in the quincentennial of Columbus's landfall in the New World? By the time of the announcement of the prize, Menchú's testimony—dictated not even ten years earlier to French anthropologist Elisabeth Burgos-Debray—had already made a name for the Guatemalan in human rights groups, in the Central American solidarity and sanctuary network, and in university multicultural classrooms. Her celebrity came relatively quickly, especially if one considers her obscure roots in the Quiché highlands of Guatemala. Menchú's family had no money, very little education, and few opportunities to work. According to her own account, Menchú had been speaking Spanish for barely three years when, at the age of twenty-three, she met with Burgos in Paris. The autobiographical elements of her testimony read like a horror story: one by one, she witnessed the torture, rape, and murder of various members of her family.

We may speculate as to why Rigoberta Menchú's story achieved such widespread success and catapulted her into the position of spokesperson for indigenous rights, especially since her text is considered by some critics such as Dinesh D'Souza—self-appointed defender of the idiom—to be of inferior quality linguistically, stylistically, and "literarily." Perhaps one answer is that Menchú was at the right place at the right time. Insurgency movements and wars of national liberation swept across parts of Central America in the late seventies and early eighties, particularly in the political hotbeds of Guatemala, El Salvador, and Nicaragua. Armed with post-Vietnam cynicism, revisionist theories of history, a deconstructionist's suspicion of power and master narratives, and the anti-elitism of postmodernism and its embrace of all things democratic, critics have turned their inquiries to the "margins" and to the "Other." There is Rigoberta.

Menchú's witness is compelling in that it presents a detailed first-hand account of someone caught in the upheavals of her time. She does not offer her testimony as the autobiography of an exceptional or heroic individual but as someone who can identify with the suffering of her people because she is one of them. In fact, she prefers to regard her story as just one of many. Problematically, newspaper reports of her Nobel Peace Prize hail her as a symbol of all indigenous peoples, an annointing she protests.

Menchú's testimony is riveting also in that it presents for the North American reader a reality far more brutal than anything most of us have ever known. Her voice has shattered a silence that has surrounded the history of Amerindians far too long. Our confrontation with "otherness" eventually leads us back to confronting ourselves. In an increasingly self-critical posture, some of us ask how we may have been complicit in perpetuating the turmoil in Central America. An encounter with this text is surely political.

Susan Sontag has acknowledged a relationship between Menchú's testimony and the contradiction between U.S. principle and policy: "I believe that the testimonios of people like Rigoberta Menchú . . . are now beginning to fill a newly created ideological space in the United States. This space has been created in large part by the long standing conflict in the ideology of the United States between the demands levied by the effort to perpetuate and extend a capitalist sphere of production, on the one hand, and a belief in democratic traditions on the other" (quoted in Rice-Sayre 54). In Sontag's view, capitalism and democracy do not mix. This conflicted space, according to D'Souza, exists and expands thanks to the arbiters of "political correctness" on U.S. campuses. Well-intentioned academics, he writes, have been duped into creating multicultural curricula such as the program at Stanford, where Menchú is now required reading. D'Souza suggests that "Menchú is really a mouthpiece for a sophisticated left-wing critique of Western society, all the more devastating because it issues not from a French scholar-activist [Burgos-Debray] but a seemingly authentic Third World source" (72). As the "consummate victim," "a modern Saint Sebastian," an "ecological saint" (72), Menchú has given a testimony that, for D'Souza, represents a subversive feminist and Marxist attack on Western civilization. The Nobel winner thus finds herself at the center of the academic debate on "political correctness" in the United States.

The growing attention paid to cultural diversity surely has contributed to the popularity of testimonies like Menchú's, but there are other reasons for the interest they have attracted. In general, testimonies are more accessible to the North American student of Latin American culture and literature than, for instance, the highly complex texts of the Boom writers. The study of testimony and of "voices from below" also coincides with a surge in interest in popular culture and in the redefinition of the literary canon. A passion for justice and peacemaking most certainly inspires many students to read "resistance texts" such as testimony as further evidence of the heavy hand of U.S. intervention in affairs of the hemisphere.

Because of the quincentennial, the field of colonial Latin American studies has proved fertile for a growing number of scholars. They remind us that testimony is really nothing new. From the time of Conquest, in which testimonies were accorded legal standing so that victims, through eyewitness accounts, could reclaim their due, testimonial narrative has expressed urgency, sought redress and justice, and challenged official discourse.

While Rigoberta Menchú's testimony is the best known to come out of Central America recently, it is by no means the only one. Claribel Alegría's *They Won't Take Me Alive* and Omar Cabezas's *Fire from the Mountain,* like many others, have been translated into a number of languages and now enjoy international readership. Publishing these texts abroad has been key to a political strategy of creating awareness among foreign readers who have persuasive powers with their own leaders and can press for policy changes.

At the same time, the testimonial novel has emerged alongside testimony per se as another form of resistance narrative. Like testimony, the testimonial novel has been translated and widely disseminated for political and cultural reasons—often reaching a reading public far greater outside Central America than within the region, where few can afford books let alone read them. With the testimonial novel, we must also deal with issues of historiography and artistic elaboration, the tensions between ethics and aesthetics, the role of the author, and the economics of production. To create the testimonial novel, writers have combined *testimonio* with narrative strategies introduced by the Boom, with various features of the old social realist and *indigenista* approaches, and with elements of magical realism and poetic lyricism. This degree of "mediation" varies from text to text, complicating attempts at classification and at times actually obscuring the testimonial elements in favor of the novelesque. When is a testimony no longer a testimony but a historical novel? Are the two forms—testimony and the novel—mutually antagonistic?

In the following chapters, I will consider novels by Arturo Arias of Guatemala, Claribel Alegría and Manlio Argueta of El Salvador, and Gioconda Belli of Nicaragua in order to formulate several characteristics and a theory of the testimonial novel as it is written in Central America. I will also argue that the primary function of testimonial discourse is the "self-representation" of the Other—peasants, indigenous peoples, women, children, homosexuals, the poor, political prisoners, guerrilla fighters—and I will examine the degree to which this Other is, in fact, present in these novels. The very fact that these voices have gained some measure of access to the novel, one of the traditionally elite genres of literature, invites questions that are frankly political: Who can and must enter literary space? How is such access achieved? Why at this moment in history must we be discussing pluralism and processes of inclusion?

My first chapter situates testimony and testimonial discourse within current literary theory and my own thinking on Third World and resistance literatures, decolonization and postcolonialism, postmodernism, nationalism, and issues of the subaltern. The second chapter briefly outlines historical antecedents of testimony and alterity in Spanish American literature and then expands these themes within the framework of the development of the novel in Central America. Subsequent chapters are devoted to specific novels by the aforementioned writers. General conclusions follow. It is my hope that this book will, in the end, draw more serious attention to Central American literature than it has heretofore received.

1

Testimony in Theory and Practice

Issues of Postmodernism, Subalternity, Decolonization, and Nationalism

The Central American testimonial novel emerges from a specific historical context of oppression, chaos, violence, and a thrust toward national liberation. Sometimes termed a purveyor of realistic or documentary discourse, the testimonial novel becomes problematic when one considers the remarks of Salvadoran resistance writer Claribel Alegría, who sounds very much like Isabel Allende and Gabriel García Márquez in saying that her country's reality "is so incredible, so incandescent, so tremendous, that we don't need to invent anything" (personal interview 1991). The boundaries between fantasy and reality blur.

The testimonial novel often becomes a field of conflict. An eyewitness who is a member of a disenfranchised community attempts to speak as an extension of, and on behalf of, that community rather than solely as an individual; however, by virtue of his or her access to the written word, that eyewitness gains status as an authorial subject possessed of the very power whose lack made the original story so compelling. One of the primary purposes of this text is the denunciation of injustice and the defense of society's marginalized or excluded, supposedly by those same people. Frequently, the referential function—to use Roman Jakobson's terminology—of the language of a testimonial text equals or surpasses the poetic (or aesthetic) function. Because language is basically social, the text turns outward, as Georg Lukács theorizes, and the writer works to restore human dignity. Ethics, urgency, and a utopian vision drive the witness/writer's production.

Some critics, like Renato Prada Oropeza, believe that all Latin American literature since, and because of, the Conquest is in some sense testimonial. Is it an exaggeration to claim, as he does, that "written discourse, whether historic or literary, has not had in Latin America any other mission than to testify [*testimoniar*] to the truth of the facts; facts which, from their origins, are dramatic and confused" (10)? (Except where translators are specifically identified in source notes, I have provided translations.) I do not dispute his general statement, especially as it indicates a historical pattern of alarming contradictions and political emergencies. However, I prefer to narrow for theoretical purposes and for clarity the definition of testimony to a specific discursive practice in specific situations of enunciation.

In this chapter I will present current theories of testimonial discourse and function as set within the crisis of the novel in postmodernity; the attendant problems of representing the marginal, or Other; the relation of testimony to decolonization and Third World literature; and the efforts of testimony toward nation building and nationalism.

Testimonial narrative especially as practiced in Central America is situated at a political, social, and economic disjuncture. Indeed, John Beverley and Marc Zimmerman note that testimony is the most influential narrative form associated with the regional revolutions of the 1970s and 1980s (xi). Part of the debate over the literary "worthiness" of testimony centers on its often blatant politicization. It can seem more a pamphlet than a work of art. As a result, testimony sometimes sees itself as devalued "anti-literature" and opposed to the traditional taste and belles-lettres sensibilities of high culture. At times it has challenged the very authority of those who establish the standards of that taste. Paradoxically, it has also been canonized by parts of the academy, as we shall see later.

Postmodernism

Postmodernism's concern with the construction of knowledge and truth and with their role in the service of power undermines the idea of the innocence of literature and culture. Michel Foucault posits that truth is not outside power as some eternal, neutral given waiting to be discovered (1980). Institutions (academic, commercial, religious, and political, among others) invested with authority have an interest in protecting and propagating their views and theories, whether for reasons of power, prestige, reputation, stability, security, continued funding, or simply survival. The old adage that "might makes right" sadly illustrates the extreme consequences of armed force being marshalled for the diffusion of a cherished ideal or principle.

Whom does a discourse serve? What are its interests? Testimony and other resistance narratives seek to expose the "connection between knowledge and power, the awareness of the exploitation of knowledge by the interests of power to create a distorted historical record," writes Barbara Harlow (116). Resistance texts confront official discourse critically and harshly, offering a rewriting of that discourse. Of course, one could argue that writers and givers of testimony expose the power grabbers and their agendas; however, these producers of testimony have their own agendas too, among which is the rewriting of history to include some of their own perspectives.

Implications for literary and cultural criticism as practiced in Western academic institutions include a challenge to activities "which are used to sustain an internationalization of the issues of development according to Western-specific models or patterns," to cite Harlow (14). This internationalization necessarily involves assimilating non-Western patterns by obliterating their differences. Deconstruction and poststructuralist practices of the postmodern period herald a collapse of the *grands récits*, the great narratives of modernity such as structuralism, capitalism, Christianity, positivism, Marxism, and Freudianism, among others, all of which have particular ends in view. Each great narrative, according to Gayatri Spivak, is a program "which tells how social justice is to be achieved" (1990, 19). And the program, she believes, must be scrutinized for what ends it privileges and what ends it excludes. Narrative has its limits: "The impulse to narrate is not necessarily a solution to the problems of the world" (18–19). Divested of its teleological properties by poststructuralists, narrative now invites theoretical questions concerning how it works rather than what it means.

The authorial, or authoritative, subject is decentered; the critic no longer reveals ultimate meaning to his or her public. Fredric Jameson speaks of "fundamental fragmentation" of the text, of the subject, and of society as he points to the need to abandon the idea of the "centered subject" and "unified personal identity" (1986, 67). If we can live with the reality of fragmentation, we can accept the existence (and coexistence) of a multitude of subjects, discourses, and identities. There is no such thing as a "politically correct deconstructive politics," states Spivak, nor can one decide to be decentered; one is always centered as the subject at the same time that deconstruction examines the limits of this centering: "Politically, all this does is not allow for fundamentalisms and totalitarianisms of various kinds, however seemingly benevolent" (1990, 104). No one has the last word, so to speak, because there is no last word. (I will argue this point later as I discuss nationalism and boundaries.) The postmodern project has displaced the "romantic hegemony of the individual originator," writes Marilyn Randall, with "the hegemony of the linguistic unconscious which betrays the subject as being essentially divided against itself" (525). Poststructuralism challenges the concept of originality, of beginnings and endings, of outside and inside, claiming that as soon as one sets limits, one has postulated the existence of its opposite—the limitless.

For Spivak, the decentering of the authorial subject signals the failure of a "rationalist project" that does not acknowledge the impossibility of self-understanding (1990, 30). While the best tools at our disposal are currently those of rational thinking, they are not "the union ticket to the truth"; rather than truth or objectivity, what is being produced is "cultural explanations that silence others" (33), a totalitarianism. While I share Spivak's suspicion of extremist rationalism (an oxymoron, no doubt)—especially when it is used as a term of value in opposition to the irrational (that is, inferior) and when it is associated with masculine behavior as opposed to "irrational" female behavior in patriarchal discourse—there is a danger of paralysis or of irresponsible defeatism if one surrenders to the fear of being deconstructed oneself or of silencing others. Why bother to critique at all? Caution and humility are appropriate attitudes for the critic at work.

On the heels of the failure of the great narratives and the decentering of the subject comes the negation of another opposition, that between "high" and "low"—elite versus popular—culture.[1] An examination of the whole concept of a literary canon is in order, which has certain implications for marginalized narrative practices, such as testimony, that do not fit traditional literary genres. Jameson judges the Western canon's rejection of non-Western texts to be parochial and impoverishing because it restricts our access to other realities (1986). It is certainly easier to digest the familiar and to congratulate ourselves on our abilities to appreciate the fine qualities of a text "close to home." At stake, perhaps, is our comfort zone. At play is a suspicion of outsiders or a fear of being shaken out of our lethargy toward what is happening in the world beyond our own private space, a lethargy perceptibly benign but possibly complicit in the exclusion and the discomfort of others.

The canon deconstructed, the European novel suffers a similar fate. In *La fuente viva* Miguel Barnet complains of its stagnation, its sterility, its insulation in noble spheres where "it will in no way interfere in human social conflicts" (1983, 15). While he may prefer to abandon completely the Old World novel, I propose an inclusive "both/and" (although not homogenizing) approach. I agree with Jameson when he says, "No one is suggesting we should not read those [canonical texts], but why should we not also read other ones?" (1986, 66).

Georg Gugelberger asks the First World to "legitimize" Third World literature—not to integrate it into the canon but "to identify with 'the wretched of the earth' and to learn from them" (506). I wonder, though, whether the very act of "legitimizing" is a paternalistic one. Who is the First World to presume its status as grantor of legitimacy? Obviously, it has done so and continues to do so, but by what right other than might? Perhaps the colonized Third World should be the one to legitimize the colonizing First World's patently illegal entry into its sphere by demanding the usual restitutions found in societies that enjoy the rule of law. Again we return to the poststructuralist project of unmasking hidden agendas, even the agendas of Barnet, Gugelberger, and other producers of literary criticism, narrative, and testimony. (My own are fair game as well.)

In his comments Gugelberger also emphasizes his aversion to integrating, assimilating, or homogenizing the Other into the hegemonic program. He recognizes the problematic nature of the term *Third World* itself and shares Jameson's caution against presumptuously subsuming a variety of cultures under one general term and theory. Gugelberger writes: "We have to look closer at the heterogeneity of Third World literature, which definition necessarily transforms into an artificial homogeneity" (509). We might remember that the French demographer Alfred Sauvy first used the term *Third World* in 1952 precisely to describe the complicated, heterogeneous nature of economic, political, and social relationships in the world and to caution against reducing tensions to a struggle between East and West in typical Cold War rhetoric.

Suffice it to say there are problems attendant to a definition of the Third World and its use as a critical term. Aijaz Ahmad, for instance, takes Jameson to task for an "empirically ungrounded" binary opposition of first and third worlds and argues that "there is no such thing as a 'third-world literature' which can be constructed as an internally coherent object of theoretical knowledge" (4–7). Walter Mignolo cites another critic of the term, Roberto Fernández Retamar, who uses it advisedly; admitting that the expression does not work well, Mignolo notes that Fernández Retamar uses it "to get rid of the idea of a homogenous world and the parallel notion of the universality of literature" (1991, 104). While Gugelberger sees "Third World" as a euphemism for "underprivileged, starving, or poor" (509), Spivak finds that "it actually reflects the site of a desire for people in the First World . . . to have a manageable other" (1990, 114). She objects to conflating the various "others." It seems to me that *Third World* is more a term to define what the First World is not than it is a term about itself. It also betrays an attitude of superiority (and inferiority) that must discuss difference in terms of rankings.

However, for lack of a more suitable, agreed-upon term, critics continue studying the Third World while offering caveats and disclaimers regarding the homogenizing tendency of the term. To their disclaimers I add my own, as I use the term reluctantly. I will say more about issues of heterogeneity and homogeneity when I discuss strategies used to represent the Other, and I will return to the topic of Third World literature as well, to consider its relationship to decolonization.

Postmodernism has rent the monolithic façade of the great narratives, exposing the vulnerability of a decentered subject and the agendas of the power brokers. It seems that nothing is uncontaminated or unbiased, nothing is sacred, everything is political. In fact, writes Jameson, all cultural products are "socially symbolic acts" (1981, 20). Literature is no longer "reflective" of a social reality (81) but performative, an act. Marilyn Randall points to the heightened political role of literature in liberation struggles where texts become political acts designed to stir the consciences of the people (532). Asked another way, the question is, state Beverley and Zimmerman, not whether ideology is present in the text but what ideology is present (4). Central American testimony offers a clear example of politically charged discourse, mostly from the Left. The Central American writer, for writer-politician Sergio Ramírez, assumes the role of an interpreter who speaks on behalf of a "collective unaware and largely silenced and buried under a heap of false and perverted rhetoric. And in this, the writer can't help but perform a political act, because reality is political" (1983, 120). Little wonder so many Central American writers spend time in jail or in exile.

The Other

From the discussion to this point, I hope it is apparent that interest in the representation of the Other has emerged as a major theme in theoretical cultural studies of postmodernism. It is not that traditional literature has ignored the Other—I present many examples of the Other as a literary theme in my historical surveys in Chapter 2—but as Hugo Achugar explains, the purpose and result of presenting the image of the Other did not question the centrality of the central subject (1992, 54). Postmodern studies have dethroned the Eurocentric subject while previously marginalized voices now clamor for attention and reach for the microphone. A new view is that they do not need to be represented but should rather represent themselves.

We can speculate on further reasons for the increased interest in the Other so apparent in North America. Again keeping in mind postmodern culture's iconoclasm and cynicism regarding authority and centered subjects, let us consider the traditional American success story—the rags-to-riches narrative that pits the "little guy" against powerful bosses, corporations, or other representatives of the establishment. The reader or viewer cheers him on to victory in the face of overwhelming odds. Recently, this type of story has lost some of its appeal. Today we may still applaud the "little guy"—the Other, the outsider—but mainly because he threatens the powers that be. He is useful as he bursts the bubbles of the high and mighty. Once he achieves status himself, we lose interest; he may even become the authority figure—the enemy—whom someone else seeks to dethrone. The anti-elitist, grassroots impulses seem to be those that provoke the most admiration.

We find an analogy to this function of Otherness in the fetishistic concept of the Noble Savage, which served as a theme in literature from the sixteenth through the nineteenth centuries (and some would argue even to the present). Hayden White speculates that the European interest in the savage Other, especially during the eighteenth century, may have been prompted by the need to assuage guilty consciences. However, White writes, it is most likely that "the idea of the Noble Savage is used, not to dignify the native, but rather to undermine the idea of nobility itself"; he believes that the true referent of the concept of the Noble Savage "is not the savages of the new or any other world, but humanity in general, in relation to which the very notion of 'nobility' is a contradiction" (129). Perhaps the true referent of our interest in the Other is not really the Other at all but the idea of equality of humankind and the contradictions posed by elitism and power within the ideals of democracy. The favorable reception of texts, such as testimony, that privilege the Other as they dismantle authority reflects the changing values and ethical postures of postmodern culture and politics.

Certainly, other factors also help explain why the Other has captured the First World's attention and imagination at this moment in history. Achugar suggests that this interest stems from the fact that the Western subject has only recently recognized the barbarity he carries within, the holocausts of which he is capable, and the magnitude of pent-up frustrations that the oppressed occasionally and justifiably unleash (1992, 55). The immediate and widespread coverage by mass media of the horrors of concentration camps, human rights abuses, torture, disappearances, domestic violence, and child abuse has heightened awareness of age-old problems and "supposes or allows the necessity of understanding the alienated, marginalized, silenced, or exterminated Other to be supposed" (55). Faced with bad news and the sight of innocent victims every day on television and in the newspapers, the audience is morally obliged to pay attention.

To follow up Achugar's observation, studying the Other affords the opportunity to study oneself. Our interest, which may partially come from a sense of guilt, can also feed the desire to understand ourselves better. R. S. Khare writes that today "a few convincing and prized ethnographers tend to be those which record a journey of self-discovery with the help of the Other" (7). Rather than a we/they split, Khare finds that a productive and ethical approach includes recognition of interdependence and reciprocity between Self and Other. This ideal(istic) result would assume that one achieves a mature self-understanding that, in my mind, values community and the interconnectedness of human beings more than the supremacy of the individual.

The next logical question is, of course, who is this Other in the context of Central America? Race, gender, class, age, education, and political preference define Central America's marginalized or excluded—all those who find themselves alienated from society's power structures or at the bottom of the social, economic, and political pyramid (including indigenous groups, blacks, women, lesbians and homosexuals, peasants, the poor, the illiterate, children, exiles, and political prisoners). "Otherness," which I would equate with Gramsci's concept of subalternity, can also refer to "the feelings of mental inferiority and habits of subservience and obedience which necessarily and structurally develop in situations of domination—most dramatically in the experience of colonized peoples" (quoted in Jameson 1986, 76).

The critic can easily fall into the trap of over-generalization, homogenization, and even fetishization of the term *the Other* (especially with a capital "O"), much in the same way that we in the First World bandy about the expression *Third World*. "The colonized subaltern subject," insists Spivak, "is irretrievably heterogeneous" (1988, 284). Chandra Talpade Mohanty warns us against constructing totalizing representations of women in the Third World (335). It is tempting and easy for First World women to assume that their agendas are universal or that Third World patriarchy and oppressions are monolithic. The 1995 United Nations Conference on Women in Beijing proved otherwise.

Illustrating this point in a 1992 interview in Chicago, Sandinista feminist Gladys Báez Alvarez outlined the diverse and sometimes opposing feminine discourses surrounding the debates ongoing in the organization that she heads, the Asociación de Mujeres Nicaragüenses Luisa Amanda Espinosa (the Luisa Amanda Espinosa Association of Nicaraguan Women, or AMNLAE). The debates cover, among other topics, reproductive rights, health care, education, nutrition, union organization, political representation, and inclusive language. Vast differences exist within their "otherness."

Sergio Ramírez cites another example of how the word *indio* has come to denominate almost all of the socially and economically (not just racially) marginalized groups of the rural areas in Central America. Very often its meaning has been so generalized in *criollista* literature that it simply means an unsophisticated, crude, or ignorant person of the urban as well as rural lower classes (1983, 39–40). "Indio" has been reduced to a general slur, thereby losing all its specifically racial referentiality.

The problem of representation of the Other continually confronts the writer, the intellectual, and the critic. "Can the subaltern speak?" asks Spivak in the title of her now-famous article (1988). Or can radical critics speak for them or represent them? She believes that as well-intentioned academics we may actually make the problem worse by focusing on what is shared and by obliterating difference. We hasten assimilation to our point of view and life-style. (To an extent, I would have to disagree. People of good will are more accepting of criticism and more amenable to negotiation than those of ill will. Good intentions are thus preferable to bad ones or to none at all. At least there is an admission of a problem, which we then can go on to address, as she does.) In fact, one of Spivak's main criticisms of Foucault is that he is a "first-world intellectual masquerading as the absent nonrepresenter who lets the oppressed speak for themselves" (1988, 292), in contrast to Derrida's less presumptuous, more critical project. Blind benevolence constitutes "epistemic violence," in Spivak's view.[2]

If we are to realize a productive multiculturalism, we must continue to be attuned to the problems in our efforts. Any time that we construct a corpus of "representative" works—as I attempt to do, to a point, in Chapter 2—we run the risk of excluding others whose inclusion might challenge or change our definitions. As I cautioned with respect to the Third World, it would be tempting to fold one's arms in despair and do nothing amid deconstructionist warnings of the perils involved in representing the Other. But that's a "cop-out," Spivak retorts. Instead, she advises, "do your homework"; never cease to critique your position as the investigating person, and you earn the right to criticize (1990, 62–63). Spivak and Jameson both recognize that "representation" comprises several different and complex operations—political, artistic, rhetorical—none of which can be divorced from the other.

The writer who represents the subaltern subject or who attempts to have the subaltern speak through the text mediates his or her presence much as have benevolent missionaries, ethnographers, travelers, and various other specialists. Jean Franco warns us to beware the writer who sees him- or herself as a redeemer and rescuer, appropriating and assimilating willy-nilly and claiming authorial rights. This person is politically and culturally dangerous (1991). I will return to the problem of representation and mediation of the Other when I consider the relationship of the agent/artist/ intellectual to the subaltern subject of testimony.

Hegemonic metropolitan texts often pay lip service to Otherness while unwittingly highlighting their own ethnocentricity. Abdul JanMohamed explains the dynamics of a colonialist text with this theory of the "Manichean allegory": "The ideological function of all 'imaginary' and some 'symbolic' colonialist literature [and, one could add, criticism] is to articulate and justify the moral authority of the colonizer and—by positing the inferiority of the native as a metaphysical fact—to mask the pleasure the colonizer derives from that authority" (1985, 84). Taking as a starting point Sartre's observation that "it is in and through the revelation of my being-as-object for the Other that I must be able to apprehend the presence of his being-as-subject" (quoted in 1983, 264), JanMohamed finds that this healthy dialectical relationship between Self and Other is petrified in a colonial situation (265). The subaltern may indeed be speaking, but no one is bothering to listen. Because he or she may be speaking not only another language but also through forms that are more familiar to him or her than to the Self (that is, nonliterary or unwritten ones), the Self does not understand that he may be missing something important. If he understands, he may dismiss it as a picturesque (read primitive) ethnic and cultural practice. (The Other/Object is "ethnic"—marked by difference; the

Self/Subject is not.) In Edward Said's concept of Orientalism, one finds a similar judgment of imperialist cultural practices: textual representations of the colonized are inevitably paternalistic.[3]

A willingness to engage the Other without feelings of moral, ethnic, or intellectual superiority—"unlearning one's privileged discourse," as Spivak would say (1990, 57), and "attempting to learn to speak in such a way that the masses will not regard as bullshit" (56), without patronizing or resorting to anti-intellectualism—does help to bridge difference and at the same time to preserve it. The colonialist or postcolonialist intellectual must divest him- or herself of privilege. To relinquish authority is undoubtedly easier said than done. The objective of both respecting and overcoming difference is, as I see it, fraught with tension. However, any process of truly democratic negotiations borders on the messy and the tenuous. But what is the alternative? If one does not relinquish authority, one risks further stoking the fires of resentment on the side that sees itself as the perennial loser.

One might expect various responses from the oppressed to authoritarian Western discourse. JanMohamed finds that the oppressed attempt to negate the West's prior negation of them; they also tend to adopt and creatively adapt Euro-western cultural forms and language to their own forms and language in their own project of negation (1985, 85).[4] Nonhegemonic groups, he concludes, also subvert the dominant discourse by exposing deep contradictions to conscious analysis; they have nothing to lose by rocking the boat of "stability and coherence" (1983, 267). Texts from the "other side" offer a site of political and ideological struggle, heterogeneity, and vitality. They are more dynamic while authoritarian texts tend toward the static.

Testimony, which rose in Central America in the 1970s in response to neocolonialism and the Cuban experience, functions in much the same way as the subaltern subject attempts to expose and resolve contradiction and effect social, political, and economic transformation. Why do the people who work the land not enjoy its fruits? ask many producers of testimonial discourse. Why does the United States, which professes beliefs in democracy and justice, not export what it preaches at home? Testimony is a protest. To claims that the United States has advanced the "cause of democracy" in Central America in recent history, resistance writers would probably answer that U.S. "gifts," the majority of which have been in the form of military assistance, have only served to polarize or eliminate political factions and exacerbate existing social and economic disparities.

Such gifts have frustrated, rather than furthered, democracy. The 1993 UN Truth Commission reports on human rights abuses in El Salvador confirm these protests.

Otherness, then, is the "epitome of objectification," in the words of Barbara Foley (243–44). Colonialism, racism, sexism, and classism dehumanize as they deny subjectivity. Testimony and oral histories serve as "authenticating apparatuses" for the Other to recover subjectivity against a background of "blended voices that attest to the historicity of a single individual" and that furnish the necessary realism for such a claim (Foley 263). The voices of the Others struggle to be heard and to gain access to the structures of power as they question the status quo and counter monologic, totalizing discourses with their dialogic and fragmented refutations. To Spivak's question of whether the subaltern can speak, I would answer yes, albeit imperfectly (since available forms are not completely adequate in conveying their message), through certain popular forms like testimony. An increasing number of previously silenced voices have penetrated cultural forums. Perhaps all do not yet enjoy the public ear, but the process has begun.

Testimony, the Nonfiction Novel, and the Documentary

Testimony as produced in Latin America is literature of and from—and sometimes for—the Other. Obviously, high illiteracy rates prevent widespread consumption of texts within Central America. The "testimonial function" is based on the Other's struggle for legitimacy and power. Not only is this struggle the referent of testimonial discourse but it is also the pragmatic function that the discourse itself accomplishes among various "literary" discourses, according to Achugar (1987, 281) and to Sklodowska (1992, 76). The testimonial text is performative.

For my purposes and interests, testimony and the revolutionary struggles of recent Central American history go hand in hand. As I begin my look at testimony, I note the importance of the Cuban revolution in legitimizing testimonial discursive practice that theretofore had lacked academic and cultural sanction. The prestigious Havana publishing company, Casa de las Américas, has awarded one of its annual literary prizes in the field of testimonial narrative. Casa de las Américas has defined as testimonial those books that document some aspect of reality through a direct source—a writer who has either experienced the events him- or herself or has compiled an account based on trustworthy reports obtained from a qualified eyewitness. Sklodowska explains that the form of the narrative is at the author's discretion, but literary quality is indispensable for the purposes of Casa de las Américas; as for its sources, testimony is most often based on personal documents or an interview (1992).

Thus, interestingly and somewhat ironically, testimony has enjoyed not only legitimacy but also hegemonic status as a discursive practice and as an object of study, first in Cuba and now in a number of U.S. universities. Rigoberta Menchú's testimony is on the multicultural studies reading lists of many first-year university students in the United States.[5] Other factors account for, or coincide with, the rapid proliferation of testimony during these years. John Beverley mentions several: (1) the importance in Latin American culture throughout its history of nonhegemonic forms of documentary literature (for example, colonial chronicles, letters of voyages, the essay, romantic biography, memoirs of military campaigns, the indigenista novel); (2) the popularity of ethnographic and sociological studies in the 1950s; (3) the warm literary and political reception accorded to guerrilla testimony in the 1960s, which corresponded to movements of armed resistance throughout the Third World; and (4) the importance given to oral testimony by the counterculture of the 1960s as catharsis and personal liberation (especially in the women's liberation movement and the base Christian communities of liberation theology) (1987, 158–59). Thus, events and conditions worldwide contributed to the growing popularity of testimonial discourse and its eventual "canonization" by parts of the academy in Latin America and also in the United States and Europe, a popularity which has also come "thanks to its ability to satisfy a demand for a discourse which is at the same time traditional and innovative, Latin American and contemporary to all people" (Sklodowska 1992, 66). It has gained acceptance in the academy also as part of the postmodern project of the deconstruction of dominant theories and practices, as an expression of the ethical interests of progressives in representing alterity and difference, and as a North American "liberal" project of solidarity and, one could argue, political correctness.

Testimony, at first glance, seems the antithesis of the elitist Boom literature that dominated the cultural scene in Latin America during the same period (the 1960s and 1970s). Beverley and Zimmerman see testimony, with its "postmodernism of resistance," more as a development or a "refunctioning" of the Boom rather than a negation of it; specifically, testimony espouses more overtly political content and finds new, more "realistic" forms of expression (117–18) as opposed to the Boom's sometimes perceived overpreoccupation with signifiers, aesthetics, formalistic experimentation, fantasy, and authorial command and celebrity.

Outside Central America and the Caribbean, the corpus of both mediated and unmediated testimonial literature is ample, especially in (but not limited to) the Southern Cone and Andean region where revolutionary movements have worked actively in recent years. I mention here the well-known work of Elena Poniatowska, Ariel Dorfman, Jacobo Timerman, Domitila Barrios de Chungara with Moema Viezzer, Florencia Varas with José Manuel Vargara, Hernán Valdés, Violeta Parra, and Angela Zago, among many others. And if I might make a brief reference to similar literature in the United States, I would call the reader's attention to testimonies by black militants, such as Bobby Seale's *Seize the Time,* and to a related genre, the "nonfictional" novel,[6] which includes James Agee's *Let Us Now Praise Famous Men* (1941), Tom Wolfe's *The Electric Kool-Aid Acid Test* (1968), Truman Capote's *In Cold Blood* (1965), and Norman Mailer's *The Armies of the Night* (1968) and *The Executioner's Song* (1979) among others. A common thread that would place them in the postmodern current is their movement away from omniscient and totalizing viewpoints. Sklodowska widens the discussion of the occurrence of this mode referring to the "ubiquity of testimony" in world literature (1992, 64); she offers not only American (North, South, and Central) but European and Soviet examples as well (1992).

Some of the most sentient features of testimony—the appeal of veracity, the claim to truthfulness, and an often journalistic-style discourse—are shared with the documentary and the aforementioned "nonfictional" novel (terms used interchangeably with testimony by some critics). What more powerful and moving statement than that issued by an eyewitness or a participant? The affinity not only to journalistic discourse but also to religious and legal testimony underlines its charged nature and force. Esteban Montejo repeatedly affirms the truth of his account in what has come to be a foundational text of the mode, *Biografía de un cimarrón* (Biography of a runaway slave): "Y no es cuento de camino, porque lo vide con mis ojos" (Barnet 1968, 172) (This is not just another folktale because I saw it with my own eyes).

Often disavowing aesthetic pretensions, writers of testimony prefer to prepare a message of urgency and import, giving the appearance of assembling details and facts hastily—although not carelessly nor heedless of accuracy, they would assure us—in order to publish a plea for solidarity amid difficult situations of oppression. The message is more important than the medium, some seem to say. Critics characterize this discourse as one of the illusion of presence. The closeness of testimony to oral history reinforces this illusion. Beverley and Zimmerman write: "Because it is the discourse of a witness who is not a fictional construct, testimonio in some sense or another speaks directly to us, as an actual person might" (177). They remind us that it is not just a matter of another category of literature or fiction. Explaining the function of journalistic discourse to lead us away from literature to immediacy, González Echevarría writes: "A journalistic account is faithful to facts, not to rhetorical modes; it deals with real people and events, not with literary characters or incidents endowed with a written history. Journalism also tends to diffuse the question of authorship. Since facts determine content, the author becomes a neutral conductor, not the generator of the text. Journalism fosters the illusion that incidents write themselves into history" (115). The illusion of the disappearance of the journalist-author plays into the postmodern project of deconstructing the author-subject.

We must note the use of the word *illusion*. For many North American readers, to whom numerous Latin American *testimonios* are directed in translation, "true" stories need to be told transparently, with little or no literary adornment or elaboration. The illusion of independence that facts seem to have—absent an obvious narrator—makes a story plausible and "objective." Fiction does not enjoy the same status of truth bearer as the documentary. Many readers consider literal truth to be the only kind.

In her study of the African American documentary novel, Foley draws conclusions that can be applied to the verification function of testimony. Such texts often seem "documentarily overdetermined" as they highlight the contradictions of a white supremacist attitude that denies full subjectivity to blacks and full authority to black authors solely because of race. The text must be assertive, Foley believes, in order to be compelling. It must persist in the "foregrounding of contradiction in the referent" (235) in order to deconstruct dominant institutions and discourses that perpetuate otherness. Episode after episode, example after example offer "proof," verifiable evidence of injustice, and build the case for the subaltern. The goal is to make believers of the readers.

Part of the verification process in testimony includes the presence and participation during writing of a sympathetic agent or intermediary (a coproducer), especially one who is well educated in the art of discourse. Often the eyewitness is illiterate and in need of a writer in solidarity if he or she wishes to communicate a written message. Achugar explains that "the presence of the voice of the mediator functions as another means of reaffirming the fact that we are dealing with authentic discourse and information" (1992, 66). The heterogeneous relationship problematizes the authority traditionally enjoyed by the writer. According to Achugar, this incursion into the *espacio letrado* (literate space) of the public sphere and the function it accomplishes are what distinguishes testimony (not necessarily at the textual level) from similar discursive practices of the past (1992, 56). There are dangers inherent in the relationship of intermediary to eyewitness, not the least of which is the trap of portraying a caricature or a nostalgic evocation of an Other who never really existed or of forcing the portrayal into a mold to serve the literary or political purposes of the intellectual, as Spivak mentioned. These problems place testimony at the "center of the dialectic of oppressor and oppressed in the postcolonial world" (Beverley 1987, 176).

Here I would note that Doris Sommer also addresses the contradiction of an intervening *letrado* (intellectual) in a people's history: "Socially responsible writers in Latin America have had to come to terms with their unrepresentativeness" (1988, 113). Rather than creating an impasse, however, testimony allows for complicity between letrado and witness. It produces a destabilization, the existence of more than one center, a space for "heteroglossia, the (battle)field where revolutionary discourse is not given but made" (1988, 122). Politically speaking, rather than a top-down operation, it is a grassroots venture of voices scrambling to be included in a democratic project. The testimonial code may not always be coherent in terms of official standards, but it is the only one available—a bricolage or patchwork of sorts, using the materials and imagination at hand. Testimony seen in this light does not just substitute the voice of the oppressed for that of the oppressor. Instead, it is an engagement of both voices and as many more as can be accommodated.

The relationship between letrado and witness must be one of solidarity (Barnet 1983, 35). Barnet describes this relationship as one of *desdoblamiento*—an unfolding—a suppression of the ego of the writer (or at least discretion in the use of the ego) (23, 36), which recalls for me Spivak's "unlearning one's privilege" and bridge building to the Other's life. The best intermediaries do not greatly interfere in the quality or meaning of the discourse; any attempts to organize the material and correct errors may detract from the spontaneity and vigor of the eyewitness account (Prada Oropeza 17). The relationship of Menchú and Burgos, which I examine more closely in Chapter 2, illustrates the problems and the possibilities that can emerge when the non-Western, nonnative Spanish-speaking subject of the oral account works with the Western subject of the written one.

Further characteristics of testimonial discourse include polyphony and a collective subject in the so-called democratization of literature. The subject, while still maintaining the first-person point of view, multiplies beyond the two collaborators—much as Foucault theorizes that the author function disappears in postmodernism (1969)—so that many gain access to the public sphere of the written text. The eyewitness, like Menchú, often insists that she speaks as only one of many who have suffered oppression, that her story is not atypical, and that many others have been silenced by the same repressive authority that beleaguers her. Very often she appears to subordinate her own singularity to the identity of the community. (We observe, however, that even though she usually does not claim to represent the whole, it occasionally happens that she does.)

As a consequence, additional voices weave intertextually in and out of testimonial literature. Theoretically, the solitary hero figure of the romantic novel disappears. Whereas the romantic hero is unique, superior, and exemplary—a metaphoric signifier, as Sommer explains (1988, 108)—testimonio's protagonist leans toward the metonymic, an extension of the collective, and in many cases the plural. This feature would distinguish testimonio from autobiography, a genre Sommer finds peculiar to Western culture. The protagonists that do emerge in testimonio are notable by their shared ordinariness. Nevertheless, these "ordinary" protagonists can sometimes be problematic as they assume an authoritative, "in-the-know" position based on their own personal experience. Very often, because of what the eyewitness has had to endure, we readers have difficulty picturing them as ordinary people.

When I first started this study, I noted that the story the eyewitnesses told had as yet no ending. Now I can say that some, though not all, are being resolved. Testimonial accounts have effectively drawn the world's attention to the crises in Central America. These documents fit into the same project as the work of human rights activists and sanctuary-solidarity groups in their appeal to moral conscience and indignation in the face of injustice. In short, they work.

In their denunciation of systemic evil and institutional violence, they offer a vision of a liberated and autonomous modern nation where the heterogeneous sectors all participate. It is not a utopian vision in a teleological sense (although some writers of testimony have espoused classic Marxism or Christianity, which are indeed utopian), but it refers to *process* rather than to a predetermined end result. It is my opinion that testimonio in form and function—inclusive, democratic, and humble—practices this process.

The form of testimony may vary, adopting narrative discourses such as autobiography, historical novel, interview, photographs, prison memoirs, diary, chronicle, letter, newspaper article, anthropological or social science documentary; it can be fiction or nonfiction. It can even coexist with poetry.[7] This variety does not indicate that testimony is just another example of a postmodern pastiche nor that it has an uncertain referent, writes Achugar; rather, there exists a certain logical indecision concerning the generic and discursive status of testimony (1992, 51). Its formal status, not its referent, is ambiguous.

Some critics have speculated about how long testimony per se will last as an avenue for the expression of the disenfranchised. Indeed, Beverley believes that its time has come and gone as a locus for the voices of the voiceless and that those voices are moving on to other, even more marginalized, forms of popular culture (1994). Subaltern study groups are examining these alternatives—graffiti, ballads, street theater, murals, to name a few—which do not depend so heavily on cultivated written form or on the intervention of an educated intermediary. Perhaps there is a sense that testimony has been co-opted by parts of the literary, political, and education establishments. With such mainstream respectability, it ceases to be subversive or marginal. Let me pursue this argument. Testimonio is not marginal or subversive just for the sake of being marginal or subversive. It has achieved an intended outcome by being read in mainstream classrooms and libraries. I am assuming, however, that there will always be a need for critical, subversive postures. This is not simply radical chic but a recognition that utopia is not around the corner even though we sometimes see progress. (I address this issue further at the end of this chapter.) In the future, testimonio may not be the vehicle best suited for critical work either because it still has limitations as a voice for the voiceless or because, as an integral and domesticated part of curriculum, it has lost its teeth as a site of struggle.

Traces of testimonio do and will remain in the novel. When one discusses testimony, as distinguished from the testimonial novel, one is discussing a matter of degree. Because generic lines are increasingly blurred in postmodernism, as we just saw above, it is easier to consider the matter of testimonial discourse and testimonial function in a text rather than the extent to which it is a "true" novel. Indeed, Sklodowska posits the idea of testimony, in the strict sense, as the "post-bourgeois novel"—an actualization (an historical genre) of the novel (a theoretical genre) (1992, 147). However, since the testimonial novel in Central America is my focus here, I will try to show what is happening to this form currently.

Beverley and Zimmerman have identified three types of testimonial novels: (1) pseudotestimonies, which are fictional; (2) novels that are written much in the style of Boom narratives but incorporate historical testimonial voices; and (3) narratives located between testimony and the authorial/autobiographical novel (178). Sklodowska proposes a typology of mediated testimony in which a variety of unmediated testimonies (for example, legal testimony, diaries, memoirs, autobiography) and other nonfictitious discourses (such as biography, interviews, life histories, and oral histories) form a pre-text, which is then mediated by an editor to create hybrid texts blending fiction and nonfiction into diverse mediated testimonies including the testimonial novel (1992, 102). In later chapters of this book examples from texts by Arias, Belli, Argueta, and Alegría will define and illustrate further the concept of the testimonial novel.

Testimony, Art, and the Novel

A discussion of any novel necessarily invites questions regarding art. In 1967 Jean Franco wrote in *The Modern Culture of Latin America* that novelists like Asturias and Roa Bastos share a similar approach "to the problem of writing a novel about an oppressed country, for both have abandoned the documentary technique, using instead fantasy, legend and myth to present the subconscious forces at work in the minds of their fellow-countrymen" (241). Each writer apparently felt realism would best be served, for an intended sophisticated international audience, by an equally sophisticated narrative approach that explored the complexity of Latin American existence.

To illustrate the point, Franco contrasts Asturias's *El señor presidente* (1946) with Icaza's *Huasipungo* (1934): "By breaking away from a mere reporting of atrocities, Asturias creates the effect of nightmare and therefore effectively communicates the horror of dictatorship. Icaza attempts honest reporting but alienates the sympathy of the reader" (173). Franco's statement is problematic, but perhaps understandable considering the date of publication, in that it presumes a universal (Euro-generated) reader with sophisticated tastes and shared ideas of what is beautiful. Nevertheless, it recalls the traditional notion that too much realism ceases to be artistic. While Icaza's novel is not testimony, like testimony it has a tendency to create the "effect of the real" with less novelistic and more transparent language. Documentary or transparent language, however, need not be devoid of art. The idea of combining art with testimony still intrigues the writer-novelist; the degree to which the aesthetic discourse is articulated with the scientific-documentary may determine the flavor of a text and even perhaps its appeal.

For Barnet, the artist-sociologist's equilibrium is rooted in exposing historical facts "without didacticism, without vulgarity," but with art (1983, 26). Art and documentation in the testimonial or nonfiction novel create a "bi-referentiality" of both fact and fiction, as Mas'ud Zavarzadeh has suggested, and "an acknowledging of the ontological doubleness of experience" (227). The traditional boundaries between the two opposing concepts have broken down in postmodern culture.

Neither can the writer divorce aesthetics from ethics (the urgency of divulging the truth of a historical phenomenon and injustice through testimony), believes Isabel Allende: "Only if we are able to say it beautifully can we be convincing" (59). (Again a caveat with regard to the word *beautifully;* I surmise that Allende is referring to her own artistic sensibilities and tastes, which many but not all of her readers share.) The testimonial novel combines with art the characteristics of testimonial discourse that I have previously described, shaping and ordering the narrative, interpreting a reality or an event by situating it historically.

Art may involve "decanting" spoken language, suggests Barnet, since the language of the testimonial novel is based on the spoken, vital word (1983, 29). (He qualifies his comments by explaining that the artist's responsibility is to refine the style and shadings of passages while conserving the tone and anecdote.) Some of the formal strategies used to mediate testimony range from mere grammatical and syntactical corrections to the use of the flashback, a change in the rhythms of the language, ruptures of chronological time, and other *nueva narrativa* techniques. Barnet specifies that the work should involve a "depersonalization" of the artist-writer-intellectual in a continual sacrifice and extinction of his own personality (1983, 25). But the more the artist elaborates, we can argue, the more "literary" or self-referential the language of the text becomes and the more it points to intervention and to the artist him- or herself. Extinction seems impossible.

Testimony, Nationalism, the Novel

In addition to the question of art and the novel, we need also to consider the relationship of history to the novel. The development of the novel in the nineteenth century accompanied the rise of the bourgeoisie and European nationalism. Structuralist Marxism sees the means of production at the base as overdetermining the cultural production of the superstructure. The historical novels told the stories of individuals who lived, loved, fought, and died against the panorama of industrializing societies and expanding empires, and they were read by individuals who possessed the ability to read the serialized versions in the newspapers or the money to purchase the books themselves and further had the leisure time to read them.

As we look specifically at the role of literature in the process of nation building, Third World novels—testimonial novels included—tend to be more political and allegorical and less psychological and personal than their Euro-Western counterparts. Indeed, Jameson proposes that we read *all* Third World texts, particularly the novel (which developed out of "predominantly western machineries of representation"), as national allegories: "The story of the private individual destiny is always an allegory of the embattled situation of the public third-world culture and society" (1986, 69).

Sommer makes a similar case, claiming that Latin American historical romance novelists combine the personal love story with the story of national politics in allegories of national consolidation: "Part of the conjugal romance's national project, perhaps the main part, is to produce legitimate citizens, literally to engender civilization" (1990, 86). She also deconstructs "the pretty lies of national romance," such as those fabricated by Mexico's PRI (Institutional Revolutionary Party), as possible strategies "to contain the racial, regional, economic, and gender conflicts that threatened the development of new Latin American nations" (92). Although Sommer refers to an earlier age, her assessment is surprisingly current in light of the events of the 1990s in Chiapas, where the indigenous population has never been fully integrated in the social, economic, and political life of the nation.

Spivak takes Jameson to task for privileging nationalism rather than deconstructing it as the other critics have done. His judgment that Third World novels are allegories of nationalism, she believes, "comes from taking the modes of production narrative [Marxism] as normative because nationalism, itself, which is very much within a certain history of European-norm is seen as an unquestioned good that these 'Third World' countries should now be aspiring to. That's a problem" (1990, 100). Is it that Jameson takes nationalism to be an unquestioned good? Or is he simply tying his analysis of the novel to its historical role in developing the national consciousness?

Just as the historical novel went hand in hand with the developing European nation-state in the last century, the testimonial novel works with similar interests in contemporary Central America. Specifically, it envisions a just nation where all sectors participate in all aspects of the national life. Because of this role, Beverley and Zimmerman have called testimony "a nonfictional, popular-democratic form of epic narrative" (174). They add that the narrator of the testimonial novel, who speaks as a member of an entire community, resembles the epic hero of old. The epic served the purpose of creating the national myth, the narrative of the people's beginnings, their founders and heroes. "At the origin of the nation, we find a story of the nation's origin," writes Geoffrey Bennington, who believes that this discovery should be enough "to inspire suspicion; our own drive to find the centre and the origin has created its own myth of the origin— namely that at the origin is the myth" (121). There is nothing but text; beginnings and endings are part of grand narratives. The nation, then, is a narrative, "a discursive formation," to quote Foucault (cited in Brennan 47).

Long before the poststructural theorists formulated their arguments, Peruvian thinker José Carlos Mariátegui reached a similar conclusion in the 1920s that "the nation . . . is an abstraction, an allegory, a myth that does not correspond to a reality that can be scientifically defined" (quoted in Brennan 49). Reinforcing Mariátegui's observation, Benedict Anderson defines a nation as "an imagined political community—and imagined as both inherently limited and sovereign" (1983, 15). Literature plays a vital role in the construction of the nation, of its myths and identity. One of the contributions of testimony and the testimonial novel for the Central American region is in the formation of a new concept of the nation, sometimes called "the national-popular," which is inclusive of all peoples within its borders.

The testimonial novel deals with the concrete and the historical; like the traditional novel, Bakhtin reminds us, it deals with discourse that is still "warm" from social struggle and unresolved hostility (cited in Harlow 82). The testimonial novel is compelling because it is a literature of emergency. But it departs from the authoritarian narrative of the traditional novel as it experiments with discourse, form, technique, and the status of the authorial subject. By deliberately incorporating popular voices and oral traditions, it challenges the standards of the canon, the criteria used to determine the "truth" and interpretation of history, and the strategies used to permit and prevent access to the written record. Resistance narratives, including the testimonial novel, make the revolutionary move from "filia-tion to affiliation," overthrowing hierarchical and hereditary bonds for collective and horizontal ones (Harlow 116). The focus shifts away from the individual, authorial, and univocal toward the communal, democratic, and multivocal.

Postcolonialism and Decolonization

In addition to the topics already discussed, testimony, the testimonial novel, and, more generally, a large part of Third World literature share a common goal of shedding their colonial past and neocolonial present as well as their racist traditions and institutions. As I have repeatedly sug-gested, Third World testimony and much other literature, for that matter, challenge dominant—in this context, imperialistic—forms, ideologies, and practices. Let us now consider testimony's strategies of resistance in its struggles to decolonize and eventually to build a nation.

From the time of the Conquest, not only did Europe colonize the territory of the New World but it also colonized its imagination (Franco in Engelbert xiv). Colonialism did not stop at silencing native voices or trying to make them conform to metropolitan standards. Frantz Fanon suggests that colonialism actually distorts and destroys an oppressed people's his-tory (Harlow 18). It deprives a people of their past, their identity. Even though following the Conquest officials moved to censor native texts, the popular imagination managed to survive at the margins mainly through oral traditions.

Despite the independence movements of the early nineteenth century throughout Latin America, however, there occurred no really revolutionary transformation of economic or social structures, no real recovery of au-tonomy. Political power was taken from the European colonizers by the Creole elites; they in turn sold much of their power to foreign economic interests, perpetuating a neocolonial status of dependency. The indigenous poor, blacks, and even mestizos stayed put.

JanMohamed compares the Latin American experience to the African independence movements of the 1950s, movements with mass support but without mass participation (1983). Jameson also notes the failed project of liberation: "To receive independence is not the same as to take it, since it is in the revolutionary struggle itself that new social relationships and a new consciousness . . . [are] developed" (1986, 81). Perhaps Jameson's view is a romantic one, especially if he is referring to armed revolutionary struggle.

Positive new social relationships and consciousness may indeed result, but so will backlash and enmity in direct proportion to the bitterness and violence of the struggle. My point is that the masses rarely felt part of, or benefited from, the independence movements of the nineteenth century. One master was merely replaced by another. Today's resistance literature and subversive cultural production, such as testimonio, are ways short of armed struggle in which the traditionally disenfranchised can educate, "conscientize," persuade, and rally in order to cause changes. The struggle must be everyone's. In this way, decolonial literature—meaning not only anticolonial writing but that which makes a conscious move *away from* or *out of* colonialism—and culture today are attempting to gain the liberation that was never won.

Afflicted with a long-lived inferiority complex, the colonized attempt to recover their identity in their own roots, their lost past. It is not a question of "rising to the heights" of European culture or importing foreign models. Culture is already there in Latin America, but the Eurocentric West has refused, or has been unable, to identify it even as it has found it. One cannot assume, caution Beverley and Zimmerman, that in Central America and other parts of the postcolonial world intellectuals and ideas inhabit the same sphere or operate in the same way as in the metropolis (37). Part of the decolonial project involves looking within for authentic modes of cultural expression; ironically, part also involves appropriating some of the very structures one wishes to overthrow—a strategy that is one of the characteristics of Third World literature.[8]

If we follow Gugelberger's definition of Third World literature, we find that in comparison with Euro-western literature, it is "more realistic than mainstream," more concrete, overtly political, combative, historically aware, didactic, and very often allegorical, and more concerned with message than with form (515). (Again, these are many of the same characteristics as testimony.) It is also "problem posing, dialogical, and fundamentally de-mythologizing" in contrast to Western literature's anesthetizing, monologic, and mythologizing tendencies (514). Literature produced under colonialism is deconstructive and subversive. A common discursive strategy is plagiarism, not because the colonized cannot think of anything original on their own but because they can better undermine the dominant discourse from within. Randall explains that when Third World writers win literary prizes for "originality" from Euro-western institutions (which have defined plagiarism as a literary crime), the whole system becomes a mockery: "The slave has beaten the master at his own game, revealing the ignorance and false authority protected by the institutional boundaries circumscribing 'appropriate' discourse" (539). Western ethics are shown to be at best meaningless and at worst unethical.

Ethics, in fact, plays a major role in decolonial writing. Writers deconstruct Western ethics for what they believe it really is—not the wisdom of the ages or eternal values but rules of conduct designed to protect the interests of a particular group: "All ethics lives by exclusion and predicates certain types of Otherness and evil," writes Jameson (1981, 59–60). For this reason, it is necessary to decenter the subject and remove the purview of ethics from his private reserve to the public and political domain for open scrutiny. Decolonial writing, resistance literature, and testimony all practice politics for ethical reasons—to transform society so that justice may be served for the Other. Since this type of writing has an activist political agenda—often anti-imperialistic and liberationist—it has occasioned official censorship and repression in many parts of Latin America. It recalls Spivak's exhortation to mix the verbal text with praxis and Jameson's assertion that all culture is political.

In a provocative article that links nonfiction and the question of the Other with capitalist production, Richard Ohmann notes that writers of texts like testimony bring a segment of life previously unknown to the reader's attention. "Of all social forms," writes Ohmann, "capitalism is the most opaque" (239). He explains that the way in which one class lives— especially the lower and working classes—is concealed from others. But because we also live in a "democratic" society, we maintain a "reformist, or a guilty, or at least a voyeuristic interest in them [the underprivileged, the masses]" (239). This kind of nonfiction prose results from the tension between capitalism and democracy. Whether the author consciously recognizes this effect or not, by introducing the subaltern as a worthy person, he or she can disturb readers' complacency and, quite possibly, mobilize their resources to anger and action.

As a practice to recover a disenfranchised people's past, decolonial literature and especially testimony provide the missing link. Part of the ethical project of testimony, according to Barnet, is that it "must contribute to articulating the collective memory, the *we* and not the *I*" (1983, 33). It fills in gaps created by dominant discourse. It also involves taking back what the dominant culture has appropriated and perverted for its own purposes. Indigenous customs come to mind here as one example. In many areas with large indigenous populations we find that official discourse (such as business or government) exploits native ceremonies as folkloric entertainment to stimulate tourism. Marginalized groups want to reclaim what is theirs.

Testimony wrests a space from the metropolis for the community. Recovery of memory represents the first step toward resistance and revolution. The community without a memory has nothing to recover, and it has lost its identity as a community. Such a loss of memory is devastating to the hopes and aspirations of the subaltern. For this reason, as we will see in later chapters, one of the tasks of testimonial discourse is to name names and create new myths of fallen heroes—names ordinarily forgotten in official history for being associated with the losing side.

The decolonial writer, especially the novelist, faces a somewhat paradoxical situation in rewriting the history of a people: Who will be able to read it anyway? How will it help galvanize an illiterate people? Ramírez answers that "like a prophet, the Central American writer can take the risk of writing for a splendid posterity" (1983, 123). But how long will one wait for tomorrow? Precisely for this reason, one of the first priorities of the cultural project in postrevolutionary Nicaragua was a massive literacy campaign so that all sectors of society could participate in the reception, understanding, and creation of culture—the collective memory and the expression of that memory.

Here one could argue that testimonial novelists, after debunking official narratives, are only substituting new myths and new fictions for old ones. Then, one might ask, what has one gained? Are old colonialist narratives to be deconstructed only to be replaced by new ones that will suffer the same fate? Or will the new narratives be qualitatively different and thus less likely to be so easily deconstructed?

Nationalism implies unity in the midst of diversity—but even within the supposed unity, some groups are more "united" than others. Nationalism implies boundaries—to keep citizens in and to keep foreigners and strangers out. Deplorably, some citizens are even treated like foreigners. Indeed, the community is only "imagined" and is merely a fiction—in this case, a lie.

The same myths and narratives that unite ironically must exclude. The multicultural state is especially vulnerable to centrifugal forces and to fragmentation. So is the two-gendered state, for that matter. Special care must be taken to reaffirm and include the different subaltern traditions within a national space—a worthy ideal but one most difficult in practice to achieve. How is this ideal to be realized? Fragmentation and Balkanization seem the operative words for postmodern times when the very concept of the nation—its artificiality and arbitrariness—is under question.

Beverley and Zimmerman identify the problem when they write that the nation is "fundamentally discontinuous, heterogeneous, and contradictory" (117), but necessarily so. These contradictions can only be addressed through negotiation if one expects to achieve any kind of long-lasting, productive accord. Once every voice is satisfied that it has at least been heard, decisions resemble compromises more than impositions.

As I conclude, this discussion brings me back for another look at the impact of the grands récits, which I mentioned earlier in the context of postmodernism and the construction of truth in the service of power. I am convinced that the master narratives have collapsed because they have not delivered their happy endings and because they have been exposed as the special-interest protection packages that they really are. I risk grossly oversimplifying issues to make my point that we see too few winners and too many losers in the master narratives—the programs of modernity for social justice—too few on the inside and too many on the outside.

The processes have been sacrificed for the ends. In the Christian narrative, the process of loving thy neighbor has been lost in the scramble to save and be saved (or be damned). The building of relationships and of community has suffered at the hands of individual piety and self-righteous judgment. For the capitalist enterprise, the process of each conducting business in one's own rational self-interest has been corrupted by the drive to accumulate ever more capital. (Besides, we do not all operate rationally.) The current rush to unregulated market economies in the United States and Latin America (and worldwide, for that matter) will fare no better than in the past unless substantial political reforms ensuring equal access and participation by all are realized. The Marxist project of dignifying labor loses its dignity as soon as some must be bludgeoned, not legislated, into redistributing their wealth. Likewise, the process of national unification rings hollow if ugly currents of racism and ethnic hatred lurk just below the surface. And all the above processes are suspect if they continue to be truly *master* narratives—emanating from the master, paternal and patriarchal—all the while excluding women or relegating them to second-class status.

The thesis that I will argue in the coming chapters is that most Central American testimonial novels, driven by a democratic vision (usually with Christian, Marxist, or socialist overtones, or some combination of the three), do hold popular-nationalism to be a positive entity, especially as imperialism's Other. National liberation is the first step. Givers, writers, and consumers of testimonial novels perceive their newly constructed myths to be vastly different from the old ones—more heterogeneous, more inclusive, with fewer Others—because they focus on the quality of the process and not on the happy ending. Hopefully, that emphasis will improve existing inequities and injustices within the national space and among neighboring states. But the process is necessarily ongoing; there is no end in sight.

2

Development of the Novel and Testimony in Guatemala, Nicaragua, and El Salvador

Before beginning a historical overview of the novel and testimony in Central America, I will briefly mention several antecedents in Spanish American literature to testimonio and to current literature that defends the subaltern. We find a variety of texts—some exemplary, some canonical, others little known—showing that in Latin America a tradition exists of unspeakable savageries committed against the so-called savages, of recognizing and protesting such injustices when they occur, and also of bearing witness to redress wrongs.

From the earliest days of discovery and conquest, the European-trained writer approached the native American as an object of marvel, of curiosity, and even of contempt. The journals, letters, and chronicles of Columbus, Cortés, Díaz del Castillo, and Núñez Cabeza de Vaca, to name just a few, grope to find words that will adequately describe the reality of the New World and its strange inhabitants. The ethnographic descriptions of Sahagún depict their customs, and the impassioned treatises of Las Casas defend their rights as human beings—truly noble savages—against the abuses of *encomienda* and evangelization.

On the other hand, defenders of Spanish colonialism, such as the viceroy Francisco de Toledo and his historians, reduced the Indians to subhuman monsters who, because they sacrificed their own and cannibalized others, deserved to be enslaved and civilized. Meanwhile, Ercilla's epic *Araucana* sings of the valor of the bellicose American tribes, indeed the honorable equals of the Spanish conquistadors.

But until recently critics disregarded native voices as enunciating subjects and spokespersons for the vanquished, leading readers to believe that none existed or that, if they did, they did not merit inclusion in a serious study of belles lettres. I do find structural and thematic antecedents (though not a coherent corpus of texts) for today's texts in indigenous writings and their variants. Texts by Guaman Poma de Ayala, Titu Cusi Yupanqui, and other eyewitnesses (see León-Portilla) give testimony to the annihilation of their cultures and to native resistance. They are often political. Guaman Poma's discursive practices overlap and vary from the juridical-theological to the religious-didactic and the subversion of official history (Adorno 87). Many modern testimonial novels, as we will see, have a similar generic and discursive mix.

A writer of the post-Conquest period who bears mentioning is the well-known Inca Garcilaso de la Vega. The Inca's *Comentarios reales* (1609) reveal an acculturated, assimilated discourse rather than a simple testimony of the indigenous Other. He represents a transition between the indigenous and European worlds; because of his work, however, he was accepted more as an exceptional intellectual than as a mainstream mestizo.

The years preceding independence saw occasional alliances between Creoles and Indians against the common Spanish enemy; that is not to say, though, that the Creoles considered the Indians to be their equals. Although they protested social injustices perpetrated against the exploited natives, Creole writers such as Carrió de la Bandera, Olmedo, Terralla y Landa, and Fernández de Lizardi saw cultural homogenization, education, and civilization as worthy goals.

A striking literary expression of "otherness" following independence is the "gauchesco genre" in Argentina. The best-known example, *Martín Fierro* by José Hernández (1872, 1879), reclaims the popular oral traditions of the downtrodden and marginalized cowboy in an effort to appeal to the consciences of the urban educated in order to effect change.

In the late nineteenth century we also find literary examples of the growing *indianismo* movement. *Cumandá,* by the Ecuadoran Juan León Mera (1871), paints a romanticized picture of Andean nature and its natives, while texts like Peruvian Clorinda Matto de Turner's *Aves sin nido* (1889) recall the criollista sensitivities to indigenous suffering and the positivist crusades to educate and civilize. But natives still, by and large, did not speak for themselves. Indianismo failed to interpellate the indigenous peoples as subjects of their own ideology or architects of their own destiny.

The indigenista movement of the early twentieth century represents another step closer to full vindication of "lo autóctono," or the native, writes Mariátegui (274). It is neither naturalist nor *costumbrista*, like so much of the *indianista* writing, yet it is still a literature of mestizos. Contradictions and *heterogeneidad* result: writers such as Ciro Alegría, Jorge Icaza, and José María Arguedas interpret their referent, the indigenous world, with a nonnative system of signs and language (Spanish) and nonnative literary forms (the novel) to nonnative readers (Cornejo Polar 1980). The text not only describes cultural and political conflict, it is itself the site of conflict.

Indigenous peoples generally remain the perennial Other within the main corpus of Latin American literature. With the exception of Sor Juana Inés de la Cruz in the seventeenth century, women have become the conscious Other in literature only in this century, along with African Americans, homosexuals, the politically alienated, workers, and the poor.

Social realism, which developed as a literary force in the 1930s, proposes an overtly socialist approach to the problems of injustice and exploitation of workers and campesinos, native and otherwise. Today's critics sometimes accuse the discourses of social realism of a heavy-handed, authoritarian, historically linear approach to social problems. Charged with being tendentious, the social realists often disclaim pretensions to aesthetics, preferring a straightforward and militant literature of action. Many writers of Central American testimony likewise preface their work with apologies for their lack of artistry. In light of theories of deconstruction, social realism has fallen into such disrepute currently that for a contemporary testimonial writer to be accused of writing in a social-realist vein is the literary kiss of death. (For a list of Latin American social-realist writers, see Gerald Martin.) Several Central American texts come to mind in a discussion of social realism: *Mamita Yunai* (1940) by the Costa Rican Carlos Luis Fallas, and *Prisión verde* (1950) by the Honduran Ramón Amaya Amador. (See Kessel Schwartz for a more exhaustive list.) We will find other examples as we discuss the development of the novel in Guatemala, El Salvador, and Nicaragua.

The literary currents I have sketched to this point, with the exception of indigenismo, have tended toward one of two options for the Other: survival by acculturation and assimilation, or destruction and disappearance. Angel Rama has examined the dynamic of acculturation-deculturation, preferring to study the actual process, which he calls "transculturation"—a term he borrows from the Cuban anthropologist Fernando Ortiz (209)—rather than the end result. Angel Rama identifies a new awareness among recent Latin American writers that goes beyond the superficial, stereotypical folklorist or criollista descriptions of subalternity. Especially effective as writers of transculturation, according to Rama, are Arguedas, Rulfo, Guimarães Rosa, and García Márquez, all of whom have transcended the need to appeal to universal (translated "Eurocentric") literary and cultural concepts. The appeal of their regionalism grows out of an ability to think and communicate as authentic representatives of a specific time and place (224). Transculturation shares with heterogeneity the creative tension that springs from cultures in conflict. It validates the voices at the margin that would ordinarily be subsumed or eliminated by more powerful voices. The testimonial novel will arise from a similar conjuncture of conflicting cultural attitudes, values, and practices.

As I move from the general to the particular, I must explain my focus on Guatemala, El Salvador, and Nicaragua. Costa Rica and Honduras have not experienced the recent revolutionary upheavals that have given rise to the new testimonial novel in the other three. This decision is not to slight either country by dismissing very real social, economic, and political injustices. Costa Rica is often touted as the "jewel" of Central American progress and democracy, a reputation that serves to mask its problems, much to the consternation of its human rights workers, activists, and economically and politically disenfranchised. Honduras, on the other hand, has profound historical scars that place it high on the list of potential hotbeds for national liberation movements. Indeed, its problems rival, and perhaps even surpass, those of its revolutionary neighbors. But it has not yet exploded to the same degree as Guatemala, Nicaragua, or El Salvador, giving rise to *letras de emergencia*. For reasons of magnitude and timing, then, I have limited the scope of this book to the three countries convulsed by revolution during the 1970s and 1980s.

One of the essential characteristics of testimony as it is practiced today in Central America is its "otherness." Somehow it seems appropriate that Central American writers have actively developed this narrative mode in recent years. The isthmus bears the dubious distinction of being the Other of the Other—that is, Third World Latin America's poor cousin. Years ago Chilean Nobel laureate Gabriela Mistral innocently baptized El Salvador "el pulgarcito de América" (the little thumb of America), metaphorically diminishing its stature in comparison to the rest of the hemisphere.

Central American literature has similarly experienced marginalization, though not because of a lack of gifted writers. External factors are to blame. Ramón Luis Acevedo has noted that "the scarce critical attention that Central American literature has received in general cannot be justified as a result of the supposed lack of literary value, it is simply due to the fact that it is unknown" (1982, 10). Economic underdevelopment together with the absence of major publishing houses, a very limited reading public (much of the population is illiterate, and those who can read often cannot afford books), writers away in exile, political censorship, and the absence of serious criticism—all have adversely affected literary production and dissemination. Acevedo notes that the novel especially, which requires time, effort, and discipline, has suffered (14). The novel in Central America has tended to lag behind its South American counterpart in major trends and innovations. Anachronistic genres coexist, and one can still find examples of historical, criollista, romantic, naturalist, *modernista,* social realist, and costumbrista narrative published today. The Boom-style novel, or nueva narrativa, which took the rest of Latin America by storm during the 1960s, arrived ten years later in Central America.

Guatemala

The novel developed earlier and the narrative tradition is stronger in Guatemala than in the rest of Central America. Conversely, poetry is scarcer in Guatemala than in El Salvador or Nicaragua.

As the seat of government for the isthmus, the Audiencia of Guatemala (so designated in 1542) under the viceroyalty of New Spain (Mexico) enjoyed special status as the political, cultural, and social capital of the area. When the first printing press arrived in 1760, arts and letters began to flourish while the rest of Central America remained an isolated cultural backwater.

The first Guatemalan novels made their appearance in the mid-nineteenth century, and modern testimonial trends developed in the midtwentieth century. Testimony and the testimonial novel, however, were not recognized as genres in their own right until the 1970s. For the purposes of this overview, which emphasizes the writer's concern with the Other, I will divide the development of the Guatemalan novel into three historical stages. The years 1846–1940 constituted the early period of historical romance, realism, naturalism, modernismo, costumbrismo, and criollismo; representative writers are Irisarri, Milla, Lainfiesta, Martínez Sobral, Soto-Hall, Arévalo Martínez, Wyld Ospina, and Flavio Herrera. (Some of these writers wrote well into the 1950s.) For them, the Mayans remained the quintessential Other, whom they either idealized or denigrated. The second period, 1944–54, the revolution, was a transitional period for literature that saw increased formal experimentation and the introduction of magical realism, a rise in social protest of the marginalization and exclusion of indigenous peoples, and the beginnings of a testimonial discourse. Major writers of this period include Asturias, Cardoza y Aragón, Monteforte, and Galich. The third period encompasses the years from 1954 to the present, with especially fervent literary experimentation beginning after 1976. This period witnessed the concurrent development of nueva narrativa and testimony. Writers of "pure" testimony during these recent years include Menchú, Payeras, Montejo, and Albizures, among others, while Monterroso is situated within the current of new narrative. Flores, Morales, Cifuentes, Arias, Lión, and Vásquez combine to a greater or lesser degree testimonial discourse with new narrative strategies. They widened the definition of the subaltern to embrace not only indigenous peoples but also women, homosexuals, the political outsider, and the urban worker.[1]

First Stage

The indio as Other has concerned the Guatemalan novelist from the beginning, which is dated by most critics in the mid-nineteenth century with the appearance of the irreverently humorous texts of Antonio José de Irisarri (who published *El cristiano errante* in 1846–47) and the historical romances of José Milla (whom Seymour Menton calls the father of the Guatemalan novel). These writers and others tend romantically to idealize the native. In 1879 the realist writer Francisco Lainfiesta published *A vista de pájaro*; in a biting attack original for its time, it elaborates "an eloquent defense of the Indian, a defense which wouldn't be repeated again in the Guatemalan novel for more than 50 years" (Menton 1985, 87). Guatemala's only naturalist writer, Enrique Martínez Sobral, takes the opposite point of view. His novel *Alcohol* shows a degraded Indian captive to all kinds of vices.

A reformist spirit characterizes both the realist and modernista novels toward the end of the nineteenth century. The novel became a political tool—modernista Máximo Soto-Hall wrote the first anti-imperialist novel, *El problema* (1899), placing himself and Central America ahead of the rest of Latin America regarding this theme. His critical spirit, however, did not extend to the plight of indigenous groups. The other major writer of the day, Rafael Arévalo Martínez, produced texts condemning the notorious Estrada Cabrera dictatorship (1898–1920). His use of animal imagery highlights the dehumanization caused by tyranny. Arévalo Martínez criticized U.S. imperialism and recognized an "Indian problem," although he showed little sympathy or understanding of them. His interest in both social themes and formal experimentation contributed to the development of more complex treatment by later Guatemalan novelists and to the beginnings of magical realism.

The criollista writers continued the experimentation with form and technique, heavily influenced by trends of La Vanguardia: surrealism, Freudianism, cinematography, cubism, the oneiric, *creacionismo,* ruptures and fragmentation in narrative sequencing, and the deformation of language. They chose psychological and philosophical, as well as social, themes for their novels. Like the great Latin American criollista novelists in vogue between the two world wars—Azuela, Rivera, Gallegos, and Güiraldes— Guatemalan criollistas slowly began seeking the typically Hispanic or Central American, relating to nature or rural life or the native campesino. The problem facing the criollista writers involved too great a distance between writer and referent, a gap that first indigenismo and later testimony would attempt to bridge. Carlos Wyld Ospina tried to capture Indian psychology and spirituality in *Los lares apagados* (written in 1939 but not published until 1958), incorporating some of their words and phrases. Acevedo judges this text to be the most successful example of indigenismo until Asturias and Monteforte Toledo (1982, 288). The other major criollista writer, Flavio Herrera, fairly ignored the plight of the Mayans or any other exploited group, preferring to turn inward to the individual rather than to the collective psyche. The novel during this period was not as potent a political weapon as it would become.

Second Stage

The year 1944 marked a pivotal moment in modern Guatemalan history and, in my judgment, the beginning of the second stage of the Guatemalan novel, a period of transition. With the Ubico dictatorship (1931–44) overthrown and a fledgling democracy installed under reformist, but not radical, President Juan José Arévalo, enthusiasm returned for the telluric novels that, different from Herrera's texts, "wanted to capture the cosmic essence of the country and protest against the injustices which the Guatemalan people suffered in silence" (Menton 1985, 208). Literary societies flourished; among them the iconoclastic Saker-ti, founded in 1947, tried to break the age-old tradition of grouping writers according to generations. Instead, it combined the sociopolitical with the artistic, emphasizing the former and favoring ethics over aesthetics (Albizúrez 1983, 35).

It must be noted here that the two Guatemalan writers of this period who had the most influence on successive generations of narrators, Generation of 1920 members Miguel Angel Asturias and Luis Cardoza y Aragón, began as poets and journeyed to Paris to steep themselves in the avant garde. Their poetry rebelled formally against Darío's *modernismo* and politically against the dictators Estrada Cabrera and Ubico as well as against the social and economic injustices brought on by the Depression. Zimmerman credits them with "an intense cultural *mestizaje*" and an acute awareness of a national identity in which "*indigenismo* [is] seen as a source for spiritual revitalization in the face of years of dictatorship, economic debilities, and strong class, caste, and ethnic divisions" (1995a, I:240).

Furthermore, while Cardoza y Aragón espoused an openly leftist ideology, he refused to embrace the aesthetics of socialist/communist governments or to advocate for conformity to a leftist, party-line literary agenda. For this position, he was criticized by Saker-ti and mistakenly labeled conservative by his critics. Both he and Asturias furthered the development of radical resistance prose in Guatemala. Though Cardoza's own work reflects a Communist-partisan linear view of history, his major contribution was to encourage artistic freedom and experimentation and to expose the "Indian question" as not an Indian problem at all but rather a problem of the entire Guatemalan people (Zimmerman 1995a, I:246).

Cardoza confined his prose writing to essays and memoirs on culture and history. He, Asturias, and Mario Monteforte Toledo continued writing throughout the dictator years but remained marginalized because of their controversial subject matter and social protest. Following the 1944 revolution, Asturias and Monteforte began to experiment with the *novela nacional,* the *novela de tesis,* and indigenismo. Adelaida Lorand judges Monteforte to be "the author who has come closest to the collective reality of the indigenous people. . . . With [him] indigenista literature would reach its culminating point thereafter descending in search of new directions in harmony with new techniques of novelizing" (124). In Monteforte's *Entre la piedra y la cruz* (1948), the rural world, the theme of land, the sacredness of corn, and the indigenous cyclical view of history form a backdrop for the story of the Indian Lu Matzar. The title of the novel situates Lu problematically between the cultures of his native world and the Christianized Western world of the ladinos. To succeed in the world, he must abandon his native ways, something he refuses to do completely. He is caught in a transcultural bind.

Zimmerman has noted that Monteforte's formal experimentation has often been overlooked (1995a, I:127). A leftist, Monteforte offers a critique in *Una manera de morir* (1957) of the inner workings of the reformist Arévalo government and the 1944 revolution itself, thus following the pattern set by Cardoza, who sought independence from dogmatism, and setting the stage for Arias, Morales, and Flores. Monteforte also contributed to the development of testimony in its realist dimension and in its move from the countryside to the city.

Miguel Angel Asturias, who won the Nobel Prize for Literature in 1967, spans the old realism and new narrative. He prefigures the Boom, combining vanguardist techniques with indigenismo, lyricism, magical realism, and social realism. His first novel, *El señor presidente* (1946), is the prototype of the Latin American dictator novel (the historical referent is the dictatorship of Manuel Estrada Cabrera). Although written in the 1930s, *El señor presidente* could not be published until after the 1944 revolution because of the author's criticism of the dictatorship. In the novel, Asturias explores ways to integrate his surrealism and vanguardist techniques with the creation of a Guatemalan national identity that included both Mayans and ladinos. The synthesis provides the prelude to Boom writing and narrative experimentation in Guatemala following the 1954 coup (Zimmerman 1995a, I:130).

El señor presidente also incorporates passages of Indian mythology. Inspired by the native sacred text, the *Popol Vuh,* Asturias penetrates Mayan cosmogony and folklore further in *Hombres de maíz* (1949).[2] He explains his interest in the native: "In any city, in any town of Guatemala, the presence of the Indian, of the authentic descendant of those ancient Mayans classified as the Greeks of America, imposes itself as a mute and meek denunciation, of violent gentleness, as an unavoidable accusation" (quoted in Osses 42).

Magical realism may seem antithetical to the author's social protest. In fact, many critics have found fault with his use of the surreal and the fantastic to deal with historical crises. Because it appeals to fantasy and subjectivity these critics fail to appreciate the gravity of magical realism. Since social realism draws on scientific and materialist analyses to explain reality, many see it as more weighty or serious. Menton describes the coexistence of the two currents in Guatemala: "In Guatemala generally, the peon and the Indian did not live in the same misery as did their counterparts in Mexico, Ecuador, and Peru. That explains the mythological and psychological orientation which is given respectively to social protest in the works of Asturias and of Monteforte" (1985, 330). Perhaps Menton is saying that a greater "misery index" gave rise to a literature of denunciation in Mexico and the Andes and that Asturias and Monteforte had the luxury of being able to play with their imaginations without guilt since Guatemala's Indians did not seem so destitute. Richard Adams indeed corroborates the "era of good feeling" toward the indigenous campesinos in 1944–54 (158), but Carol A. Smith is quick to point out the "uniquely brutal treatment of Indians by the modern Guatemalan state" (2).

I find Menton's analysis a bit ingenuous. It takes more than an era of good feeling to redress centuries of injustice. There is and has long been plenty of misery to go around in the indigenous communities, whether in the Andes, Mexico, or Guatemala. In fact, one can argue that magical realism and fantasy are by far some of the most compelling ways in which a writer can deal with the nightmarish quality of life, both public and private, in Latin America. I can think of few other pages in all of Latin American literature as moving and as chillingly terrifying as those of *El señor presidente*. At any rate, the concurrent orientations seen in both social realism and magical realism underline what some critics see as anachronistic tendencies that have persisted in Guatemalan literature.

Also part of this transitional period but quite different from Asturias's magical realism or Monteforte's indigenismo was some of Manuel Galich's work. Galich wrote, according to Beverley and Zimmerman (198), the first genuine testimony in 1949, *Del pánico al ataque*. His text, which contains elements of the *pensador* or intellectual essay popular in the late nineteenth and early twentieth centuries, documents student unrest during the Ubico years.

With the fall of the Arbenz government in 1954, many illusions and ideals faded. Successive dictatorships came and went in the 1950s, 1960s, and 1970s. Guerrilla warfare broke out in the mountains and in the city streets as Indians, suspected of "communist" involvement or sympathies, became the targets of disappearances, tortures, and assassinations by paramilitary death squads or by the regular armed forces. The first wave of guerrilla resistance following the 1954 coup failed in the 1960s, a failure that would provide the impetus for a change in literary production. Many writers were driven underground or out of the country. What was written sought radically new forms that would more adequately reveal Guatemalan reality.

Third Stage

The third period in the development of the Guatemalan novel began slowly following the tremendous repression of the 1950s until it finally exploded in a flurry of new narrative activity in the 1970s. The linear, realist, and totalizing narratives that corresponded to the failed project of the old Left gave way to innovative writings structured "to replicate the destruction of Guatemalan society, portray its social chaos, and pose the difficulty of grasping the meaning of life itself when it is degraded by war and tragedy" (Zimmerman 1995a, I:150). Writers concerned themselves with both aesthetics and ethics. Most of the Guatemalan writers who experimented with new narrative strategies—Flores, Morales, Cifuentes, Arias, and others—lived and worked outside Guatemala. Critics have generally favored their work, in terms of quality and importance, over that of their compatriots who remained at home.

The production of nueva narrativa, inspired by the works of Boom writers Fuentes, Cortázar, Vargas Llosa, and García Márquez in the 1960s, did not arrive in Guatemala until the 1976 publication of Marco Antonio Flores's *Los compañeros*. Multidiscursive, lacking an authoritarian narrative voice, freed from mimeticism, fond of linguistic play, resembling more a pastiche or collage of forms than a linear narrative sequence, the new novel forces the reader to work as hard as the writer to create meaning. Here it seems appropriate also to mention the impact of short story writer Augusto Monterroso. Master of irony, satire, and humor, Monterroso exposes bourgeois foibles and hypocrisies in *Lo demás es silencio* (1978) and *Mr. Taylor & Co.* (1982). While he does not write testimonial novels, his influence on these novelists is enormous. His narrative resembles a pastiche of genres and discourses. More will be said about new narrative following the discussion of testimony.

Testimony. At the same time that the new novel was taking shape, testimony emerged as a vigorous new literary concept and form. Testimonial writers of the third period not only consider the Indian question but continue to explore other manifestations of marginalization and exclusion as well. In my opinion, the best example of Guatemalan testimony per se (testimony written without fictionalization or excessive regard for aesthetic value, as opposed to the testimonial novel) is *Me llamo Rigoberta Menchú, y así me nació la conciencia* (I, Rigoberta Menchú) (1983).

Menchú's voice represents the "Other of the Other"—the female Indian marginalized several times over by virtue of race, gender, and language. In her introduction, collaborating transcriber Elisabeth Burgos Debray writes that "the voice of Rigoberta Menchú allows the defeated to speak (1984, xi) . . . [she] learned the language of her oppressors in order to use it against them" (xii). Since winning the Nobel Peace Prize in 1992, Menchú, it can be argued, is no longer marginalized. Nevertheless, she is still not welcome in her native land, either by government officials who are suspicious of her ideology or by many fellow Mayans who feel that her international tours have distracted her from business at home and that she has lost touch with indigenous concerns in Guatemala.

Burgos explains the process she followed in recording and editing Menchú's testimony, a process that could become problematic depending upon the degree of intervention by the editor: she organized the five hundred pages of transcript into thematic areas; deleted her own questions, thus turning the text into a monologue; cut some of the repetitions; and corrected gender mistakes: "It would have been artificial to leave them uncorrected and it would have made Rigoberta look 'picturesque,' which is the last thing I wanted" (1984, xx–xxi). She wishes to avoid any hint of the costumbrista, or the folkloric. When an interlocutor like Burgos must edit oral testimony, Philippe Lejeune cautions against overcorrection, a maneuver that may result in a condescending, patronizing treatment of the subject. Balancing concerns for readability by the reading public with the desire to preserve the "presence" of oral discourse, the interlocutor walks a fine line between the purely scientific and the purely literary representation of the Other: "Respect for the Other imposes a minimum of adaptation," writes Lejeune (293–96). Elzbieta Sklodowska has also problematized the mediation of testimony, pointing out that Burgos has relegated any metadiscourse and dialogue to the margins of the text (that is, Burgos's introduction); the result emphasizes the harmonious relationship and solidarity between Burgos and Menchú (1992, 118). We readers can legitimately ask, "Whom are we really hearing here, Burgos or Menchú?"

Within the text, Menchú repeatedly emphasizes to Burgos her role as representative, not as individual and certainly not as hero: "Mi situación personal engloba toda la realidad de un pueblo" (1983, 21) (My personal experience is the reality of a whole people) (1984, 1).[3] She speaks as an orphan but realizes she is not the only orphan in Guatemala: "Yo me decía, no soy la única huérfana que existe en Guatemala, hay muchos y no es mi dolor, es el dolor de todo el pueblo" (1983, 261) (There are many others, and it's not my grief alone, it's the grief of a whole people) (1984, 236). She emphasizes her relationship to her community as metonymic, as contiguous, as only one of many. Much critical work has tended to agree. It seems to me, however, that her insistence on her own representativeness—that her situation encompasses the whole reality of a people—is actually metaphoric. She can and does speak for all Indians; her experience is totalizing. Perhaps she really wants it to be taken both ways.

Menchú takes the moral high ground, defending her participation in the struggle as a Christian. Her testimony thus bears much in common with the discourse of religious testimony. Presenting an idealized, perhaps nostalgic view of her native world, she insists that Indians know how to live communally, sharing what they have and working together peacefully. They are not sexist, judgmental, or homophobic (1983, 86). Women, she feels, have a moral obligation to participate in any movement for liberation. She remembers her mother's advice: "No te obligo a que dejes de sentirte mujer, pero tu participación tiene que ser igual que la de tus hermanos" (1983, 243) (I don't want to make you stop feeling a woman, but your participation in the struggle must be equal to that of your brothers) (1984, 219).

At the time she wrote her testimony, Menchú was working as a community and labor organizer. Since then she has traveled throughout the world as an activist, speaking on behalf of indigenous people and their struggle, work that continues to this day. Occasionally, she returns to Guatemala, heavily guarded, to protest abuses of indigenous rights and to accompany returning refugees seeking repatriation. But some groups remain skeptical either because she is not of their tribe or because they perceive her as having been co-opted by the outside world.

The strength of Menchú's testimony, for Beverley and Zimmerman, lies in the "matching of form and content . . . and in the sense of life and community it narrates. Testimony is, first of all, a written transmission of voice and memory" (202). The voice is collective: "The act of narration involves a love of and an identification with the people; it is a ceremonial form of representation in which the relation between spirit and body, individual and community, human beings and nature are defined and affirmed. These relations are depicted early in the text as Menchú speaks of the ceremonies that accompany birth and the progressive initiation of the child into the history of the group, its ancestors, its own special *nahual* or spirit double, the meaning of corn, the value of ceremony and ritual" (202–3). The ritual of the testimonial text is "performative," joining one voice to many, bringing the past forward to the present.

As she closes her book, the dignified Menchú confirms that she still guards several secrets of the community as well as her own Indian identity and name. The sacred, innermost private space must remain inviolate. Sklodowska observes, nevertheless, that Menchú has had to reveal some of those secrets in her political activism. She has been partially "ladinized" and "transculturated," paradoxically, in order to serve the interests of her community—in a sort of "Malinche syndrome" (1992, 125). Menchú's narrative act of love has in some ways separated her from the community, both as source and recipient of her love.

Other notable Guatemalan testimonies include Mario Payeras's *Los días en la selva* (1983), a lyrical account of the author's own experience as a guerrilla; Víctor Montejo's *Testimony: Death of a Guatemalan Village* (1987), about the slaughter of small-town inhabitants by a military unit; and Miguel Angel Albizures's *Tiempo de sudor y lucha* (1987), which narrates from a worker's perspective the 1984 Coca Cola strike in Guatemala City. Almost all of the above testimonies have been translated into English and many other languages. This fact, however, does not signal best-seller status as it did with the translations of the major Boom novels in the 1960s. Rather, it is a strategy to reach an international reading public with political clout who might express outrage when confronted with eyewitness accounts and with information regarding its own government's complicity in perpetuating the injustices.

Testimonial Novel. The persistence of anachronistic narrative modes into the present—which has long characterized the Guatemalan novel—combined with different narrative and discursive strategies, has produced generic overlapping and a confusion of forms. The inclusion of testimony into literature results in "composiciones heteróclitas," mixed genres of great vitality (Rama 482). Several examples follow.

Los compañeros (1976), by Marco Antonio Flores, marks the first time the forms and techniques of nueva narrativa combine with testimony in Guatemalan literature. The new novel seeks linguistic, stylistic, and formal renovation, at times becoming an ideologically subversive "anti-novel" (Morales 1986b, 81–82). Arias has attempted to explain the two somewhat divergent tendencies, testimony and nueva narrativa, that coexisted in the 1970s. He finds that the first approaches an authoritarian voice without melding completely as it documents its victimization by forces of oppression, whereas the second is a series of "more literary" discourses that allegorically play with possible historical variants (1990d, 11). In the testimonial novel the two intertwine in various levels of discursive play and tension. From its innovative language, slang from the pop culture (some of it imported), fragmentation of narrative sequence, lack of punctuation and traditional syntactical structure, free association, chaotic alternation of a fragmented narrator, and interior monologue, to its audacious sexual imagery throughout, *Los compañeros* exudes insolence. Nothing is sacred for this negative, iconoclastic text. Edwin Cifuentes's *El pueblo y los atentados* (1979) shares Flores's irreverence and verbal acrobatics, as do Morales's *Los demonios salvajes* (1978) and *Esplendor de la pirámide* (1986), which sometimes erupt in rebellious obscenities.

I find interesting the complete omission of the "Indian problem" in *Los compañeros*. Indigenous people figure obliquely and only as fuel for linguistic jokes and word games. Granted, the venue here is the urban battleground of the marginalized middle class, but the omission for me is significant because it further highlights the selfishness, limited vision, and dashed illusions of failed revolutionaries who lack discipline and commitment. Absorbed in their urban world, they are indifferent to the rural Maya-Quiché groups who also demand a voice within the project of national liberation. The novel succeeds; medium and message become one. This novel is an example of what Rama calls the urgent political protest novels that "do not aspire to simplify but rather heighten the complexity of society and its incredible degrees of distortion" (483).

Flores shares the social commitment of his contemporaries elsewhere in Latin America, especially Mario Vargas Llosa, who found hope in the Guatemalan and Cuban revolutions, only to lose it as the United States in concert with local militaries and elites mounted counterrevolutions. Perhaps Flores failed to understand the changes that other contemporary writers were making, away from a hard-line leftist project to a more inclusive and democratic approach where there is space for indigenous peoples as well as any other marginalized group. After all, Morales's *Los demonios salvajes,* from the same period, pays no attention to the indio either and imitates Flores's linguistic insolence. But Morales had opted for the new approach.

One of the youngest of Guatemala's currently acclaimed novelists, Arturo Arias (born 1950), author of *Después de las bombas* (1979), *Itzam Na* (1981), *Jaguar en llamas* (1989), and *Los caminos de Paxil* (1990), is the subject of Chapter 5. His work tends to follow the same vein as Cifuentes's in its carnivalesque tone and linguistic experimentation and shares with the aforementioned novelists many characteristics of the Boom novel. He criticizes Flores's intransigence, bitter denunciation of the Left, and consequent withdrawal from activism. In the tradition of Cardoza y Aragón, Arias like Morales is eager to flex his creative muscles; he goes on to explore new narrative possibilities within a deconstructive, inclusive, postmodern politics.

If the reader is looking for an "authentic" indigenous voice among Guatemala's recent novelists, perhaps Luis de Lión serves as the closest example. Beverley and Zimmerman note that Lión is only a partially ladinized Indian who has "emerged as one of the first poets who could present Indian perspectives in his work firsthand" (163). He exemplifies Rama's transculturated writer. His novel *El tiempo principia en Xibalba* (written in 1972, published in 1985) makes a general protest against the living conditions of the indigenous community and the discrimination they suffer at the hands of the ladinos. The novel does not present testimony about a particular historical event; rather, it creates a mood that is poetic, oneiric, and erotic using at the same time new narrative techniques. Lión paid the price for his literary activism. He was "disappeared" in the early 1980s. Another important indigenous voice is Gaspar Pedro González, who wrote the novel *La otra cara* (1992) in a Mayan language. R. McKenna Brown sees this text, which is both a compilation of oral traditions and the fictional life story of a Mayan male, as a complement to the testimony of Rigoberta Menchú (1).

The 1989 novel of Miguel Angel Vásquez, *Operación Iscariote*, bears mention as one that speaks in the voice of a peasant turned torturer and military man (among a number of other voices). As we see in texts of Arias and Morales, and later of Salvadoran Manlio Argueta, this representation has become increasingly interesting and important as writers explore this dimension of "otherness" in relation to power. *Operación Iscariote* remains within the current of the testimonial novel, although by this time much other Guatemalan narrative has moved in an even more introspective, lyrical, and subjective direction.

One of the most recent testimonios to appear—a significant event since the current "testimonial era" is waning—is Mario Roberto Morales's *Señores bajo los árboles* (1994). Morales leaves cosmopolitan "Boomism" to return to what he calls the *testi-novela*. In it, Morales, whom Zimmerman has called "a free thinker par excellence" (1995a, I:279), criticizes the Left from within the Left. Again, he follows in Cardoza's footsteps by going beyond literary models of the past—in this case, party-line testimonio—to create new forms. By "testi-novela" Morales means a hybrid text combining the mythic and the concrete, the ethic and the aesthetic, orality and literature: "The *testi-novela* is a specific type of novel structured around testimonies. It constitutes a collective creation in which the professional writer acts as a facilitator/organizer—deliberate and interested—of the voices and their truths" (1995).

I find the actual term *testi-novela* somewhat problematic since as a neologism it highlights (one hopes unintentionally) the male qualities of testimony. In Latin, "testis" is the word for both witness and testicle, implying that the giver of testimony necessarily has testicles, is male. This limitation is precisely what current theorizers, including Morales, have wished to avoid in their attempts to extend testimonio to many voices, including those of women (Craft 1996b). At any rate, if we can move beyond the word itself to Morales's theory, his explanation emphasizing that the testi-novela is a "borderlands genre" situates it nicely within my working and flexible definition of the testimonial novel.

Several observations need to be made regarding *Señores bajo los árboles*. In experimental mode, each of the three sections of the novel is entitled a "fragment." Stream of consciousness, the lack of punctuation, and a conclusion that recalls the introduction combine to create a feeling of "life on the run" and of circularity. At times the narrator is the same person who, in the middle of a monologue, dies. Nevertheless, he continues speaking. In death, the spirit of the deceased accompanies the next victim who is about to be killed, welcoming him or her to the "other side" in a technique highly reminiscent of the speaking dead of *Pedro Páramo*.

Regarding content, the various narrators (men, women—all indios) repeatedly protest the abuses perpetrated by both the army and the guerrilla fighters. *Señores* has the most brutal sustained descriptions of campaigns of scorched earth and extermination that I have ever read in a testimony. Fortunately, the text is mercifully short. It is clear that the Indians are caught in the middle and mostly wish to have nothing to do with either side. The testi-novela is their collective voice raised to protest and prevent the destruction of their communities and way of life; it is also an appeal for Indian unity.

Finally, we need to acknowledge two Guatemalan American writers who publish in English and do most of their work from the United States, Victor Perera and Francisco Goldman. Texts of both show cosmopolitan influences. Perera's *Rites* (1986) and *The Cross and the Pear Tree* (1995) examine, among other issues, being Jewish in a Latin American context. Goldman, much like Arias, experiments with new narrative techniques, superimposed texts, and labyrinthine plots in *The Long Night of White Chickens* (1992). But like Perera, Goldman is far less insolent and humorous than Arias. This novel definitely falls within the Guatemalan tradition of psychological introspection; however, it is resistant to totalizing (and dehumanizing) political projects as much as it is to totalizing novelistic discourses (see Craft 1996a). It is my opinion that *The Long Night* represents the most wide-open and dynamic text in the current Guatemalan corpus.

To conclude, while the Guatemalan novel has developed along the same general pattern as that of other Latin American novels—albeit following somewhat later—and it precedes its other Central American counterparts, particular features distinguish it from the rest. Testimonial discourse and function combine with nueva narrativa to highlight the popular struggle and to mark the revolution of 1944 as the defining moment of Guatemalan history in this century. All else leads up to it or, after the coup in 1954, is "fall out" or an attempt to restore it.

In addition to this historical and political orientation, many critics have observed that the novel of Guatemala tends toward an exploration of the interior or psychological ramifications of conflict (for example, parts of Asturias's *El señor presidente* and the works of Herrera, Arias, Morales, Vásquez). Furthermore, sardonic humor, irony, and linguistic play characterize the Guatemalan novel (such as those of Morales, Arias, Cifuentes) more than that of Nicaragua or El Salvador, perhaps due to the lasting influence of the first "novel" of Irisarri in the nineteenth century. As we find in Andean novels and those of El Salvador and Nicaragua, the "first Other" of the Guatemalan novel is the Indian and the campesino. Because of the increasing intrusion of testimonial discourse into novelistic space during the last twenty-five years and its use as a mouthpiece for the voiceless, that focus has been widened to include a great many other subaltern groups—women, Jews, and children, to name a few.

Current criticism of Guatemalan literature has especially emphasized the shift of the last twenty-five years from the linear discourse of realism to the fragmented, nontotalizing presentation of new narrative and postmodernism. Many disparate voices clamor to be heard in the national arena. Arias, Morales, and Zimmerman have increasingly looked to the influence of Guatemala's towering giants of twentieth-century letters, Cardoza (all the more notable when one notices that Beverley and Zimmerman paid scant attention to him in 1990) and Asturias, to explain that Guatemalan literature has had a tradition of free thinking, experimentation, and resistance and that writers have rebelled at party narrowness and censorship. This assessment is even more important now as the new Left of Guatemala, Central America, and beyond distances itself from the old fatigues of a stale and discredited Marxism and attempts to redefine iself and set its course in a far less certain world.

Nicaragua

Poetry and the short story, not the novel, have defined Nicaragua's literary history. For various reasons, the novel developed quite late in Nicaragua, if we compare it to that of Guatemala, while testimony emerged at about the same time.

Oral tradition emanating from the indigenous communities provides the base for Nicaragua's earliest literature. The Nicaragua and Chorotega tribes composed songs and created pictographs depicting the tragedy of conquest, some of which were collected by Las Casas, who visited the area in 1535 (Arellano 1982, 19). Narrative literature began with orally transmitted short stories, *cuentos de animales* (animal stories) featuring characters from Indian folklore and *cuentos de aparecidos* (stories of apparitions) combining both indigenous and Spanish traditions. Sergio Ramírez has reported that in this vernacular literature, which is anonymous and collective, a storyteller assumes the role of eyewitness in an early form of testimony (1976, 9). If one can find a "moral" to these stories, it is surely that intelligence and wits prevail over brute force in the fight to survive. Lest this mention of indigenous influence mislead the reader, we note that the pre-Columbian heritage in Nicaragua has been more limited than in Guatemala, Mexico, and Peru (Borgeson 407).

Very little literary activity marked the colonial period and the first half century of independence. In March of 1881, one journalist registered a complaint in Nicaragua's *Gaceta oficial:* "If we lack literature it is because we don't have any wise men, writers, scholars, et cetera" (Arellano 1982, 27). Arellano makes the point that most of the capable men of letters in the nineteenth century, who also doubled as politicians, had no time to devote to writing because the business of running the country consumed them. (We will see a resurgence of this argument following the revolution of 1979.) Eventually, learned societies and other institutions such as libraries and newspapers dedicated to the advancement of culture and education in general—albeit *criollo* and Eurocentric—began to appear in the late 1800s.

In considering the development of the novel in Nicaragua, especially as it pertains to the representation of marginal social sectors, I will divide my study into four stages. First is the period 1878–1930, which is notable for early attempts at novelizing in the romantic, criollista, costumbrista traditions with little or no concern for the subaltern. A corpus of this period includes the narrative texts of Gámez, Valdéz, Guzmán, Fletes Bolaños, Cuadra Chamorro, Chamorro Zelaya, and finally Rubén Darío. The second period, 1930–59, saw the beginning of the quest for the "national-popular," the rise of regionalism and social realism in novels, the influence of the vanguardia in literature, the role of increasing North American dominance in politics and culture with the sellout by Somoza to U.S. interests, and the resistance of Sandino. Several prominent names associated with this period include Robleto, Román, Quintana, Manolo Cuadra, Pablo Antonio Cuadra, Coronel Urtecho, and Cardenal. The third period, encompassing the years 1959–79, was characterized by ferment and struggle leading up to the revolution. Experimentation with nueva narrativa strategies began in 1969 with Chávez Alfaro and later Ramírez; the same period gave birth to testimonies by activists Tijerino, Guadamuz, Borge, and Cabezas, although many of the testimonies could not be published until after 1979. During the fourth period, post-1979, the nature of testimony and the role and status of the writer changed following the successful revolution. Ramírez and Belli, among others, wrote testimonios and testimonial novels in an effort to rewrite history. They joined many of their contemporaries to broaden the concept of the Other to include women, political prisoners, homosexuals, and the poor, as well as indigenous peoples. With the 1990 electoral victory of UNO (National Opposition Union, a coalition of political parties formed in 1988 to oppose the Sandinistas), we are currently witnessing a post-Sandinista adjustment in the role of the writer, culture, and art in national life and soon will be able to add another chapter to this discussion. Some of the same writers who worked within the revolution are now questioning the "openness" of the Sandinista project, especially as it concerns the participation of women and indigenous groups in the nation.

First Stage

The early "novelists" chose the costumbrista narrative mode as their favorite. The first Nicaraguan novel, *Amor y constancia* (1878) by José Dolores Gámez, is primarily romantic and anachronistic; it is followed by the romantic and "folletinesque" novels of Carlos J. Valdéz and Gustavo Guzmán, which Arellano judges to be out of touch with Nicaraguan reality (1982, 130). Other attempts in the early twentieth century include costumbrista and picaresque novels by Anselmo Fletes Bolaños, Pedro Joaquín Cuadra Chamorro, and Pedro Joaquín Chamorro Zelaya. Ramírez calls the renowned modernista poet Rubén Darío "the first Nicaraguan narrator" (1976, 10). However, Arellano judges two of Darío's three novels, *El hombre de oro* and *Oro de Mallorca,* to be failures (1982, 129). Not everyone agrees. His first novel, *Emelina* (1887), is his only complete one. He wrote it for a literary contest in a record ten days in collaboration with his friend Eduardo Poirier. Although *Emelina* bears all the marks of a less than first rate, thoroughly conventional romantic *folletín,* it is most likely a playful parody not to be taken too seriously (Acevedo 1982, 184). Darío's irony, elegance, and humor—combined at times with lyricism—anticipate his first important book of poetry, *Azul* (1888).

Apparently distracted by other professional and diplomatic responsibilities, Darío never finished his second novel, *El hombre de oro* (1897), several chapters of which were published serially in *La Biblioteca* of Buenos Aires. This novel (which coincides with his triumphant collection of poems *Prosas profanas*) is considered by many critics to be aesthetically refined, musical, mature, elegant, and exotic. In it, Darío juxtaposes the Christian and the pagan, the spirit and the flesh (Acevedo 1982, 188). Some passages of the text tend toward the intimate, confessional, and autobiographical.

No evidence exists that Darío ever finished his last novel, *Oro de Mallorca* (1913) either. Here the autobiographical and existential are foremost; the tortured man of letters broods over the condition of his soul in a direct, simple, and natural style much more representative of the later periods of his life (compare *Lo fatal* and *Cantos de vida y esperanza*). Acevedo concludes that the great Nicaraguan poet had the potential to be a fine novelist but that circumstances as well as his temperament as a writer prevented him from achieving that literary goal (1982, 198).

All in all, the Nicaraguan novel made its debut late and slowly in the shadow of modernista poetry. Few writers could devote themselves to the long hours and discipline of creating a novel, even the great Darío; and when they did, most could scarcely find a market to publish their works.

Second Stage

By the 1930s, realism and regionalism characterized the novel, in large part because of the vanguardists' rejection of the modernistas' universalizing, elitist tendency. In addition, a variety of factors contributed to a narrative literature of social realism including social and economic upheaval, a search for a national identity (led by writers Pablo Antonio Cuadra, Ernesto Cardenal, and José Coronel Urtecho and by the military-political leader Augusto César Sandino), a series of foreign interventions including that of the United States, the concomitant sellout by nationals (under the Somoza dynasty) to these foreign interests, and the frustrations experienced by Nicaraguan idealists in their search for freedom and democracy. Osses has noted the unending polarities faced by the Nicaraguan people with their "virtue of dreaming and fighting" (72). The Nicaraguan social-realist novels, writes Acevedo, find their inspiration in the novels of the Mexican revolution, written generally between 1925 and 1940, in terms of political referent, treatment, collectivization of characters, and narrative structure (1982, 296). The testimonial tendency in Nicaragua dates from the insurgencies of this era (Beverley and Zimmerman 179). In general, however, the writer is still the man of letters looking from the outside into the world of the peasant farmer or *peón*.

Hernán Robleto's *Sangre en el trópico* (1930) carries the subtitle "La novela de la intervención yanqui en Nicaragua." In an account flavored by testimony and a documentary style, Robleto captures the prevailing anti-American sentiment of his time, writes from personal experience to denounce U.S. intervention in his country, and decries U.S. racism against blacks and Indians in Nicaragua as emblematic of its dehumanizing foreign policy against marginalized or excluded peoples. It is one of the first novels to examine successfully and dramatically the difficult realities of Nicaragua.

One of the most important texts of the second stage is vanguardist José Román's *Maldito país*, a "proto-testimonio" and bildungsroman rather than a true novel (Beverley and Zimmerman 179). It follows the resistance leader Augusto Sandino in the mountains in February of 1933 as he fights to oust the Americans from his country. Román, a journalist, composed the text based on interviews with Sandino at the time but did not publish it until 1983. Sandino had initiated the contact because he understood the power of the written word to gain the world's attention in order to denounce the abuses of U.S. imperialism.

At times Román reminds us of an ethnographer taking note of the strange ways of the natives (102). Far from an "objective reporter," however, he praises Sandino for being one of the few Nicaraguans of his era to defend the rights of the Miskitos and Zambos of the Atlantic coast, to civilize them, and to incorporate them into national life (104–5). Sandino's men also impress Román. After observing their hardships and dedication, he is convinced of their moral and physical superiority, the purity of their motives, and the justness of their cause. Román leaves the mountains a changed man himself. To endure the rigors of the jungle, Román writes that "you have to be a real man and have real balls to put up with this" (152). He is a precursor of Cabezas's "new man."

Following Sandino's assassination on February 11, 1934 (shortly after the United States exited Nicaragua), by National Guard troops under Anastasio Somoza García, Román refused to edit and complete his text. He explained that he wanted to honor Sandino's wishes that the book be published first in Nicaragua. Postrevolutionary Nicaragua recovered the text, which in many ways reconstructs and narrates the origins of the new

Nicaragua by contributing to the myth of the hero Sandino. The text also served as a model for the modern testimonio, which enjoyed hegemonic status following the 1979 Sandinista revolution.

Another vanguardist, Manolo Cuadra, who helped found the Partido Socialista Nacional (Communists), wrote some of the earliest testimonies in Nicaragua, especially significant because they filled a void in *narrativa social* (Ramírez 1976, 13). In *Itinerario de Little Corn Island* (1936), he narrates the adventures of his own political activism and imprisonment, and his *Contra Sandino en la montaña* (1945) documents the experiences of Sandino and the peasant rebellions of 1926–33.

His writing shares territory with that of Román. Manolo Cuadra's work is of special significance as it reflects his distancing from fellow vanguardists, anticipating the bourgeois vanguardists' split following the 1979 revolution. Greg Dawes describes the instabilities and contradictions among the ideologically heterogeneous vanguardists of the 1920s and 1930s: while Sandino's peasant rebellion was not quite compatible with the political and aesthetic ideology of the vanguardists, his nationalism and his posture vis-à-vis U.S. intervention were indeed (37). For a time nationalism was the "tie that binds." But writers such as Pablo Antonio Cuadra and Coronel Urtecho moved toward the extreme right while in the end Manolo Cuadra and his friend, the poet Joaquín Pasos—after an early fleeting attraction to fascism—pursued the opposite course.

At the same time, a few writers practiced social realism. The best-known example of the genre in Nicaragua, *Bananos: La vida de los peones en las bananeras* (1942) by Emilio Quintana, both attacks the exploitative United Fruit Company in Central America and reveals the deep, nationalistic pride of the narrator. Early and mid-twentieth century writers like Quintana and the vanguardists forged a strong nationalism that separated the beloved native Nicaragua from the ugly reality that consumed it. The social-realist cycle came to a close in the mid-1950s. By and large, the novel stagnated until the late 1960s.

At the same time, the prestigious vanguardist writers Pablo Antonio Cuadra, Coronel Urtecho, Cardenal, and others founded a cultural journal, *El pez y la serpiente* (1961). In their search for a national literature, they privileged poetry (Darío, the modernistas, and the vanguardists), the essay, the short story, and a few short novels. Ileana Rodríguez writes that, at first, the scope of the journal was valid "but very partial, sectarian, and elitist, within a national context of a high illiteracy rate" (1986, 10). Ideologically, the group espoused nationalism, Catholicism, and anticapitalism. They favored an idealized, mythologized indigenismo in the formation of an autochthonous Nicaraguan nation; thus, they validated folkloric and native literature by subsuming it into "superior" (Western) art forms. Rodríguez judges this posture to be paternalistic albeit well-intentioned: "The writer is still shut up in his study: he creates a landscape and he speaks inventing it, taking it from other books. He invents the peasant and makes him appear to be 'the national soul.' The Indian is the landscape, the folklore, a business of the spirit" (1986, 50). For Rodríguez this approach belongs to nineteenth-century costumbrismo. Ramírez compares it to European Orientalism (1976, 11) and criticizes the objectification of the Indian. Arellano, on the other hand, finds an overall positive contribution from the vanguardia: "It achieved . . . a rebirth of the national in which our culture was defined and benefited . . . it gave a firm impulse to the development of the Nicaraguan nationality" (1982, 83). Perhaps this stance with regard to the Indian did sharpen the definition of a Nicaraguan nationalism, as Arellano maintains, but in my opinion it did so at the expense of the indigenous people who tended, at the stroke of the pen, to become folkloric caricatures or fictional representations of some artistic desire. The national self-definition still remained exclusive. At any rate, these differences, along with those already mentioned, would contribute to the split over ideological differences in the 1979 revolution.

Third Stage

Meanwhile, other tendencies were at work. In the aftermath of the student massacre at León and the Cuban revolution, both occurring in 1959, many writers turned their attention to urban problems. El Frente Ventana, the literary counterpart of the FSLN (Sandinista National Liberation Front) formed in 1961, believed that the poet should commit him- or herself to the struggle for liberation. Ventana met plenty of resistance, especially from the bourgeois Generación Traicionada, a group oriented more toward foreign cultural forms than toward native ones, a stance Arellano finds "irresponsible . . . out of touch with national reality" (1982, 80). Later the Grupo Gradas emerged from the tragedy of the earthquake that rocked Managua in December 1972 and issued a manifesto equating the struggle for culture to the struggle for social change; they rejected "the commercialization of the intellectual or artistic work and classist literature; equally, foreign meddling in our culture, proposing [instead] the full participation of the popular sectors in its programs and activities and the implementation and support for every cultural current which would be within the reach of the people" (Arellano 1982, 84). They set the stage for the emergence of popular literary forms—notably poetry—and for the development of testimony as an authentic expression of the marginalized and excluded sectors of society.

Testimony. The texts that follow have as their historical referent the turbulent years of FSLN activity leading up to the 1979 revolution. (Most of these testimonies could not be published until after that date.)

In a mediated testimony, FSLN leader Doris Tijerino tells her story in *"Somos millones . . . "* (1977) to Margaret Randall, who first published it in Mexico. As a respected female cadre, Tijerino offers a strong feminist perspective and underlines the triple exploitation of women in Nicaragua by capitalism, imperialism, and machismo (7). Shouldering more than a woman's traditional responsibilities during war, working to free political prisoners, and advocating for children's rights, Tijerino gains a complete picture of herself as an equal to any man. Her defense of society's victims extends to the black population of the country, which has suffered racial discrimination, and even to members of the National Guard's lower ranks, who, for lack of better employment opportunities, have been manipulated into killing their fellow citizens.

Among other testimonies of the years of Sandinista struggle, we find Carlos José Guadamuz's *Y . . . "Las casas quedaron llenas de humo"* (1982), which traces the life of one of the fallen heroes of a military action on July 15, 1969. Although he disclaims any literary pretensions, Guadamuz's testimony reads like an epic as he creates the legend of Julio Buitrago, who died fighting single-handedly against tanks and hundreds of National Guard troops. He expands the legend also to glorify the courageous women of the struggle. The heteroclitic text ends with pen-and-ink sketches and poetry composed by other imprisoned Sandinistas. Likewise disclaiming artistic intent, Roberto Fernández Retamar writes in the now-famous preface to Tomás Borge's *Carlos, el amanecer ya no es una tentación* (1982): "This writer is as much an author as García Márquez is a refrigerator salesman." Many critics, however, have praised Borge's literary capabilities and his adaptation of elements of nueva narrativa to the mode of testimonio. Written in prison like many others, this testimony documents the life of Carlos Fonseca, FSLN cofounder and martyr. What I find interesting here is the alternation of a Marxist social discourse with Christian imagery and metaphor, evidence of the important role liberation theology played in the revolution. Omar Cabezas's well-known testimony, *La montaña es algo más que una inmensa estepa verde* (1982), recounts his transformation during the 1960s and 1970s from a middle-class student in León to a revolutionary "nuevo hombre" (new man), one who finds himself suddenly in a position of power after the 1979 triumph. Hugo Achugar notes that the text need no longer promise future deliverance; rather, it performs the transformation, and the subject becomes invincible (1987, 282–83). The new man is born from his period of preparation in the mountains, a time of suffering, sacrifice, and self-denial. He becomes part of a concrete reality emerging from a dialectic of historical forces. For Beverley and Zimmerman this text is a speech-act (186). Julio Cortázar has praised Cabezas's language: "It's evident that the language of the book which is as much oral as it is written (something which is rare) creates in the reader an immediate relationship with you as both author and protagonist of the story" (quoted in Osses, 162). With an inclusive message and an appeal for Indian support, Cabezas invokes the name of the historical Subtiavan Indian leader, Adiac, incarnated in Sandino. (The same was done in poetry by Leonel Rugama.) Other important pre-victory prison testimonies include those written by Daniel Ortega and Ricardo Morales-Aviles.

Testimonial Novel.—Let us now turn our attention to the development of testimonial discourse and function in the novel, which occurred simultaneously with the production of the texts discussed above. The publication of Lisandro Chávez Alfaro's *Trágame tierra* in 1969 marks a turning point in Nicaraguan narrative with its incorporation of Boom-style techniques. Ileana Rodríguez notes the mixture of historical discourses—that of the chronicler, the popular singer, the transcriber-copyist, and the journalist—with nineteenth-century romantic and criollista literary tendencies juxtaposed against a twentieth-century critical dialectics (1985, 86–87). With *Trágame tierra* the Nicaraguan novel finally came of age. Arellano considers it "the best work of its kind, if we understand by 'best' the most complete narrative, the most conscious novelistic structure and the most effective interpretation of Nicaraguan reality" (1982, 138). The setbacks and failures of the FSLN in the late 1960s provide the backdrop for this novel. Chávez Alfaro tells the story of a father and son, Plutarco and Luciano Pineda, whose differences not only attest to a generation gap within their family but also configure the conflict at a national level. Whereas the primary plot exposes national conflicts, a secondary plot introduces questions of the Other. A homosexual transvestite, "la Viqui," receives frank treatment from the author, who, much like Guatemalan writers of the same period, approaches questions of sexuality head-on. A tragic ending reinforces the denunciation of Nicaraguan reality.

The short-story writer Sergio Ramírez, who was Nicaragua's vice-presi-

dent under the Sandinista government, published his most highly acclaimed novel, *¿Te dio miedo la sangre?*, in 1977 just before the revolution.
In it he creates a panorama of the Somoza years in a dictator novel without
the dictator. This Boom-style narrative challenges the reader to follow six
interwoven but separate plot threads as Ramírez re-creates Nicaraguan
society, especially the more colorful, less savory, or less fortunate aspects of
it. Beverley and Zimmerman find that the myriad of narrators create the
illusion that they are all telling their own stories directly rather than
through one narrator (182), precisely a key element of testimonial discourse. Guerrillas, exiles, National Guardsmen, bartenders, musicians, prostitutes, defrauded political has-beens, Miss Nicaragua, campesinos, street
vendors—all populate Ramírez's narrative, which he punctuates with black
humor: a doctor's prized possession is a jar of Rubén Darío's brains; nuns
raffle off orphan girls to good Catholic families who come to their Sunday
charity sweepstakes; Colonel López gets caught with his pants down at a
Managua brothel. The novel ends on a bleak note with no victory in sight.

Kathryn Kelly observes that Ramírez demystifies both Somocistas and
Sandinistas by unveiling the myths that surround both; while the first
group creates its own self-glorifying myths, the people create the myth of
the second group in their need to escape an ugly reality. In the end, "all are
mortal. Nobody is a god on the earth" (214–15). Claudia Schaefer finds a
note of hope, however, in the title itself. She asks, "Doesn't blood signify
life as well as death?" (151). Heroes may no longer exist, but perhaps
ordinary people can forge new life out of past bloodshed.

Fourth Stage

Whether testimony can retain its vitality is questionable now that the
political emergency has passed. With the electoral victory of the anti-
Sandinista coalition in 1990, testimonial discourse may follow new directions dependent on ideological shifts and concrete experience.

The political, social, economic, and cultural context for literature has
thus changed dramatically between *¿Te dio miedo la sangre?* and Ramírez's
newest novel, *Castigo divino* (1988). Since the vanguardist movement,
Nicaraguan writers have been searching for a national identity and art
forms to express it. The revolution of 1979 officially recognized that art can
no longer be the property of a privileged few but must belong to all. Ernesto
Cardenal, minister of culture under the Sandinista government, describes
the overall cultural project as "the democratization of culture." Nicaraguans sought not only political independence from foreign (particularly

U.S.) domination but cultural independence as well. Ramírez once re-marked sardonically that Nicaraguans were tired of the mountains of *Reader's Digests*—in his opinion the best example of U.S. cultural medioc-rity—that used to be shipped to them each month (Steven White, 6). The revolution stopped that flow. The new dominant ideology also announced that artistic creation alone was not enough; it had to serve the revolution. The literacy crusade, the efforts to publish books at inexpensive prices, and the poetry workshops (*los talleres*) grew out of the new project. The chapter on Belli will discuss the conflict that arose among the Sandinista leadership regarding the workshops, especially among the women.

Pablo Antonio Cuadra, editor of the opposition newspaper *La Prensa*, who once had allied himself with the more militant practitioners of Sandino nationalism and then moved to the right, believes that, once installed in power, the Sandinistas betrayed their mandate to establish democracy and freedom. He wrote: "We are going the wrong way from the cultural point of view, when an ideology must impose itself, with the negation of freedom and criticism, the essential elements of the creation of culture" (1985, 117–18). Cuadra complains that by practicing censorship and proclaiming that art is worthless unless the common worker can understand it, the revolu-tionary government is moving culture to the lowest common denominator instead of educating the people to understand it at a higher level.

Ramírez, on the other hand, defends the Sandinista cultural project stating that the revolution was laying the foundations for a new culture "with lots of creative freedom, without dogmatism, without sectarianism, encouraging freedom which is the very dynamic of the revolution" (Marga-ret Randall, 40). His defense is at odds with Cuadra's protest against sup-posed strict prescriptions for literature and art. Cuadra's conflict with the Sandinista cultural program crystallizes the problem posed by testimony, a discourse traditionally devalued by more polished literary voices. Can the voice of the Other make itself heard and respected in the presence of powerful institutionalized discourses, or are the two mutually exclusive?

Ramírez moves in a new direction with his postrevolutionary novel *Castigo divino*. Seymour Menton classifies this text as a "new historical novel" (1993, 3) because its referent is a more removed past than what one finds typically in documentaries or testimonies; the loss of immediacy creates a more escapist, less engaged tone. In his novel, Ramírez recreates the hypocritical bourgeois milieu of León in the 1930s but also takes his reader all over Central America.

The narrative operates on several levels—the familial, the national, and the regional. It poses the question of how far each entity will go in order to protect its vested interests. The reader follows the efforts of the prosecution to build a legal case against a man who is accused of poisoning his wife, his lover, and her father. Ramírez constructs the plot—which resembles a "whodunit" mystery of a detective novel—through a series of court depositions, documents, letters, and testimony by witnesses and the accused, all connected by third-person narration. The reading becomes tedious as we witness the same crime through a multiplicity of narrators—nevertheless a rather ingenious twist in the adaptation of testimonial discourse. The truth, however, becomes more complicated rather than more clear. The voices represented in *Castigo divino* are no longer the "voices from below," which have characterized testimony to this point. In keeping with the argument presented above, I would question whether *Castigo divino* is accessible to "the masses." Ideologically, it falls within the boundaries of the revolution; stylistically, formally, and linguistically, it is obviously the work of a highly educated mind and may prove difficult for someone who lacks appropriate training.

A group of texts that need to be mentioned includes what Beverley and Zimmerman call the "neo-testimonios . . . texts based on testimonial materials, but very much controlled and worked up by an author with explicitly literary goals" (186). Among others written in the late 1980s, Gioconda Belli's *La mujer habitada* (1988), which I examine in Chapter 6, falls into this category.

Nicaraguan novels and testimony since the late 1960s through the period of the revolution have concerned themselves with the formation of a national-popular narrative in order to rewrite history and to penetrate its complex reality. This interest marks a continuation of the attempts by writers of the 1930s to liberate culture, as well as society, and to find, to create, and to celebrate that which is authentically Nicaraguan. Only recently, with the publication of Ramírez's *Castigo divino,* has the novel moved beyond the national boundaries to include the rest of Central America in a panorama of interrelated tragedies.

El Salvador

A history of military, political, social, and economic repression has stunted the development of the novel in El Salvador, the smallest and most densely populated country of the Central American isthmus. At the same time, repression has provided plenty of material for personal and political testimony.

If Luis Alberto Sánchez once called Latin America "a novel without novelists" (quoted in Toruño 392), El Salvador is the metaphor incarnate. Juan Felipe Toruño remarks that while El Salvador has much to novelize, "what has been missing . . . has been the desire, the dynamic, the love in order to cultivate the genre" (394). His judgment, I believe, falls short; it lacks a critical awareness of environments that can favor or discourage literary production, especially that of a genre like the novel.

Like its neighbor Nicaragua and in large part Guatemala, El Salvador has suffered from a dearth of readers because of high rates of illiteracy, an almost nonexistent internal market for books and thus few publishing houses, censorship of written literature and the mass media, threats to writers who challenge the system, and the departure of most committed writers into exile. Moreover, the fact that Salvadoran writers generally have been unable to make a living from literature, and instead have to supplement their incomes with other employment, leaves them very little time for any literary pursuit, much less the long hours needed to write a novel. It takes more than authorial desire to make a novel in El Salvador.

Other factors conspire against it as well. Borgeson observes that "literature has been, all too often, an escape from national life: a false and dangerous refuge in the picturesquely romanticized countryside and the unrecognizably idealized *campesino*" (517). While poetry has fared better, the novel in El Salvador developed only in this century.

In presenting an overview of the novel and testimony in El Salvador, I will approach Salvadoran literary history in four stages. First were early attempts at the costumbrista and precriollista novels dating from 1895 to the mid-1920s; important names from this period include Ambrogi, Gavidia, Guevara Valdés, Delgado, and Leiva. Following that were the years of the 1920s to 1940, a period of ferment, violence, and the Matanza; Masferrer and Farabundo Martí are the two most prominent thinker-politicians from this era, while Salarrué dominates Salvadoran narrative. A contemporary is Claudia Lars, the first major female poet in Central America, who later wrote narrative as well. The third period, from 1940 to the mid-1960s, was distinguished by the criollista and social-realist period of González Montalvo, Rodríguez Ruíz, Castro, and Martínez. The last stage, from the mid-1960s to the present, is marked by renovation; prominent writers include López, Alegría, Escobar Galindo, Mendoza, and Lobato. Members of the social-activist writers of the Generación Comprometida included Cea, Lanzas de Chápez Muñoz, Argueta, Armijo, and López Vallecillos, while the Círculo Literario Universitario gave El Salvador its best-known poet, the iconoclast Roque Dalton. During this time, writers experimented with nueva narrativa and testimonio. Names associated with testimony include Mármol (mediated by Dalton), Cayetano Carpio, and Martínez.

European-style culture came late to El Salvador. The conquistadors, most notably the Alvarado brothers, wrote several accounts. The colonial period produced few narratives with the exception of moral and ecclesiastical histories, didactic texts, and lives of saints written by clergy.

First Stage

Certain citizens began to publish newspapers actively after 1840. Others established the University of El Salvador in 1841 although they could not open its doors for several years for lack of funds. In 1871 the Biblioteca Nacional was founded, and the increased interest and availability of books led to the formation of the first scientific-literary society, "la Juventud," dedicated to the renovation of romanticism and to the introduction of modernismo.

The initiator of the precriollista novel in El Salvador was in fact a short-story writer, Arturo Ambrogi (Acevedo 1982, 342). In 1895 he published *Cuentos y fantasías*, a glimpse at the harsh conditions of the campesino's life complete with examples of his crude language. Francisco Gavidia, the most prominent of all literary figures in El Salvador at the time and a friend of Rubén Darío, experimented in both narrative and poetry. Antonio Guevara Valdés and Manuel Delgado were among the first writers actually to attempt novels; the latter's *Roca Celis* (1906–8) merits Acevedo's designation (1982, 130) as the first Salvadoran novel although it resembles more a legal treatise than novelistic discourse. José Leiva wrote *El indio* (n.d.) about the morally and intellectually exceptional Indian Juan, who faces much discrimination despite his accomplishments: "The work poses the problem of racial prejudices and the separation of castes, but it is also distinguished by its costumbrista pictures which confer upon it a peasant flavor" (Acevedo 1982, 131). These texts did not enjoy huge success. In general, realism and naturalism were forbidden currents in Salvadoran literature of the early twentieth century. Borgeson mentions a certain Juan Montalvo Society that worked to heighten awareness of social issues among Salvadoran readers (521). But activism met with official government resistance and punishment.

Second Stage

The world plunged into the Great Depression in the late 1920s and 1930s, and El Salvador saw prices of coffee, its main export crop, tumble. As the labor movement coalesced worldwide, its agitation spread to Central America.

Socialist theoretician, essayist, orator, and journalist Alberto Masferrer took up the cause of the campesino, who especially suffered as a result of the falling coffee prices. Toruño calls Masferrer the "voice of justice" (207); Gallegos Valdés describes him as "the defender of the working classes" (99). Masferrer's writing covers many periods and movements from romanticism and modernismo to the vanguardia, and it encompasses both prose and poetry. He campaigned in 1929–30 for the election of Arturo Araujo to the Salvadoran presidency. Araujo won the office by a sizeable majority in March 1931, only to be overthrown the following December by the military strongman Maximiliano Hernández Martínez, who had the blessings of the United States government. In January 1932 the Salvadoran Communist leader Agustín Farabundo Martí called for a peasant-worker rebellion in defiance of the coup. Hernández Martínez crushed the revolt within forty-eight hours, massacring over thirty thousand Indian peasants in the western part of the country near Sonsonate. Masferrer, completely demoralized, was forced into exile.

In a concerted effort to wipe out any trace of the "Matanza of 1932," as it has come to be known, elites in league with the military rulers ordered that all newspaper and other accounts of the events be destroyed. This modus operandi has served as a model for the official repression of all succeeding subversive expression since then (McClintock 100). Alegría refers to this "silence" and her difficulty in finding information about the Matanza as she pieced together the events for her novel, *Cenizas de Izalco* (interview 1991). Official denial has not expunged the Matanza from the popular memory, though; it has remained the galvanizing moment of the national conscience and a point of departure for current protest literature.

At the time, however, writers could ill afford to broach the subject directly. Although his narrative establishes no direct historical referent, Salvador Salazar Arrué, or Salarrué as he is better known, composed many short stories and novels that are saturated with violence. Many critics consider Salarrué, a member of the Generation of 1920, to be "the first modern Central American writer to develop a major narrative voice" (Beverley and Zimmerman 119). Even though he and Claudia Lars were writing at the same time as other vanguardists in Latin America, they did not belong to the movement "for reasons of form and style" (Borgeson 523). Best known for his *Cuentos de barro* (1927) and *Cuentos de cipotes* (1928),[4] Salarrué bridges the gap between costumbrista realism, magical realism, and regionalism. He draws his characters from the humble of the earth, replicates their rustic vernacular, and simultaneously paints the Salvadoran countryside. In *Cuentos de barro*, Salarrué likens himself to a potter working with clay, making realistic little figures of animals and people and shaping them with harsh, rhythmical slaps of the hand. After firing them in the oven, he pulls out some that are a bit crude and twisted, scraped and cracked; others come out whole, still others in pieces (8). His realism is often quite lyrical and metaphorical.

Perhaps Salarrué's most important legacy to Salvadoran literature is the masterful incorporation of indigenous and peasant slang into his texts. Indeed, Roberto Armijo finds that the use of the vernacular was Salarrué's way of exalting the indigenous people whose way of life he saw threatened by an unfriendly government (386). Roque Dalton would inherit this love of spoken language, brilliantly weaving it through poems and later testimonial writings, such as *Miguel Mármol* (1971) and culminating in *Las historias prohibidas del pulgarcito* (1974). After Dalton, Manlio Argueta also turned to the expressive idiom of the peasants in order to capture voices of rural El Salvador.

Salarrué wrote several novels that, while they do not equal his short stories in critical acclaim, have exerted a major influence on contemporary Salvadoran novelists. In the first, *El cristo negro* (1927), Salarrué subtly exposes the contradictions of culture—especially with respect to religious beliefs and practices—which were born at the Conquest with the imposition of one culture on another. With humor, irony, and paradox, Salarrué suggests that the good (Spanish) are actually evil, and the evil (Indians) good. The Other obviously interests Salarrué, but his cannot be considered a literature of overt protest or resistance.

Third Stage

The major Salvadoran novelists who followed Salarrué shared his love for the land and rural life but not the philosophical approach he developed later. Writers of the Generation of 1940 and particularly poets of the Grupo Seis (1940–41) expressed more militantly their social and political goals to "fight for what is human, raise the conditions of man who is subjected to poverty to the level of the person who is somewhat comfortable in life: a rebirth of the idea of the *minimum vital* of Masferrer" (Gallegos Valdés 371). They believed that aesthetics must be wedded to a social message. This conviction inaugurated the criollista period of the late 1940s and the 1950s in El Salvador—much later than the criollista novel in other parts of Latin America and another anachronism so characteristic of Central American letters.

Ramón González Montalvo, the major criollista novelist of this period and a student of Ambrogi, called attention to the simultaneous violence and beauty of the rural world. In his first novel, *Las Tinajas* (1950), he interpolates many tales of Salvadoran folklore, such as "la Siguanaba" and "el Sembrerón," into the main narrative, imitating rustic speech patterns and colloquialisms after the fashion of Salarrué. (These stories would surface again in the popular imagination of the 1970s and 1980s.) Acevedo credits González Montalvo with a successful representation of and identification with the Indian (1982, 351). Less picturesque and more brutal, González Montalvo's second novel, *Barbasco* (1960), emphasizes the collective struggle of the peons against the *latifundista* in the manner of the social realist and indigenista novels of Icaza, Ciro Alegría, and Amaya Amador (Acevedo 1982, 354). The author denounces injustice, especially sexual exploitation, perpetrated by cruel and powerful characters, both men and women. Acevedo has praised González Montalvo's ability to avoid exotic, picturesque, or idealized portraits of campesinos (1982, 363).

A contemporary of González Montalvo, Napoleón Rodríguez Ruíz published *Jaraguá*, a criollista and costumbrista novel, in 1950. Flirtations, love triangles, *cuestiones de amor*, threats of suicide over unrequited love, peripeteia, and anagnorisis combine to make this novel more an anachronistic romance than an example of social realism. Rodríguez Ruíz creates a world populated with landowners and peons who get along, men who worship their women, and Indians who face their destiny stoically.

Other criollista novels of interest include Carlo Antonio Castro's *Los hombres verdaderos* (1959). The author, an anthropologist and expert in Mayan languages, develops the theme of indigenous wisdom and traditions. Finally, social worker and writer Yolanda C. Martínez examines racial issues in two novels, *Sus fríos ojos azules* (1964) and *Corazón indio* (1967).

Fourth Stage

A member of Grupo Seis and of the Asociación de Escritores Antifascistas— an organization that included González Montalvo and Gallegos Valdés and opposed the politics of Maximiliano Hernández Martínez—the Salvadoran critic and theorist Matilde Elena López signaled the changes about to occur in the Central American novel. In her *Interpretación social del arte* (1965) she documents a revitalized realism: "Formal resources of the modern novel such as the interior monologue and the discontinuity of time are increasingly integrated in the realistic novel constructed just a few years ago to conform to classic canons" (quoted in Gallegos Valdés 375). The novel

Cenizas de Izalco (1966) by Claribel Alegría and her husband, Darwin J. Flakoll, is an example of the new mode described by López. Its historical referent is the Matanza of 1932. (I discuss this text further in Chapter 3.) Alegría never affiliated with any one literary generation or group; she emerged alone between the Grupo Seis and the Generación Comprometida. More examples of the renovated novel include those by David Escobar Galindo, Miguel Cobos, María Elena Mendoza, and Carlos Lobato.

The iconoclast Generación Comprometida coalesced in 1956, following "one guide: Neruda; one problem: the social" (Gallegos Valdés 415). The social function of literature interested them, not art for art's sake. Born in the 1930s, these writers were entering adolescence when explosive events of 1944 awoke their political consciences (the October revolution in Guatemala; the coup against Hernández Martínez in El Salvador). López Vallecillos describes the group's credo: "The work of art necessarily must serve, must be useful to today's man. . . . Literary movements which have had as their formula the writing of much in order to say nothing, have fondled words, and have diminished the value of the high content of the letter" (quoted in Toruño 427). A member of the Generación, José Roberto Cea, explains the importance of leaving a testimony to "the concrete historical moment in which the creator was being developed" (quoted in Osses 129). Group members also dedicated themselves to resisting the imitation of foreign models and to developing their own; all genres awaited their renovation.

In his critical appraisal of the Generación Comprometida, Toruño described the group's members as young and impetuous, dogmatic in their own right, impulsive, and in need of maturity—as if to say "boys will be boys." But he admitted (1957, 430) that it was too early to judge them. The Generación Comprometida included Cea, Irma Lanzas de Chápez Muñoz, Manlio Argueta, Roberto Armijo, and López Vallecillos, among others. Some of them concurrently joined Dalton to form the Círculo Literario Universitario Salvadoreño, which shared many of the same philosophical and political theories about literature and that still exists today.

Testimony. Modern Salvadoran testimony fits ideologically into this current. The mediated testimony of Miguel Mármol by Dalton and the unmediated accounts by Cayetano Carpio and Ana Guadalupe Martínez offer perhaps the best-known examples.

Dalton interviewed Mármol, a founder of the Salvadoran Communist Party and a survivor of the Matanza of 1932, in Prague in 1966 and published his testimony in 1971. Mármol's life, as it unfolded during the first half of this century, paralleled that of the Salvadoran working class. The relationship of interlocutor to witness is problematic, as we have seen, and Dalton recognized the challenges.[5] An educated, accomplished writer himself, he acknowledged the temptation to reshape the narrative with stylistic uniformity but hesitated because the person giving the testimony did not organize his account in that way (1982, 31). Like many other mediators of testimony, Dalton assures us within the text that he has faithfully transcribed Mármol's words and has done so in the colorful, idiomatic expressions of everyday El Salvador.[6] Dalton poses the theoretical problem of "novelizing testimony" because what truly interests him is not simply "reflecting" reality but "transforming" it (34). In the end what we have is his urbane wit, irreverence, iconoclasm, ideology, and machismo coupled with Mármol's earthiness. As he finishes his story, Mármol further problematizes his own account and, by extension, Dalton's, admitting that what he has given us is only half a disclosure; he still harbors some secrets, a claim similar to Rigoberta Menchú's closing words. If readers expect "the whole truth and nothing but the truth"—the mimetic code and reader contract of testimony—they may be disappointed.

While Mármol represents the classic communist, Dalton is the new militant whose ideology is forged after the Cuban revolution and during the turbulent 1960s. Beverley and Zimmerman explain the conflict: "Dalton, who was educated to be a lawyer, notes his 'natural tendency to complicate things, which bristles seriously at Mármol's tendency to simplify them'." (190) The first purpose of the Mármol testimony is to record an eyewitness version of the events of 1932, hushed up for so long in official annals. But the project does not stop here. Dalton defines his goals as clearly political— to elucidate and denounce reality, to rewrite history, to confirm "the profoundly national character of the Salvadoran revolutionary struggle inspired in Marxism-Leninism" (1982, 33). That Dalton may disagree with Mármol is not the point; Mármol and the organized workers of his day are part of Salvadoran history. For Dalton, identifying Mármol and like-minded individuals is necessary because there is no rallying, mythical figure like Nicaragua's Sandino to define El Salvador. These historic events informed Dalton's own decision to advocate and participate in the armed struggle for national liberation.

Besides Dalton's *Mármol,* the unmediated testimonies by Cayetano Carpio and Ana Guadalupe Martínez represent other important accounts of the period. Salvador Cayetano Carpio, a baker and union organizer, and later a guerrilla commander, wrote *Secuestro y capucha* about his imprisonment for politically subversive activities in the 1950s during the Osorio dictatorship. His interest in the peasant turned guard is shared by fellow Salvadoran Manlio Argueta, as we shall see, and by Guatemalans Arias and Vásquez.

Ana Guadalupe Martínez of the ERP (People's Revolutionary Army) wrote *Las cárceles clandestinas de El Salvador* (1978) following her release from jail in a prisoner exchange. In her text, apologies for artistic short-comings no longer matter; in fact, "literariness" has become a liability. Literary pretensions are not a necessity of the revolution but rather part of the petit bourgeois theory and fiction of the revolution (15–16). Her mention of the "petit bourgeois" may be a veiled reference to Dalton and a reaction against his cultivated style of writing. Dalton was murdered in 1975 as a result of a schism within the ERP. In her testimony, Martínez seems to be waging war on two fronts: against the government and against dissident party factions.

While the three texts just presented illustrate the various characteristics of testimony as it has been written recently in El Salvador and elsewhere, they are limited to representing only a few of the voices of the Other: the woman, the worker, and the urban guerrilla. The indigenous peasant figures only obliquely in Mármol's testimony and not at all in the other two. Guatemalan and Nicaraguan testimonies—especially those of Menchú and Tijerino—do incorporate Indian and peasant voices to a greater degree. Salvadoran novelist Manlio Argueta fills in that gap with his most recent work.

Testimony, the Novel, and Poetry. The experimentation with narrative that began in *Miguel Mármol* leads Dalton in several directions. His work will influence or parallel developments in Alegría's and Argueta's testimonial novels.

Dalton's *Pobrecito poeta que era yo,* written over a ten-year period and published posthumously in 1976, is what Armijo has called "an open novel" (388)—that is, it blurs genre lines. I see it as both a bildungsroman and as a Boom-style novel. What the novel gains in aesthetic qualities it loses in immediacy; it is only marginally testimonial. In this text, thought to be partly autobiographical, the narrators pose the question of what it means to be a poet in El Salvador today. (The historical referent is the 1960s and early 1970s.) Narrative voice is fragmented as are space and time. Ariel Dorfman calls this fragmentation "narrative violence" (in Acevedo 1986, 75), a testimony to the internal violence racking the poet and the external violence afflicting Salvadoran society. We will see a similar angst regarding the writer's relationship to his or her society in all four writers who are studied in this book.

Another of Dalton's literary experimentations, *Las historias prohibidas del pulgarcito* (1974), is a fragmented collage of poems and prose poems, newspaper clippings, advertisements, obituaries, proverbs, songs, and other selections, again attempting to "construct" the nation. I mention it here because, even though it appeared before *Pobrecito poeta,* many critics consider it Dalton's most creative and important work. The chaotic presentation, ironies, and contradictions "[make] fun of the effort to construct a monolithic national narrative" by decentering canonical linear histories (Beverley and Zimmerman 132). It approximates more the discourses of Boom writing and less the straightforward presentations of testimonio. Militant, antidogmatic, and demystifying, Dalton's text criticizes the totalitarian (utopian, paternalistic) Left as much as it does the bourgeoisie. It is, in part, a continuation of his attack on the old Left, begun in Miguel Mármol, and on the ideological divisions that were destroying its effectiveness in the struggle. *Las historias prohibidas* also presents Dalton's vision of the nation, which is more inclusive and realistic, less nostalgic and idealizing than hegemonic versions. In "Poema de amor" from *Las historias prohibidas,* the poetic "I" addresses the nation, a motley assortment of hardly ideal types: thieves, contrabandists, the hungry, peasants, artisans, drunks, beggars, "los hijos de la gran puta" (children of the grand whore), and "los eternos indocumentados, / los hacelotodo, los vendelotodo, los comelotodo" (511) (the eternal undocumented, the do-it-alls, the sell-it-alls, the eat-it-alls). He urges them to unite, despite their differences, in armed insurrection against the powers that oppress them.

The trend we see in Dalton's work also indicates what was happening to other writers of El Salvador. Armijo notes the shift from poetry to prose and the pastiche-collage: as poetry attempted to rescue history, myth, and "our collectivity," it found its rhythms fairly inflexible and could not obtain the profundity and extension of its intentions" (387). Narrative and the novel, with its seemingly infinite discourses, extended the possibilities.

Following Dalton's death, we find a move away from his sophisticated (elitist, in the opinion of unashamedly "antiliterary" writers such as Martínez) style. Cea, especially in poetry, and Argueta shift their gaze to the campesino. They and Alegría "feminize" the struggle, incorporating testimonies from Salvadoran women and certainly surpassing Dalton in this regard.

Unlike Nicaragua, El Salvador has no postrevolutionary stage per se. Like its northern neighbor, Guatemala, El Salvador has experienced the frustration of its popular insurgencies and a war-weariness that has settled over its devastated towns and countryside. Well ahead of Guatemala, however, El Salvador is moving slowly but steadily to demilitarize itself and to accommodate and incorporate the disaffected Left into the democratic project.[7] It appears that the UN-brokered peace accords of 1991 have affected the literary, cultural, and political climate that gave rise to testimony and the testimonial novel. So have the demise of the Soviet Union, the defeat of the FSLN in Nicaragua, and a less aggressive U.S. foreign policy. The emergency has passed and with it this stage of resistance literature. To be sure, there is still much rebuilding to do, land to be distributed, jobs to be created. Old antagonisms remain, but we can express a cautious optimism at hopeful signs of reconciliation and healing.

3

Claribel Alegría

Family Ties/Political Lies

We begin our look at specific writers and their texts with Salvadoran writer Claribel Alegría because her work appears first and continues throughout the same periods of political crisis that Argueta, Arias, and Belli have experienced. Like many of her compatriots, Alegría began her literary career as a poet but turned to the novel when poetry no longer sufficed to describe the national reality. Marc Zimmerman has called her one of the "essential forgers" of the poetic system in Central America, "the one who most fully internalizes the work of the women writers who matured prior to the 1960s" (1994, 222). From poetry and autobiography to short stories, novels, and testimonies, Alegría's work does not merely reflect literary trends of the day but rather creates new ones to express the changing realities that surround her, other women, and fellow countrymen.

Born in 1924 in Estelí, Nicaragua, Alegría moved with her family to Santa Ana, El Salvador, when she was still an infant because of political problems plaguing her father, a supporter of the Sandino insurrection. Alegría considers herself a Salvadoran, although the histories of both countries are interwoven throughout her life and her texts. She married North American writer Darwin J. Flakoll, who coauthored some of her novels and translated much of her work into English. Flakoll died in April 1995. Alegría has spent most of her recent life outside El Salvador in self-imposed exile.

The trajectory of Alegría's professional career follows a transformation of consciousness. "The subjectivism that is generally associated with feminine literary discourse [in her early years] is converted to objectivity with regard to an unjust world and identifies with the struggle for rights of the abused underdogs of society" (Acevedo 1992, 20). Margaret B. Crosby pinpoints the mid-1960s as the definitive moment of change for Alegría (26). Her novel *Cenizas de Izalco* (1966), coauthored with Flakoll, heralds her coming to consciousness and signals the beginning of what she has called her "letras de emergencia" (letters of emergency). I would note that Alegría's conversion to social and political activism was not unique for times rocked by worldwide upheaval. Alegría herself has explained her politicization as a result of Castro's victory in Cuba in 1959. Until that time, she had written off Central America as "sin remedio" (hopeless) and doomed to eternal dictatorship. The triumph of Castro gave her hope that reality could be otherwise (interview 1995). The assassination of Salvadoran Archbishop Oscar Romero in 1980 was also decisive, provoking in her feelings of revulsion. Each calamity propelled Alegría on to firmer convictions and hardened her resolve and resistance.

As a child Claribel would write poetry while hiding in her closet—her family thought she was "loca" because she preferred writing to "more feminine" pursuits (interview 1991). At the impressionable age of eight, she witnessed the tragic effects of the 1932 Matanza, which was forever to mark her writing. In my opinion, that moment is the first in a series of defining political crises, each one successively reinforcing the radicalization set in motion by the previous one. Alegría's life and work are a continual processing of that seminal event. That tragedy and the crucial events to follow in El Salvador, Central America, and the Caribbean awakened her sympathies for the victims of injustice, especially women, children, and the poor. Her feelings of solidarity with the voiceless deepened in proportion to her mounting political outrage at oppression. She continued to write love poetry, moving from the intimate expression of a woman in love to the very public declaration of one who loves her people. Writing has been her way to react, to fight back against injustice. Her choice of genres has corresponded to her "conscientization"—from the autobiographical "I" to the collective "we," from the private, the lyrical, the feminine, and the familial, to the public, the testimonial, the feminist, and the political.

For the first forty years of her life Alegría mostly wrote poetry. She claims she belonged to no particular literary group or "generation" in El Salvador. Only one other person, Dora Guerra, began to write poetry at the same time, but she soon disappeared from the literary scene, leaving only a small book of poems. When Alegría arrived in Washington, D.C., in 1944 to attend George Washington University, she studied with the Spanish poet, Nobel laureate Juan Ramón Jiménez, whom she credits with teaching her discipline and with helping select books for her first published collection,

Anillo de silencio (1948). It seems fair to assume that Alegría's work was influenced not only by the master's lyrical warmth and simplicity but also by the melancholy spirit of his elegies and quite possibly by the move toward narrative in the prose poems of his *Platero y yo*. Like Alegría, Jiménez's roots were in an upper-class family; and like her, he expressed great compassion for suffering people.

One is tempted to look for influences among other Salvadoran and Latin American poets. Alegría's favorite Salvadoran woman writer, Claudia Lars, was a friend and classmate of her mother at the Colegio de la Asunción. Alegría notes that she and Lars shared a deep passion for poetry, but that in general Lars's poetry is more classically formal while her own is more colloquial (interview 1995). Deep sensibilities, intense lyricism, tenderness toward children and the dispossessed, and melancholy in the face of death—all of which characterize the writings of Lars—also mark Alegría's.

Several parallels can be drawn between the two writers, although I will resist any temptation to say that Alegría was "influenced" by Lars. In later years, Lars increasingly wrote political poetry (in the context of the 1969 Soccer War with Honduras). One finds a similar alarm in Alegría at the eruption of civil war in El Salvador, the contra war in Nicaragua, and the exacerbation of hostilities by the United States. The tumultuous 1960s were defining years for the two, and here their concerns overlap, although Alegría no longer lived in El Salvador. Both developed a strident antimilitarism, a distaste for what they perceived to be hypocritical values in North American culture, and a distrust of U.S. imperialism. And both express in their writing the problematic nature of their own biculturalism—in Lars's case her Irish and Hispanic heritages; in Alegria's, her transcultural marriage. Lars's preoccupation with *la nueva mujer* (the new woman) "at the center of societal evolution and harassed by the expectations of those around her" (Wycoff 61) is a precursor to Alegría's feminism. While distance of time and place precludes any "cross-fertilization" between the works of Lars and Alegría, similar historical circumstances arising from a culture of violence, machismo, and authoritarianism produce areas of shared thematic interests.

Alegría sees herself primarily alone as a Salvadoran writer. Although she maintained an active correspondence with Roque Dalton, she never knew him personally. Of fellow Salvadoran writers Roberto Armijo and Manlio Argueta, Alegría writes that they have been good friends but are too far apart in age and experience to have been influenced by her work, or she by theirs. She counted Armijo among the members of her social and literary circles in Paris in the early 1960s, which also included Julio Cortázar, Carlos Fuentes (who, by the way, urged her to write the story of La Matanza, which resulted in *Cenizas*), Mario Vargas Llosa, and Mario Benedetti. She met Argueta later and, with him and others, toured the United States in 1985 under the sponsorship of solidarity groups to bring attention to the role of U.S. foreign policy in the problems of Central America. Argueta concurs with Alegría's assessment of her position in Salvadoran letters: "She is unique, completely alone"; her personal and conversational verse is at the opposite end of the spectrum from Dalton's intellectual production (interview 1995).

She does admit to certain other influences outside her homeland and beyond Jiménez and has attributed to poets Emily Dickinson, Walt Whitman, T. S. Eliot, and Robinson Jeffers the colloquial tone that she has adapted to her verse (Namer 41). Alegría especially admires the work of Peruvian poet César Vallejo and acknowledges his contribution to her own. She has learned much from his "manipulation of the word: he turned it, loved it, crushed it" (interview 1995).

Highlights of Alegría's politically conscious poetry include *Sobrevivo* (1978), which won the Casa de las Américas prize; the bilingual edition of *Flores del volcán* (1982) translated by Carolyn Forché and widely read by North American students; and *Mujer del río* (1987), translated by Darwin Flakoll, which combines poetry and the testimony of peasant women eyewitnesses to lament the Sumpul River massacre of 1980 and other similar tragedies. She and Flakoll also edited and translated a bilingual anthology of poems by revolutionaries fighting in her country's struggle, *On the Front Line: Guerrilla Poems of El Salvador* (1989).

Moving to Alegría's narratives, we find a subtle blend of the autobiographical and the testimonial. The young woman from a provincial bourgeois family matures through the experience of political and cultural exile. Her militancy and feminism grow as she witnesses the nightmarish events of twentieth-century El Salvador unfold. While her life and career may indeed be exemplary, focusing on the "I" at a time like the present in El Salvador would appear egocentric, irrelevant, and immoral. Conventional autobiography simply cannot adequately relate the oppression of her people or the marginalization of women by a patriarchal and militaristic oligarchy. Testimonial discourse offers her a way to include voices of the community.

Doris Sommer has studied the nature of both autobiography and testimony by female writers and concludes that the basic difference between the two is the "testimonial's insistence on showing relationships" while autobiography remains focused on "one isolated being speaking for other isolated readers, not for a community" (1988, 129). The insistence on relationships is a major goal of women's testimony: "to raise the reader's consciousness by linking her to the writer's testimony" (Sommer 1988, 130). Along with the other goals of testimony, such as the denunciation of injustice and the recovery of a lost popular history, Alegría's novels—some more than others—explore the gender relationships within the Salvadoran family, gender and class relationships in the community, political relationships in the international arena, the literary-cultural-linguistic relationship between writer and reader, and the extent to which one set of relationships may be dependent on another.

While Sommer notes that identification between reader and writer is neither necessary nor possible because the situations of enunciation that give rise to testimonial discourse are often so extreme as to be beyond most readers' experience, she explains that both reader and writer understand that language, albeit imperfectly, "always relates to the world"; and "apparently incompatible codes, such as Catholicism and communism, militance and motherhood, are syncretized to produce a flexible field of signification and political intervention" (1988, 130). Only through language can one achieve communication. Alegría's texts interpellate the reader not by empathy from shared experience (metaphor) but by language that establishes solidarity amid difference (metonymy) at what Sommer calls "a respectful distance" (1988, 130). Through a developing testimonial discourse, Alegría joins the personal to the political; her story follows that of her country and that of its female Other.

Furthermore, Alegría is no different from many other socially committed writers Sommer described to us earlier. They all have had to resolve to some extent their own feelings of inadequacy and unrepresentativeness (1988, 113). Alegría, after all, was born into the privileged elite and had little in common with the Salvadoran peasants or working class. She and other writers have had to face the often unpleasant realities of their countries, to decide the "whether" and the "how" of political engagement, and then to choose their weapons, so to speak. They risk losing any status and security they have enjoyed. Argueta, Arias, and Belli all struggle with this issue. Dalton agonized over this problem and ultimately threw his lot with the armed militants. After an equally wrenching period of soul searching, Alegría decided that her writing should serve her militancy.

Three narrative texts will be the focus of the rest of this chapter: two written in collaboration with her husband, *Cenizas de Izalco* (1966) and *No me agarran viva* (1983); and one, *Luisa en el país de la realidad* (1987), that bears Alegría's name only. Other important texts in Alegría's narrative corpus include the coming-to-consciousness novel *Despierta mi bien despierta* (1986) and three novellas known together under the Spanish title *Pueblo de Dios y de Mandinga* (1986) and later in English as *Family Album* (1991), a collection that shares some historical, autobiographical, and testimonial ground with the aforementioned texts and that could also be used in the discussion of women in the Central American revolutions. Also of note are the "political chronicle" *Nicaragua: La revolución sandinista* (1982), written with Flakoll and documenting the years 1855 to 1979 in her country of birth, and *Para romper el silencio: Resistencia y lucha en las cárceles salvadoreñas* (1984) by both Alegría and Flakoll, a testimony of political prisoners including a student leader.

Darwin J. "Bud" Flakoll

A Bud

> Todos los que amo
> están en ti
> y tú
> en todo lo que amo.
>
> —*Claribel Alegría*, *"Amor,"* Sobrevivo

The first time I met both Claribel Alegría and Bud Flakoll was at the Latin American Studies Association Congress in Washington, D.C., in April 1991. I had made arrangements to meet Claribel in her hotel room for the interview. As Bud opened the door to greet me, I realized that I had probably made a major gaffe in not including him in the interview as well. In my eagerness to track down the major women writers of Central America, I had doubly marginalized him—both by gender and by nationality. Nevertheless, Bud graciously received me and removed himself to a corner of the room, where he proceeded to work on some papers and answer a few questions that Claribel directed to him for clarification. Some time later Claribel explained to me that Bud would not have been offended "because he was quite humble" and never sought the limelight (1995). Family members have described him as "low key" and supportive.

My embarrassment finally prodded me into delving more into his background to understand what interests and experience he brought to the transnational collaboration. My only regret is not having done this research while he was still alive. I make a special point of including information on Bud Flakoll not only because the sheer number of times his name appears on a book cover demands attention and because he deserves more recognition than he has received, but also because I would like to offer, in some small way, *un homenaje*—an homage—to his important contribution.

Born in Wendte, South Dakota, in 1923, Darwin J. Flakoll grew up in San Diego, California. He received his undergraduate degree in history (his special interest was World War I) from San Diego State University in 1942 at the age of nineteen. During his years in college, he edited the student newspaper, the *Aztec*, and worked as a police and general assignment reporter for the San Diego *Union*. Following graduation, he joined the Navy as an officer, spending the war years on a destroyer escort engaged in antisubmarine warfare in the Atlantic.

Following his discharge from the military, Flakoll enrolled as a graduate student at George Washington University, where he met Alegría. Apparently he knew some Spanish at that time but did not attain proficiency until well after their marriage on December 29, 1947. The couple had four children. Flakoll returned to the world of journalism, where he worked as Washington correspondent for the Western Reporters News Service, reporting back to client newspapers in Albuquerque, Santa Monica, Bakersfield, Pocatello, Tacoma, and other cities.

A perusal of news clippings with his byline reveals a thorough and mature understanding of the wranglings between Congress and the Truman administration over such disparate issues as the control of the California coastal tidelines, the sloppiness and extravagant waste of the Atomic Energy Commission, the Columbian Basin projects (including irrigation dams, fisheries, pollution and silt control, and reforestation), states rights versus federal control in various disputes, and the nascent arms race with the Soviet Union. His style is crisp, clear, and occasionally wry and just a bit scornful. In the tidelands article from the Santa Monica *Outlook* (no date available), for example, Flakoll opens in exasperation: "For the umpteenth time in the past few years Congress this week set about unsnarling the oil-saturated tidelands question. . . . Chances for a compromise settlement look dim as both sides are wholeheartedly convinced of their righteousness."

For a young reporter in his mid-twenties, Flakoll made his way quickly into the circles of power. One newspaper photograph shows a beaming Flakoll in black tie at a White House Correspondents' Association dinner honoring President Truman. By far the youngest man at the table, he is surrounded by two congressmen, a major general, and three other journalists. Alegría reports that her husband's assignments frequently took him to Capitol Hill, where he once interviewed then Congressman Richard M. Nixon.

In 1950 Flakoll entered the foreign service. The U.S. State Department sent him and his family to posts in Mexico, Chile, Argentina, Uruguay (where he was second secretary at the U.S. embassy in Montevideo), and finally Paris in 1962 ("Darwin Flakoll" B5). Throughout the 1950s and into the 1960s, Flakoll and Alegría forged friendships with local and exiled intellectuals and writers in their various stations. Both were exhilarated at news of the Cuban revolution in 1959 and then extremely disappointed following the U.S. Bay of Pigs invasion. The idealistic Flakoll admired and respected John F. Kennedy and attributed the debacle to bad advice from the president's counselors. U.S. foreign policy throughout the sixties in Latin America and Vietnam further discouraged him to the point that he finally felt, like many other Americans of that era, betrayed by the same government for which he had fought so proudly only two decades earlier. "He was very proud to have fought against Hitler and fascism," but the anticommunist hysteria in pursuit of Castro "disillusioned him" (interview 1995). After resigning from the U.S. State Department, Flakoll dedicated himself to writing and translating.

In an obituary by Luis Rocha, the newspaper *Nuevo Amanecer Cultural* of Managua notes that Flakoll "was a diplomat until, because of his differences with certain aspects of the policies of the State Department, he resigned his job to return to journalism which again sent him to various parts of the world" (7). The same obituary also pays tribute to the contribution of "Claribud"—"one cannot speak of them except as a couple, an inseparable couple"—to the cultural life of Nicaragua where they had relocated in 1979. Both were members of the editorial board of *Nuevo Amanecer Cultural* and founding members of the Centro Nicaragüense de Escritores (Nicaraguan Writers' Association).

Alegría credits Flakoll with the genius of her narrative. She states that his background as a reporter provided much-needed guidance as she undertook her first novel, *Cenizas de Izalco,* in collaboration with him: "He was the pilot, I the co-pilot" (interview 1995). Perhaps militant feminists will cringe at a perceived "dependency." However, she was no more dependent on him than he on her. "Claribud" was a unit that brought out the best of both the poet and the narrator.

Cenizas de Izalco

Written by Alegría and Flakoll in 1966, before the rise of testimonio as a narrative mode in its own right, *Cenizas de Izalco* best approximates a historical novel, according to Alegría (interview 1991b). Acevedo notes that *Cenizas* marks the beginning of the contemporary novel in El Salvador;

Cenizas is also one of just a few Latin American novels with a double author (1988, 77). While focusing on political themes, as did the earlier social-realist novel, *Cenizas* experiments more than its predecessor with style and form. In fact, it became a "parting of the waters," according to Arias (1994, 25), both ending social realism and supplanting poetry with narrative as the aesthetic vehicle of choice for many writers of the 1960s, including Dalton and Argueta.

While *Cenizas* incorporates autobiographical elements of Alegría's child-hood and narrates the intimate world of the protagonists, the text moves beyond simple autobiography by fragmenting the authorial voice, ruptur-ing the linear flow of the narration, and fictionalizing characters and some events; it also includes a testimonial account of La Matanza of 1932. As a "hybrid" text, then, it occupies a generic middle ground.

Unlike autobiography, which insists on singularity (Sommer 1988, 108), *Cenizas* is told by two "first-person" narrators, Frank and Carmen. *Cenizas,* however, does not quite approximate testimonial pluralism either. The "I" of *Cenizas* differs from the "I" of testimonio in that the latter "does not invite reader identification because experiences are so different" (Sommer 1988, 108). In *Cenizas* I do find some attempts at universalizing experience, especially that of women. Moreover, *Cenizas* does have a historical and political agenda like testimony but is more personal and intimate than most testimonies. Thematically, the text examines the oppression of women and the degradation of the poor, although it does not necessarily link the two. *Cenizas* certainly describes injustice, but it does not probe that dimen-sion of relationships as deeply as does Alegría and Flakoll's later testimonio, *No me agarran viva.*

At the beginning of the novel, Carmen Pierson, one of the two narrators and a wife and mother in Washington, D.C., returns to her hometown of Santa Ana, El Salvador, for her mother's funeral. The mother left instruc-tions before her death that the writings of Frank Wolff, a North American who had visited her family many years earlier and whose diary and letters had been entrusted to her, should be given to Carmen. The text develops as we, along with Carmen, read through these papers. Carmen interweaves musings on her own problems, her memories of her mother, and recollec-tions of the friends and relatives who come to the funeral with the texts of Wolff's diary and letters.

Humor and lyricism mixed with bits of popular, oral tradition (such as the legend of the Siguanaba—albeit a "cleaned up," more properly bour-geois version than the one we will find in Argueta) enhance the play of signifiers and the artistic or "literary" quality of the narration. Frank Wolff's alcoholism, his journey to Central America to "find himself," his meeting and falling in love with Carmen's mother, Isabel, Isabel's romantic longing to be free from the stifling atmosphere of Santa Ana, and her final refusal to leave husband and home to follow Frank are the elements that provide the narrative core.[1] Carmen's thoughts and attempts to understand both Isabel and Frank punctuate the writings; her flashbacks and her tendency to begin reading the diary wherever she opens it upset the chronological development of the text. Finally she attempts to bring some order to her query: "¿Qué vería mamá en Frank? ¿Se sintió atraída por su mundo, por su aura de autor con éxito, o sería un insatisfecho impulso maternal que nunca halló eco en papá? Es mejor que vuelva atrás" (54) (What was it Mother saw in Frank? Was she attracted by his worldliness, the aura of the successful author? Or did she feel, perhaps, an instinctive maternal impulse that went unfulfilled in her relationship with Dad? I'll have to start at the beginning) (1989, 45).[2]

In the course of her reading, she also wonders what moved her mother, after so many years of secrecy, to pass her the diary "como un golpe repentino en la cara a través de la tumba?" (150) (like a sudden slap in the face from the other side of the grave) (1989, 121). Armed with these questions, the text works toward a climax that it achieves on two levels: the personal, with the "one-night stand" of Isabel and Frank; and the political, with Frank's eyewitness description of the massacre at Izalco.

Alegría relies on her own memory and the testimony of survivors of the Matanza to reconstruct the horrific events of 1932. Only seven years old at the time, she remembers vividly the parade of peasants, their thumbs tied behind their backs, being thrashed by a military officer and led to the barracks across the street from her house. An Indian woman from Izalco who worked in her home cried every day as she recalled dreadful scenes that continued to haunt her. Officially, the dictator General Hernández Martínez and the authorities permitted no accounts to be printed in the newspapers; they expunged all evidence from historical documents. Alegría refers to this excision as a "cultural lobotomy" (interview 1991b). Because of the scarcity of written information, she had to reconstruct the massacre using the eyewitness accounts that she gathered in much the same way that Dalton reconstructed Marmol's testimony. She thus links the private to the public by combining her own experience of this major upheaval in modern Salvadoran history with that of many others.

The circumstances of Isabel's and Carmen's lives parallel autobiographical details of Alegría's early years in El Salvador: the passion for reading and writing, the longing to escape from provincial Santa Ana, the spurning of bourgeois society's frivolous roles for women, and the compassion for her country's downtrodden. One mourner at the wake says of Isabel that "de joven era conservadora . . . pero es curioso, con la edad se fue haciendo izquierdista. Tenía un gran corazón" (163) (she was very conservative when she was young but it's curious: the older she got, the more she turned to the left. She had a very generous heart) (1989, 133). The same could be said of Alegría herself.

In *Cenizas de Izalco,* Alegría and Flakoll approach descriptively rather than prescriptively the problem of the Other as they portray unequal gender relationships and political, social, and economic discrimination. Theirs is certainly a voice of protest in the face of injustice. However, the final chapters of the novel—in which we witness the tragic massacre at Izalco, Isabel's farewell to Frank, Frank's return to alcoholism and self-destruction, and Carmen's realization that she is as trapped in her marriage to Paul as was her mother in hers—do not synthesize the disparate strands of oppression into any overarching cause, explanation, or solution, nor do they transcend the inauthentic existence lived out by each character. The last page signals unfinished business as the shovelfuls of dirt thrown onto Isabel's grave cover up, rather than reveal, everything.

Explicit signs of society's machismo are plentiful in the novel. Within the family, Alfonso's affairs with other women hurt Isabel deeply even though she is fully aware of society's forgiving wink at an adulterous husband and quick condemnation of a wife guilty of the same transgression. Both Church and society demand she forgive him; but no matter how hard she tries, she cannot (166). Ironically, one of the mourners at Isabel's funeral wonders how Alfonso will cope now that his wife is gone, "Tan unidos que eran" (29) (They were so united) (1989, 23). The English translation adds: "You don't see marriages like that any more" (23). The reader recognizes their unity as only a façade.

Men have control of women's bodies, as Paul demonstrates when, against Carmen's objections, he tells her to get an abortion (162). Carmen also complains because Paul dismisses her as being "too emotional" in contrast to his "superior attitude" of self-satisfied equanimity. He sees her as a doll: "Si me viese más como a un ser humano, puede ser que algo se salvara de nuestro matrimonio" (90) (If he'd only treat me like a human being, we might be able to save something of our marriage) (1989, 73). Even Frank, who understands Isabel's need for freedom, sets out to "charm and impress her" as the experienced man of the world (51). His anecdotes of Parisian nights and discourses on culture entertain his novitiate with a world she can only envision in her dreams. Unfortunately, most women are not encouraged to dream.

In a conversation with Frank, Isabel criticizes the education of women, which emphasizes decorative accomplishments like learning to play classical music on the piano, walking prettily, and crocheting. Moreover, their mothers teach them to prepare various exquisite dishes but never any plain, everyday food. The young man finds the product of this training adorable until, after the wedding, he realizes that his bride "no es misteriosa, sino simplemente sosa" (139) (is not really mysterious, merely insipid) (1989, 111). Society expects women to find fulfillment in marriage, ideally in a marriage with comforts and status provided by a respectable husband like Isabel's. Yet marrying even a "remotely acceptable" man is superior to spinsterhood, as witnessed by the shriveled "Blind Virginia" and the immobile and bitter Señorita Soto, "una araña que nunca atrapó nada" (21) (a spider that never trapped anything) (1989, 17). In Santa Ana there is no room for old maids (31), concludes Carmen. A woman has little choice in the macho culture. Life either leads to marriage or it leads nowhere.

After marriage, a woman gains satisfaction only through a low community profile with regular attendance at Mass and generous almsgiving, the major expectations of her public persona. In Isabel's day Salvadoran women could not vote. Unwelcomed in political discussions, they assumed the role of mediators by steering conversations to noncontroversial, safe subjects (50). As a result, not much communication took place. Social intercourse was an exercise in sterility as women were locked into their acceptable topics and men into theirs. Frank's comment that "no tiene que gustarle lo que eres, pero no puedes escapar de ti" (187) (you don't have to like what you are, but you cannot run away from the fact of yourself) (1989, 154) acknowledges the impossibility of change or transcendence.

A variety of implicit signs define gender differences and the relationship of each to the other. Alegría emphasized, in my interview with her, that she does not feel capable of writing fiction from a man's point of view. She explained that her husband wrote the majority of the thoughts and words attributed to Frank and that she added only a little. It is possible to detect stylistic, lexical, and discursive differences in the male-narrated, as opposed to the female-narrated, passages. Deciding, however, what constitutes male discourse may prove difficult since the male author, Flakoll, differs not only in gender from Alegría but also in nationality. And since so much of the conflict of the novel hinges not just on the gender gap but also on the culture clash as well between Frank and Isabel and Carmen and Paul, the reader may attribute the discursive differences to a conscious effort—rather than to any "natural" tendencies—of the writers to portray "femininity" or "masculinity" and "North Americanness" or "Salvadoranness."

With these caveats against attempting too vigorously to interpret why the textual differences exist, suffice it to say that a number of examples do highlight a divergence in discourse most likely based on gender. Perhaps the most obvious is the sense of control that the masculine "I" of Flakoll/ Frank's narration exerts on his life and in his text. As he describes a youthful winter trek through the high sierras, Frank begins almost every sentence with an action verb or verb of strong desire in the first person. The preterit yields to the conditional to express volition: "Decidí . . . tenía que regresar . . . comencé a hacer una lista . . . estaba anhelante por establecer contacto . . . llegaría . . . pasaría . . . almacenaría . . . esperaría . . . conviviría . . . comenzaría . . . me encontraría" (64) (I decided . . . I had to return . . . I began to make a list . . . I had a hunger to establish contact . . . I would arrive . . . I would spend . . . I would stack . . . I would wait . . . I would live . . . I would begin . . . I would find) (1989, 52–53). Frank has the luxury of choice and decision. When he contemplates a career decision, he wants to "hacer algo útil, algo que yo creyera importante" (61) (do something useful . . . something I felt was important) (1989, 50), "algo vital" (102) (something vital).

In contrast to Frank's attitude of aggressive adventure, Isabel relates to Carmen her feeling of being buffeted by forces beyond her control, of being in exile in Santa Ana. Even though she has lived there her entire life, "me siento como de paso" (63) (I've always felt as if I'm only passing through) (1989, 52). Later she tells Frank she envies his independence: "Un hombre como usted es libre, puede darse el gusto, sentir el hormigueo de la aventura, pero una mujer . . . " (113) (A man like yourself is free to search for new experiences that give zest to living, but a woman . . .) (1989, 89). She fails to verbalize the rest of the thought.

Illustrating another difference, Frank can put distance between himself and his problems in order to consider them objectively. His images are telling as he describes his actions: "Revoloteé, di vueltas alrededor de mi pasado como un zopilote al acecho, marcando sobre la arena mis vacilantes huellas" (I circled and hovered over the desert of my past like a dispassionate buzzard marking my own staggering tracks in the sand), gaining an "objetiva altura" (objective altitude) with which to judge his sins (58).

Frank prefers to rationalize his relationships and to manipulate people by depersonalizing them. That way he can keep his distance: "Manejaba palabras y no seres humanos" (66) (I dealt with words, not with humans) (1989, 54). Whenever he feels emotionally threatened, alcohol offers him refuge. To him, home is a concept; to Isabel, home is a network of relationships, a collection of nostalgic memories of time spent with loved ones (46–47).

Unlike Frank who gains objectivity and distance from his problems, Isabel turns inward to her books, plants, and dreams, soul-searching as if trying to unlock some dark personal secret. Her ever-present keys jingle metaphorically at her hip, reminding us of her role as "woman of the house" and of the fact that they, like the stifling role of women, are passed from one generation to another (Acevedo 1988, 79). Carmen notes that she and Isabel have lost their illusions and innocence while both Frank and Alfonso still make empty plans like naive young boys (69–70). Isabel's "visions" are too subtle for her husband's tastes (24). She observes that Alfonso operates empirically in a world he can see and touch, relying on "skill and knowledge" to solve his problems; he is crushed when his skill and knowledge as a physician fail to save the life of his sickly son Neto (26). The aggressive rationalism of masculine discourse claims a lofty position in contrast to Isabel's and Carmen's "more lowly" intuition, passivity, and emotion because as women they think with their bodies, not just with their brains. In a man's world women's ways of perceiving reality—again, "too emotional" in Paul's words—are not just different but inferior. Woman is clearly the Other of macho sangfroid.

The result is a negation. Carmen concludes that she may think about herself too much—a disturbing, ironic conclusion in itself because there may be nothing really to think about—"un pensamiento circular dando vueltas alrededor de un cero" (171) (a circular thought orbiting around a zero) (1989, 141). If she peels away the labels of "Patient, Forebearing Wife," "Understanding Wife," or "Wife and Mother of His Children," what will she find? Who after all is she, she asks. She fears that she is repeating a cycle, confronting the same emptiness as did her mother. Each one fails to define herself outside a dependent relationship.

Perhaps women of this novel find neither authenticity nor transcendence because they must truncate their public image. Isabel and Carmen recognize that they lack something without being able to identify exactly what it is and how they may obtain it. Unlike the later *No me agarran viva*, in which Eugenia takes charge, controls her own life, and still responds meaningfully to those around her, Isabel and Carmen do not communicate within their marriages nor do they achieve independence. Bound by their own patriarchal codes, the men of *Cenizas* have access to both the public and the private spheres, but by and large they cannot integrate the two (the possible exception being the North American missionary, Virgil). They may possess power in the community and in the family, but they do not transcend stereotypical roles in order to assert self-defined character, to admit weakness and error, to understand women, or to include women in official discourse.

While Frank genuinely shares Isabel's interests and establishes an intellectual and emotional bond with her, he never escapes his North American or male arrogance nor his ultimate dependency on alcohol, especially when he fails to convince Isabel to leave everything and go with him. Frank attributes Isabel's refusal to her own dependency and weakness, never admitting that Isabel may have seriously considered her options, limited as they are, and come to the conclusion that by choosing him she would only be trading one form of bondage for another. Isabel explains to him that the very foundation of the relationship is as important to her as her actual passion: "¿Cómo podríamos construir algo duradero sobre una base de traición, de huida, de culpa," she asks (199) (How could we build any kind of life on my betrayal, my abandonment, my sin?). In Flakoll's translation, she accepts responsibility for the adultery. (The Spanish text apportions blame more evenly.) She refers as well to her other responsibilities and obligations to her family, admitting that, because of her own insecurity, she finds refuge in the stability, if not excitement, of her marriage to Alfonso. She knows that she is a prisoner to society's conventions; had these granted her freedom and access to the public spheres of education, employment, and politics, she might have chosen differently.

Forming the historical backdrop to the love story between Frank and Isabel and to the search for authenticity by both Isabel and Carmen, the political events of 1931–32 in El Salvador run parallel to, but do not intersect, the private lives of the women of *Cenizas*. Alegría and Flakoll move beyond the problematics of gender to another aspect of subalternity, the injustices of classism and racism. They paint a strongly negative picture of El Salvador: a fiefdom of coffee barons who exploit children (38); a death camp where half of the babies born in the country die before they reach the age of one year (104); a land of squalor where the poor must live like animals (86); a country of confused priorities that "no podrá prosperar hasta que sus niños no se alimenten mejor, hasta que en vez de cantinas se construyan escuelas" (38) (can never be great until its children get enough to eat and its people build fewer cantinas and more classrooms) (1989, 30). Complicit with the powers that be, the Church does nothing to improve the lives of the suffering poor. Its practice of sending out a priest once a month to the peasant communities to preach conformity only serves to reinforce the status quo.[3]

The liberal Alfonso[4] complains of the country's militarism and its attendant brutality and disregard for human rights. Berating an army officer for beating a bound prisoner, Alfonso admonishes him for a cowardly act: "A un hombre indefenso no se le pega, coronel" (36) (You don't hit a man whose hands are tied!) (1989, 28). When the civilian president Araujo is overthrown by a group of military officers who install General Martínez, Alfonso cynically observes that every country gets what it deserves, and El Salvador has the theosophist madman Martínez (124).[5] Poverty, disease, death, and exploitation of the masses have created a situation ripe for revolution. After Isabel expresses her fears of a bloodbath of vengeance in the event of a popular uprising, family friend Eduardo—the novel's voice from the far Left—asks her to try to understand: "¿No odiarías vos también si hubieras sido explotada toda tu vida y encima de eso te trataran peor que a un animal?" (50) (Wouldn't you feel hatred too if you had been exploited, trampled on by the oligarchs, and treated like an animal all your life?) (1989, 41).

Throughout the novel the rumblings of the volcano Izalco—home of the indigenous god Chac, who demands human sacrifice for sustenance—bode doom and disaster. Its ultimate blast coincides with the insurrection, just as it did historically. The ashes of Izalco, explains Acevedo, are metaphorically the ashes of past rebellions, the only thing left along with memories of intense passion (1988, 87). Many years later Alfonso still laments the legacy of violence of El Salvador's military rulers, who committed terrible crimes in the name of "national defense" (94).

Eduardo's voice, as remembered by Frank, is almost prophetic as he tries to understand the causes and propose solutions to the basic injustices of Salvadoran society. "You must read the Communist Manifesto, Isabel. . . . You'll find practical Christianity there" (1989, 41).[6] He invites Frank to accompany him on a tour of Farabundo Martí's experimental farm, where corn and beans are replacing worn-out coffee trees (1982, 120) so that the peasants can grow their own food instead of cultivating coffee for export and for the profit of the landowners. Eduardo here is critical of capitalism and its exploitation of workers. However, he does not find fault with the

United States for its capitalism or imperialism; rather, he blames the U.S. ambassador for his cozy relationship with top Salvadoran army officers (1982, 154). No link is established in the text between El Salvador's political and economic woes and the U.S. presence there. Isabel knows the situation is bad, but a revolution, in her mind, is unthinkable (1982, 50).

Isabel concludes that Santa Ana is to blame for her own stunted development. The various narrators describe it as a place where dates mean nothing (1982, 16) and nothing has changed in the last thirty years (1982, 154). It is stifling, fenced-in, underdeveloped, a boring, dead city, "Sodom and Gomorrah," a "corner of Hell"—a mythic, Comala-type place. For a woman there is no way out. As a child Carmen equated departure with death: "¿De qué otra manera podría una irse de Santa Ana?" (63) (What other way was there to get out of Santa Ana?) (1989, 52). George Yúdice comments that in *Cenizas,* "death serves as a metaphor for the suffocating social conditions which keep people from defining and liberating themselves" (1985, 954). This remote provincial town of an "absurd little country" (48) epitomizes the stifling nature of private space. Isabel is determined to send her own children away for their education. But no matter—Carmen's brother Alfredo remains a dissipated spoiled brat, and Carmen herself finds Washington, D.C., and her marriage to Paul, "the perfect Organization Man" (1982, 34), just as confining as Santa Ana. To her own chagrin, Carmen realizes she is becoming her mother, even imitating Isabel's smallest gestures: "Ella no está aquí, pero nada ha cambiado" (156) (She has gone, but nothing has changed) (1989, 127). The reader suspects that even Isabel before her death understands the reason for Carmen's unhappiness—in time to pass her the copy of Frank's diary but too late to make much difference. But while she does not yet realize that one can struggle to overcome the roots of her alienation—machismo and discrimination against women—she does recognize it as a problem that goes beyond El Salvador's borders, that even the "good life" in the United States offers no cure for feeling like or being the Other. In this respect, Alegría the author proposes a common experience based on gender to which even a reading audience in another country can relate. However, Carmen and Isabel are practically alone in their awareness of their subalternity, or at least they perceive themselves as singular. In their minds, all women suffer to be sure: the spinsters remain isolated and despised, although there is no indication within the text of any "conscientization" on their part nor is there any bond other than sympathy established between them and Isabel and Carmen; the frivolous high-society ladies have unwittingly conspired with the machista practice of silencing them, and do not seem to share Isabel and Carmen's awareness and malaise.

Alegría has called *Cenizas* her "catharsis" (interview 1991b), a testimony to the personal frustrations she felt growing up as a woman and a gifted poet in Santa Ana, and to the political frustrations of seeing her people suffer injustices. She combines elements of autobiography, testimony, and historical discourse to delineate both the public and the private spaces of small town life in El Salvador. Sensitive to the needs of women, the poor, and the oppressed, she expresses her anger at sexism, classism, and racism in this her first novel. But her narrators show no real understanding that perhaps all three are linked, that there may be a way out of Santa Ana that leads to life.

Acevedo has written that *Cenizas* suggests the convergence of interests among three marginalized social sectors—the poor, the upper-class woman, and the alienated North American—and that it posits a "harmonization within the margin" (1988, 78). I disagree. Certainly it is easy to read more into the novel, to see it as a first step toward the creation of revolutionary alliances, especially now that we have the benefit of later novels from Alegría and Flakoll that do indeed connect the various Others. But taken on its own, the novel ends in frustration precisely because there is no link, no way out. Acevedo contradicts himself later, observing that none of the three sectors have a clear awareness of future possibilities. The end is "a painful and violent reaffirmation of the 'status quo'" (1988, 78). No productive relationships are established.

In a fine reading of *Cenizas* as an example of cultural dialogism, Arias studies the culture clash between North and South, First World and Third World, Frank and Isabel. Arias sees in the text an effort to overcome the "Yankee Go Home" hatreds of the 1960s in Latin America and to negotiate a relationship. This novel, for Arias, attempts to "break the stereotypical attitudes about U.S. citizens and their involvement with the political affairs of Central America" (1994, 34). For readers south of the border, changed attitudes may indeed be the principal result.

The text speaks to me first, however, at the level of gender, second at the level of nationality—but both within the frame, of course, of a crime against humanity. Without erasing differences, Isabel and Carmen's bourgeois status and womanhood—with all they entail—level the cultural field enough so that I believe their lives reach across borders to touch many different women. Women can, in fact, relate to the very process of negotiation and conflict mediation mentioned by Arias because it has been one of their traditional responsibilities in the family. So while it seems that within *Cenizas* the relationships go nowhere, the bonds that are established are extratextual—with women and other readers of good will, no matter where they are.

No me agarran viva: La mujer salvadoreña en lucha

In 1983 Alegría and Flakoll wrote and published *No me agarran viva,* their text that most closely approximates testimonio in the strict sense. As Alegría herself states, she has only "slightly novelized" the story (interview 1991). She and Flakoll collected a variety of personal testimonies from friends, relatives, and acquaintances of "Eugenia," the nom de guerre of Ana María Castillo Rivas. A guerrilla leader, Eugenia died in an ambush during the general offensive launched by the FMLN against the Salvadoran government in January 1981.

Alegría and Flakoll novelize the testimony to the extent that they assemble the testimonies in a coherent order, connecting them with a third-person narration and prefacing them with a chapter of suspense-thriller fiction describing the ambush and death of Eugenia and her three *compañeros.* Since none of the guerrilla commandos survived the ambush, the details of this chapter, including the dialogue, are pure speculation. No information, to my knowledge, was ever furnished by the military squad that perpetrated the assassination. One of Eugenia's friends, Isabel, had monitored a radio transmission from a military unit that pursued and finally intercepted a pick-up truck that matched the description of Eugenia's; however, that sketchy information is the extent of any eyewitness report. The narration that begins with a fictionalized account of Eugenia's death ends with that news from Isabel along with the testimonies of Eugenia's husband, Javier, her commander, Ricardo, her sisters Marta and Ondina, and letters in Eugenia's own hand dated only days before her death.

Between the fictional first chapter and the testimonial ending, Alegría and Flakoll incorporate a multitude of voices that describe Eugenia's upbringing in a bourgeois milieu: a Catholic education, an activist faith, and political concientización on a trip to Guatemala where she worked with the poor. We follow her subsequent enlistment into the forces for the liberation of her country, her marriage to a compañero and the birth of their daughter, as well as her everyday joys and frustrations. At times, we view the same event through different eyes, a narrative strategy that undermines any attempt at a "definitive" version. Each voice attests to Eugenia's diligence, sense of responsibility, and organizational skills.

Lest she appear exceptional, however, Alegría and Flakoll write in the prologue that while Eugenia is a model of self-denial, sacrifice, and revolutionary heroism—a problematic martyr role, as Mary Jane Treacy notes, if it just consigns women to their traditional function of long-suffering servants of sacrifice (1994, 88)—she is "un caso típico y no excepcional de tantas mujeres salvadoreñas que han dedicado sus esfuerzos, e incluso sus vidas, a la lucha por la liberación de su pueblo" (9) (a typical, not exceptional, case of so many Salvadoran women who have devoted their efforts, including their lives, to the struggle for the liberation of their people). (Further translations of *No me agarran viva* are by Amanda Hopkinson.) Alegría and Flakoll balance her (typically female?) self-effacing, self-erasing tendencies with qualities that make her human and accessible yet no less feminine to the reader. The narrators list her flaws in order to underscore her ordinariness—her asthma, allergies, aches and pains, fragility, myopia, and refusal to wear glasses (perhaps a concession to vanity). Rather than a metaphor—the unique, superior woman in a hierarchy of women—Eugenia exemplifies the metonymic participant in the struggle and a "horizontal" extension of a group of many women and men.

The narrative polyphony goes beyond Eugenia's story to recount a host of women's testimonies from El Salvador. The two-part title of the testimony identifies the first-person direct object "me" of the "No me agarran viva" as part of the whole, "La mujer salvadoreña en lucha." In addition to Eugenia's two sisters who join her in the guerrilla movement, several school chums—Isabel, María Elena, and Nadia—document their own involvement, adventures, and misfortunes in the events leading up to the insurrection of 1981. Other women such as Cayetano Carpio's wife, Tulita, and Ana Guadalupe Martínez tell their stories here, which are indicative of "miles y miles de vidas abnegadas, anónimas y a la vez combativas" (110) (thousands upon thousands of lives denied, lives at once anonymous and combative) (1987c, 117). If they happened to have worked with Eugenia, they include that information.

The third-person narrator who connects the various episodes bemoans the fact that many stories remain undiscovered because all the witnesses are dead (77); nevertheless, examples of female heroism abound. Alegría calls these women "precursoras" who have opened the eyes of the rest of El Salvador's women: "They began to tell us that we were worth as much as our male compañeros" (interview 1991b). Here Treacy's commentary would push the equation: womanly traits are actually worth more than their traditional male counterparts; the male project of armed insurrection has failed, but the female warrior/mother has succeeded in "overcoming death and destruction" by affirming life and love (91). In the same vein, Ileana Rodríguez's "sentimental narratives" are the "narratives of success" in this novel because, although Eugenia may fail politically, she testifies to the power of love—for husband, child, friends, orphans, country—hopefully to heal the deep social wounds (1994c, 51).

Solidarity—bonds of love and respect—remains the key to productive relationships among women and their sympathizers, according to several of the female voices of the text. Friendly doctors and nurses conspire to keep newborn "guerrilla" babies out of the hands of the National Guard. The issue of child care preoccupies Eugenia and others as they creatively combine their responsibilities as mothers with their duties as revolutionaries. At times men must play the supporting role. One of Eugenia's last letters to her husband, Javier, contains a long list of instructions regarding the feeding schedule, medicine, diapering, and discipline of their daughter, Ana Patricia. Juxtaposed with her declarations of love for Javier and with her revolutionary rhetoric, the mundane details of babysitting are just as urgent. In a reversal of traditional roles, she counts on him to step into the domestic arena while she goes off to war. Militancy and maternity—one of Sommers's syncretized "incompatible codes"—can coexist fruitfully with support from friends and family. (The narrators have not chosen their armed resistance lightly or eagerly, they maintain, but only as a last resort after exhausting all peaceful means.) Eugenia metaphorically joins the two seemingly incompatible roles with language that she, a woman, understands: "Hoy nos adentramos al momento más difícil, dolores de parto para un renacer feliz y gozoso" (134) (We've now advanced into the hardest part, birth pains for a blissful and joyous rebirth) (1987c, 137). She compares the long and painful labor of childbirth to the agony that precedes the birth of a renewed country.

The repeated insistence by the narrators on Eugenia's sense of responsibility toward her child appeals to the sympathies of readers, especially women, who might otherwise share precious little with a Salvadoran guerrilla fighter: "En ningún momento dejó las tareas, pero tampoco descuidó a la niña" (94) (She never for a moment neglected her duties, nor did she disregard the child) (1987c, 103). Again, language reconciles traditionally conflicting kinds of activity and reaches a reader who understands simultaneous professional and domestic demands. At two in the morning, we find Eugenia reading, writing, calculating, stuffing envelopes, washing, ironing, cooking, and doing sentry duty (56). Some critics might see a "superwoman" discourse in the almost breathless enumeration of endless chores.

I propose, instead, a metonymic reading that is designed to reach most women who daily juggle such schedules. Eugenia is typical, not exceptional. The text also explores the relationship between today's militant Salvadoran women and future generations. The compañera Marina explains her motives in the struggle: "Yo lucho . . . para que mis hijos no tengan que hacerlo, o que si luchan que sea para defender lo que nosotros les vamos a heredar" (122) (I'm in the struggle . . . so that my children won't have to be, or if they do it'll be in defence of what we've handed on to them) (1987c, 127). Another woman explains that maternity has collective, historical dimensions and not just personal, individual ones (99). The former, that is, the collective, ranks higher on her moral scale than the latter, the individual, an attitude that many of the guerrilla women share. In further moral self-examination, the women consider whether even to have children while they are so deeply involved in dangerous activities, much as Gioconda Belli's characters do in *La mujer habitada*. Javier and Eugenia postpone parenthood for a while, although Eugenia admits to her husband that one of her greatest disappointments was not having become pregnant earlier (72). Like Eugenia, Ana Guadalupe Martínez makes a personal sacrifice by postponing motherhood in the interest of the common good. When asked whether she would like to have children, she replies, "yo creo que todas las mujeres aspiramos a tener hijos y bastantes" (100) (I think that all of us women hope to have children, and quite a few of them) (1987c, 109); and like many of her compañeras, she plans to adopt children of the future generation—the burgeoning number of children orphaned by the war.

The women's testimonies in *No me agarran viva* respond to the machista discourse prevalent in all strata of Salvadoran society by proposing new ways of relating to men. Eugenia's sister Marta proclaims the cause: "Hay que levantarle la cabeza a la mujer oprimida" (84) (Oppressed women have to raise their heads) (1987c, 96). Both men and women have to be cured of machismo (74).

Theoretically, within the revolution no difference exists between men and women: "Pero una cosa son las bases teóricas y otra cosa es la historia del país, el desarrollo que desde que nacen traen hombres y mujeres" (81) (But basic principles are one thing and a country's history another, a development that involves men and women from the time they're born) (1987c, 93). The compañeras who give testimony realize that they will not eliminate machismo overnight; nevertheless, it is disappearing (81). The female militant is playing an increasingly more substantive role in both the

theoretical and practical work of national liberation, not only as a collabo-
rator but also as a combatant and a supervisor (80). As participants, they
wish to enjoy the "spoils of war"—peace, justice, equal opportunity—as
much as their male counterparts. They will have earned them. Eugenia
believes that through their incorporation into the revolutionary struggle,
women will free themselves (74), just as Belli's women achieve freedom
"through necessity."

Eugenia's liberation, according to Yúdice, offers the key to feminine
identity for the protagonists of Alegría's other stories (1985, 956), the
identity that Isabel and Carmen of *Cenizas* were seeking but could not quite
pinpoint. In measured rhetoric, the women of *No me agarran viva* demand
equality: "Es una lucha constante que uno debe llevar sin caer en actitudes
equivocadas de querer decir que la mujer es mejor que el hombre, porque es
exactamente igual que el hombre" (81) (It's a continual struggle one has to
carry on without falling into erroneous positions of wishing to declare
women superior to men; woman is exactly man's equal) (1987c, 94). They
are equal, but each gender brings a special gift to the relationship. According to Nadia, women add understanding, tenderness, and a note of happiness to the workplace (82). Some have even convinced their compañeros,
like Javier, to assist in domestic duties (83).

Changes in gender relations go hand in hand with a new socioeconomic
formation, observes Marta, as she links women's liberation to the defeat of
capitalism and imperialism. In an industrial society, "la mujer era aplastada,
violada, usurpada" (85) (the woman was crushed, violated, usurped) (1987c,
96). There is no hope for woman to realize her potential. In this text the
discourses of socialism and women's liberation are inseparable.

Javier explains that Eugenia's feminism has deepened her awareness of
her people and renewed her solidarity with them. When she joins the
Fuerzas Populares de Liberación Farabundo Martí (the Farabundo Martí
Popular Liberation Forces, or FPL), she has to swear an oath of solidarity
with the poor (57). She overcomes a vertical relationship of paternalism
and charity in which the more fortunate traditionally stoop to help the less
fortunate: "No era cuestión . . . de ayudar a aquella gente a levantarse, sino
más bien de sumergirse en la vida de ellos, surgir con ellos a una nueva
alternativa" (40) (It wasn't a matter of undertaking a project in a spirit of
paternalism . . . to help these people get on their feet, but rather one of
submerging herself in their lives, in order to rise with them in pursuit of a
new alternative) (1987c, 60). Such a relationship implies an intimacy based
on time spent together and shared experiences, a *convivir* with the people

to learn from them (53). If change is to occur, Eugenia realizes, it must come from within. The people themselves must resolve their problems.

As agents of history and as the proverbial architects of their own destiny, the "masses" need to mobilize for grassroots participation (95). To underscore this point, Javier narrates a lengthy historical analysis of the rise of El Salvador's popular organizations during the 1970s (43), a phenomenon described by historians as key to the politicization of the Salvadoran workers and peasants and to the growth of the revolutionary movement. Eugenia, like other women from the bourgeoisie, rethinks her attitudes and praxis vis-à-vis the poor and the working classes. To this end, Eugenia sees all her personal relationships in a political light. While she misses Javier intensely during the time she must spend away from him, she consoles herself, perhaps feeling guilty for a passion she considers selfish: "El dolor de nuestra separación es poco comparado al dolor de nuestro pueblo" (136) (I believe the pain of our separation is small compared with that of our people) (1987c, 139). Solidarity with the people takes on sacramental proportions as she elevates it to the position of cornerstone of her marriage. In a romantic gesture, she dedicates her marriage to the revolution and militancy (64–65). She will feel most proud if her own daughter grows up to be a "digna hija de su pueblo" (135) (a fitting child of her people) (1987c, 138).

The testimonies of *No me agarran viva* also note the new relationship that an activist Church has established with the poor, much as Argueta will describe in *Un día en la vida*. By syncretizing the two apparently "incompatible" codes of Marxism and Christianity, the narrators again appeal to a reading public that may know only one side of this double-edged moral, ideological, and political discourse of liberation theology, "la nueva pastoral de la Iglesia" (26) (the church's new pastoral concern) (1987c, 48). The occupation of the cathedral, which Javier describes as its conversion into "una tribuna de denuncia hacia el pueblo y hacia el mundo" (45) (a public forum for the people and the world) (1987c, 65), shocks some people as an act of desecration. But the Church justifies its "option for the poor" and its prophetic role as the fulfillment of a biblical mandate. For siding with the oppressed, the Church suffers persecution and becomes a target of the ultraright, which charges that sympathetic priests are communists and subversives (61). Javier documents the martyrdom of priests and the awakening conscience of Monseñor Oscar Romero (91). The Church assumes a major role in conscientizing the poor, according to compañera Marina: "Empezamos un análisis de la vida. Así fue como fuimos adquiriendo conocimientos" (118) (I started from the basis of my own experience. . . . That's how one gains consciousness of how to organize) (1987c, 122). The torture and killing of priests made a lasting impression on Alegría. She still recalls with horror the campaign of terror she witnessed on a trip to El Salvador in 1979 when people put signs in their windows reading, "Haga patria, mate un cura" (Be a patriot, kill a priest). She also marks the 1980 assassination of Archbishop Romero as a turning point in her own conscientization: from that point on she would write to denounce evil. Her narratives after that date show an awareness of the relationship between the writer, the woman, the militant, and the Other.

In a look at another type of relationship, the narrators examine the imperialistic exploitation of Central America by the United States, the arrogance of the superpower toward its "traspatio" (its backyard) and its irrational fears of "el peligro comunista" (the red scare) (22). A theory of dependency offers only a partial explanation for the unjust imbalance (31). The narrators find the Salvadoran people to be victims of a double exploitation, both by these foreigners looking out for their own interests and by the local oligarchy profiteering from the greed and fears of the foreigners. "Progress" has come at the expense of the common people. Deconstructing common euphemisms by showing that things are not what they seem, the narrators engage in some conscientizing of their own. For example, they show how Kennedy's highly touted program, the Alliance for Progress, actually encouraged underdevelopment in the hemisphere.[7]

While the Alliance encouraged the industrial modernization of El Salvador, it failed to ensure the parallel improvements in the agricultural sector that would raise the standard of living of common Salvadorans and permit them to buy the new products and support a domestic economy dependent on increased consumption (28–29). Instead, the landed oligarchy refused to raise the starvation wages of the farm workers. A "new world order" is certainly needed, the narrators argue, one that is based on horizontal relationships of justice and caring, not on a vertical power paradigm that encourages greed and plundering.

The testimonies of *No me agarran viva* thus emphasize relationships of metonymy rather than of metaphor. Eugenia is an example, by extension rather than exception, of the many voices of resistance in El Salvador, especially those of women. Alegría as author is another example of a militant voice—if we relate this testimony to her personal text—that raises its protest via the pen rather than the gun. The voices seem to be telling us that there are many creative ways to fight the war. The polyphonic narrative structure decenters the traditionally singular authorial voice of the text and becomes, in fact, more democratic with the inclusion of heterogeneous voices. Furthermore, in this text Alegría/Eugenia have transcended the gender limitations imposed on them by society, limitations that thwart Isabel and Carmen in *Cenizas;* they have in the same struggle fought for the lifting of barriers for all members of El Salvador's subaltern classes. Like other testimonial texts, the function of this one is to demand action and to denounce machismo, imperialism, and other forms of oppression. By recombining seemingly conflictive discourses of maternity and militancy and of Christianity and communism, this testimonial narrative creates Sommer's "flexible field of signification" to help describe unjust relationships and propose new, more just ones, to increase understanding of the present reality in El Salvador among readers, and to promote solidarity among the reading audience and the narrators.

On the heels of her testimony, Alegría published a collection of novellas, *Pueblo de Dios y de Mandinga* (1986), which was later translated by Amanda Hopkinson in 1991 as *Family Album.* It includes "El detén" (The Talisman) (1977), "Album familiar" (Family Album) (1982), and "Pueblo de Dios y de Mandinga" (Village of God and the Devil) (1985). The stories speak to the many tensions—autobiographical, sexual, cultural, political, and textual—that have marked Alegría's work. "Album familiar" narrates the "conscientization" of a bourgeois Central American woman living in Paris who is radicalized by the Sandinista triumph in Nicaragua. "Pueblo de Dios y de Mandinga" describes the eccentricities of several outrageous characters—similar to some we will meet in *Luisa*—in a text that approximates magical realism and departs from the testimonial/political mode. Slim and Marcia, a presumably autobiographical couple, return to her native Central American country when tourists overrun their island paradise in Mallorca.

In a series of memories, nightmares, conversations, and stream-of-consciousness monologues, "El detén" presents the confessions of a troubled young woman, Karen, to her spiritual director, Sister Mary Ann, and to a psychiatrist to whom she only alludes. Karen lives in a world of extremes; she is sexually abused by her mother's lover, misunderstood by her father, and trapped between the wanton permissiveness of her mother and the accusatory finger of the Church. The primary focus of the novella is on the construction and destruction of female subjectivity in an upper-middle-class milieu that spans both U.S. and Latin American cultures. It is a tale of female *desengaño,* an awakening to brutal reality, a theme that has characterized much of Alegría's writing. As the Reverend Mother reminds Karen, "El mundo no es un cuento de hadas y debes prepararte para enfrentarlo mejor" (12) (The world isn't a fairy tale, and you have to learn to come to terms with it) (11; translation by Amanda Hopkinson).

In 1986 Alegría also published her novel *Despierta mi bien despierta,* a love story that is loosely testimonial and only barely autobiographical. The author turns once again to the theme of writing as she narrates the brief but passionate affair of Eduardo, a poet and guerrilla fighter, and Lorena, a wealthy married woman ten years his senior, who meets him in a university workshop on the novel. The text is important for our study in that it asks to what extent women's liberation is dependent on national liberation.

The events of August 11, 1977, which are reported in the *Los Angeles Times* under the headline "Nueve rebeldes guillotinados en San Salvador," provide the historical point of departure.[8] Slowly conscientized to the hell on earth that is her country through her contacts with Eduardo, with her own mother who works through the Church with the poor, and with various activist priests including Monseñor Oscar Romero, Lorena learns that the murder of the nine rebels reported in the *Times* took place at a slaughterhouse owned by her husband. Narrated by Lorena in the second person and the past tense, the novel follows her political and personal coming of age. Forsaking the role of a passive housewife, Lorena challenges her husband's complicity in the crime, his autocratic rule, and the tyranny of machismo in general: "Soy mayor de edad y me mando sola" (34) (I'm a big girl now and can take care of myself) (my translation). When her husband strikes her, she leaves home, suffering no second thoughts.

At the personal level she attains an exhilarating independence; politically, however, she is about to be baptized into the dreadful consequences of challenging the power structure. Leaving the university workshop, she enters her car and is surprised to find a large package on the seat wrapped in newspaper. She opens it to find the head of her lover, Eduardo. The novel ends at that moment leaving the reader to wonder whether Lorena's liberation has achieved much at all. Until the country is freed, she and many Others will continue to suffer.

Luisa en el país de la realidad (1987)

In *Luisa* Alegría returns to the generic hybrid of autobiography-testimony–historical novel that characterizes most of her narrative work. Although the cover of the English translation bears the title *Luisa in Realityland* followed by the description "A novel by Claribel Alegría," the author has experimented with the narrative form. She punctuates the pithy anecdotes of Luisa Solórzano—an autobiographical character whom a third-person narrator follows, although not chronologically, from the time she is seven years old until she reaches grandmotherhood—with generous passages of poetry to create a literary pastiche. (In this novel Alegría does not even bother to change the name of Luisa's husband. It is Bud, Darwin Flakoll's nickname.) Much of the text is dialogue, which gives the sense of heteroglossia; at one point, the narrator includes her- or himself in a "we": "We never saw Wilf again" (19). Temporal, spatial, even "generic" ruptures situate this text well within nueva narrativa. Alegría herself enters the text in a passage of poetry: "the earth is my body / and I am the body / of the earth / Claribel" (18).

Like the narrative, her poetry is both personal and political. Alegría writes in a line of verse near the end of the English version of the novel: "I have freed myself at last" (137),[9] as she integrates the two directions, thereby resolving a struggle she has been waging textually since *Cenizas.*

The artful blending of poetry and storytelling—what Alegría has felt called to do since childhood and what she feels she does best (interview 1991b)—represents her contribution to the revolution of the Salvadoran people. Like many Central American writers who have had to deal with the supposed conflict between public militancy and the private activity of writing, Alegría comes to terms with both by putting one at the service of the other. *Luisa* pays homage to storytellers and poets, to the "locos" and "locas," as she herself was called when as a child she sought solitude to write. The narrator establishes the theme of storytelling and the tension between truth and fiction: "En la familia de Luisa abundaban los mitómanos, incluyéndola a ella por supuesto" (71) (In Luisa's family there were many fabulous liars, including herself, of course) (53; translations of *Luisa* are by Darwin Flakoll). P. J. Eakin reminds us that autobiography draws as much upon creative fictionalizing as it does upon remembered fact in its attempt to reconstruct the past: "Autobiographical truth is not a fixed but an evolving content in an intricate process of self-discovery and self-creation" (quoted in McGowan 117–18). Fictionalizing is not the art of escapism; on the contrary, storytelling is Alegría's way to define herself as she looks back at her own life and her strategy to confront the tragedies of history as she considers the fate of El Salvador.

Luisa/Claribel remembers well-known Salvadoran writers possessed of great imagination—for example, Salarrué, who in addition to being a great storyteller and painter "sabía también desdoblarse y ver el aura de las gentes" (166) (also knew how to bilocate and see people's auras) (124), and Roque Dalton, Salvadoran militant writer par excellence, whom she never met but with whom she shared dreams through correspondence in exile (125). Alegría's mentor and favorite writer, Julio Cortázar, telephones Luisa with a personal prophecy, and Nicaragua's José Coronel Urtecho writes her a political one: "Vos vas a ver la liberación de Centroamérica" (141) (You will live to see the liberation of Central America) (105). Not to dwell on the literary elite, the narrator also includes Luisa's fondness for Carmen Bomba, the marketplace porter, beast of burden, and poet whose memory refreshes her. Every afternoon after work he would get a bit drunk "para coger valor" (to arouse his courage), and he would stop at the windows in his neighborhood "a soltar las rimas que había compuesto ese día" (175) (to recite the verses he had composed that day) (131). Luisa/Claribel is seeking inspiration from her forebears.

Turning Lewis Carroll's *Alice in Wonderland* on its head, Alegría incorporates the fabulous and the fantastic to tell a story that is frightfully real. The opening anecdote of the novel establishes imagination as a theme. Through the eyes of seven-year-old Luisa, the narrator introduces Wilf, a free spirit on his way from Germany to Brazil to teach philosophy. He is sidetracked in Santa Ana for a year, having fallen in love with Luisa's Aunt Olga, who does not reciprocate. According to Luisa, Wilf speaks twenty languages, dresses occasionally in kilts—for which Santa Ana's citizens predictably ridicule him—and, clad in black tie and tails, reads Faust in German by candlelight to anyone who cares to listen. Following the Matanza, he leaves as mysteriously as he appeared, but not without thundering, "¡La naturaleza no perdona!" (18) (Nature doesn't forgive!) (15).

Equally colorful figures populate Alegría's text: the familiar Siguanaba, Cipitío, and *cadejos* (magic dogs) of Salvadoran folklore; Luisa's mother, who hears ghosts at night; the deaf-mute who amuses everyone with her gestures; Tata Pedro, who spends his life looking for buried treasure; the dog Cuis, who reads the mind of its mistress, Aunt Elsa; Luisa herself, who loves to paint because she thinks it is magic and who "[miente] sin titubear" (154) (fibs without faltering) (115) if it will create a good story; and finally Luisa's friend the gypsy, a bubbly, wild, adventurous, "mad creature" with a utopian streak and a sad face (108).

It seems that the "locos" are the only people able to dream of a better world. Another of Luisa's friends, Manuel, has a "crazy grandmother" who cooks for the soldiers at the Golden Bridge and smuggles arms to guerrillas under the load of mangoes in her handcart (137–40). Luisa also remembers "la loca Pastora que con ojos desorbitados y el bastón en alto, predicaba la desigualdad social en las esquinas polvorientas de Santa Ana" (123) (crazy Pastora, wild-eyed and brandishing her cane as she harangued against social injustice on the dusty street corners of Santa Ana) (92). No one takes seriously these quixotic prophets who dare to challenge the establishment. By dismissing them as "locos," relegating them to the margins, the Santanecos need not heed their condemnations of the misery and violence all around.

Alegría does not need to invent a historical frame: from the sixteenth century Conquest and the sellout by the Malinche, who "le entregó al invasor/ su continente / con su amor lo entregó / con su locura" (101–2) (handed the invader / her continent / out of love / out of madness) (75), through the Matanza and Farabundo Martí's activism, to the modern-day torture chambers of Chile, Nicaragua, and El Salvador, Alegría fictionalizes only the details of an ugly reality as she works her craft.

Victims of the abuse of power relate incidents that are even more horrifying because they are so widespread, so commonplace. Alejandra, a Chilean friend of Luisa, describes the interrogation she underwent in the "Blue Theatre," a prison in which she was forced to witness the mutilation of a suspected subversive. Another friend, Carlos, tells Luisa about the rescue of a pregnant woman from a well into which she had been tossed by the military along with the bodies of twenty other "compas." When they pulled her out, she was covered with maggots. She died several days later, completely insane. Unfortunately, the *locura* (craziness) that results from persecution is the fatal, rather than the fertile, variety. This reality is more shocking than any fiction Alegría could invent.

Feminism as a discourse still plays a dominant role in defining the Other in *Luisa*. The "I" of the poem "En la playa" (At the Beach) laments the Chinese custom of binding women's feet. Actually, in patriarchal society, "no son los pies los que atan / es la mente" (68–69) (it's not that their feet are bound / it's their minds) (51). The problem extends beyond China.

The feminine voice of *Luisa* differs from the personally anguished lost souls like Carmen and Isabel of *Cenizas*. What emerges is a voice of confidence, irony, and sophisticated perception, even though it belongs to a seven-year-old girl. Several humorous examples illustrate Luisa's sensitivity to "women's issues" and her forthright reaction to them. The child Luisa and her family offer shelter to her Aunt Filiberta, who, after suffering beatings from her husband, comes to stay with them at least three times a year. Typically, several days pass, the abusive but repentant husband sends a serenade to woo back his wife, and she dutifully responds "con una sonrisa que no se sabía si era de alegría o de vergüenza" (58–59) (with a smile that wavered between happiness and shame) (44).

The never-ending cycle makes an impression on Luisa. When she celebrates her first communion, her aunts tell her she can make any wish she desires. At the moment of swallowing the host, Luisa prays silently: "Niñito Jesus . . . yo no me quiero casar, no me gusta cómo son los hombres con las mujeres, pero quiero tener un hijo, niñito Jesús. La Chabe dice que sólo las mujeres casadas pueden tener hijos, por eso yo te pido con toda mi alma que me case y que cuando tenga el niño mi marido se muera (52) (Dear little Jesus . . . I don't want to be married; I don't like the way men treat women, but I do want to have a baby, Dear Jesus, and Chabe says that only married women can have babies. So that's why I ask you with all my heart to let me get married, and as soon as I have my baby, to let my husband die) (39). When she is ten, Luisa—because she has heard that whores are evil—approaches one out of curiosity and pokes her head into her curtained quarters: "Si fuera mala no tendría tantos santos en la pared" (32) (If you were bad, you wouldn't have so many saints on your walls) (24), Luisa tells her. The whore offers her a candy as Luisa notices the picture of a young boy on the shelf. After she learns that the boy, presumably the whore's son, died of dysentery, she felt "ganas de abrazarla" (33) (like hugging her) (25) with compassion. Luisa's young male friend tells her she is stupid for entering the woman's house because "whores are bad," to which Luisa responds: "El malo eres tú" (33) (You're the bad one) (25). The evidence, she finds, contradicts society's stereotype.

The narrator's and Luisa's critical eye extends to other situations that oppress sectors of Salvadoran society. The plight of the poor confronts the child Luisa as she talks with her playmate Memo. Having listened to her grandfather's stories of Paris, Luisa tells Memo she envies the fact that he lives in "El mesón Versailles"—the Versailles Tenement—the oxymoronic name of a Santa Ana shantytown. He does not understand. Later he brings her a little bird he caught to put in her cage, but she tells him birds should be free. As he twists his filthy toes, he explains that he cannot let it go: "Es que, es que . . . mi mamá la quiere matar porque hoy no tenemos qué comer" (44) (It's just that . . . my ma wants to kill her because we don't have anything to eat) (34). The reality of poverty only heightens the absurdity and the insensitivity of her comments on "Versailles."

Luisa also learns first hand about the insecurity and fragility of children orphaned by the Matanza. One of them, Felix, stays with her family until he is frightened away by the dire threats of Delia, the maid who is at the same time an "evangelista or algo por el estilo" (83) (some kind of evangelist) (61). The narrator makes several such comments about the hypocrisy and uncharitable spirit of certain brands of Christianity. The poem "Operation Herod" condemns soldiers who toss babies into the air onto bayonets; the "Personal Creed" of revolution and the resurrection of the oppressed replaces the traditional Apostles' Creed; and the story of Sor Ana Teresa's vows in her "marriage to God" is critical of the stern practices of the traditional Church. Little Luisa attends as maid of honor. While she is waiting for the bridegroom (God) to appear, Luisa is shocked when the mother superior hacks off Teresa's beautiful chestnut hair. Luisa concludes that God obviously did not attend the ceremony because he never would have allowed such a haircut (42). She cannot imagine a God who dislikes beauty.

Luisa wakes up to injustices beyond the borders of El Salvador as well. After high school graduation, she travels to New Orleans, where she reacts indignantly when she sees a sign reading "No dogs or Mexicans allowed" at an exclusive restaurant. Her friend's mother tries to soothe her ruffled feelings: "Cálmate, *honey* . . . tú eres salvadoreña" (171) (Calm down, honey, . . . after all, you're Salvadoran) (128). Luisa probably wonders whether the bigots are really going to take the time to distinguish between Mexicans and Salvadorans. And, after all, it matters little. Racial prejudice is blatant. She experiences the dehumanizing effects of discrimination, racism, poverty, war, and machismo as both victim and witness.

Luisa/Claribel has straddled both worlds. No stranger to dehumanization and death, she has been able to maintain a somewhat privileged existence in a corner of hell. Toward the end of *Luisa,* she charts her life in the poem "From the Bridge." Life as "turbulent water" flows below carrying images from her past—loved ones, her own silhouette as a child and adolescent, former students now dead who were the victims of political torture, her own children. She retraces her journey: "I remember you well at that age / you wrote honeyed poems" (138). But reality shatters her cocoon and she is forced to "search for order in chaos." The only thing she ever seems to find, however, is death, "a sinister / and well-planned disorder" (139). Justice and happiness are illusions. Only the "stench of carrion" hangs in the air. She is looking for redemption, as both Carolyn Forché and Marcia Phillips McGowan have remarked (McGowan 112). Writing and storytelling, love and solidarity—which she learned through *No me agarran viva*—will transcend death. Zimmerman has called "From the Bridge" the "subjective centerpiece" of Alegría's book and life work—"a central auto-biographical, aesthetic/political statement, tying [her] own development as a daughter of the Central American bourgeoisie to her achievement of self-understanding and full self-expression" (1994, 215). She metaphorically bridges the poles of her existence: from the personal to the political, from poetry to testimony, and from the individual to the compañera in solidarity.

Through her growing awareness and concern for the Other, she is visionary. *Luisa* establishes a relationship, a paradigm of oppression, which the final poem, "The Cartography of Memory," blasts to pieces. This hymn envisions "a rebellious / contagious peace / a peace that opens furrows / and aims at the stars" (152). It will be a peace "of a different kind" (151), a peace not of somnolence and repression but of justice. Interestingly, this poem, as well as "From the Bridge," appears only in the English version—the language of exile? Or perhaps it is the language of the audience she wishes to win over to the cause of Salvadoran liberation. The seed metaphor speaks to the deaths—"heads dangling like seedpods"—that will not have been in vain because seeds are sprouting into "plants [that] had never been seen in the country" such as liberty, justice, and conscience. The seed refers also to her "first seedbed of memories" and her longing to return to her "roots," to come full circle. The closure will represent both a private and a political fulfillment since she will not return until the "love that seeds dreams" has restored and redeemed her country. Perhaps then she can write the poem in Spanish.

The poetic "I" combines her dreams of a return from exile with her hopes for a better future for all. While she longs to rest in the shade of the comforting old ceiba tree in her garden and to recover nostalgically the good times past, she knows that the greater reality will and must be different: "The jasmine won't be there / nor the araucaria./ Nor will there be a fortress / in front of my house / nor children / flaunting their misery / nor mud shanties / with tin roofs" (150–51). A return to what is past is impossible, even undesirable. Crossing over has brought great pain yet represents the only mature response possible: "Come, love, let's return / to the future." Luisa/Claribel has awakened to reality, and there is no turning back.

When in her dream, "The Final Act," the lights come on in the darkened theater, she realizes that "the play is over . . . and all the people have left"

(*Luisa in Realityland* [or 1987b] 141). This is no fiction. But in a marvelous irony, she can use her powers as a poet and storyteller to break out of the confines of a Santa Ana mentality, envision a future full of life, and join the struggle for change.

Much of Claribel Alegría's writing is a mapping of her own passage from privileged child of Santa Ana to woman and writer in solidarity with a community. This trajectory will frame the historical and literary experience of the other writers I will highlight in this book. Alegría and Flakoll use their writing to link the insurrection of the 1970s and 1980s to the indigenous uprising of 1932 and the subsequent Matanza, a defining moment in all the texts. They recover lost history and lost popular voices in a rewriting of that history from the point of view of its disadvantaged. Also at play are cross-cultural tensions and gender conflicts within the struggle for dignity and justice.

Alegría and Flakoll's later work, most notably after 1980, shows a keen awareness of the relations of oppression and of the relationships among various marginalized groups of people in the struggle for national liberation. They also realize that they are particularly well suited to cross borders to address an international audience in order to make El Salvador's martyrdom known to the world. The later texts show more of Alegría's hand, again especially in the incorporation of poetry and the feminist perspective. The woman's voice grows stronger and more confident; her liberation is a function of her activity in the liberation of an entire people. Some like Eugenia serve in the capacity of gun-toting compañera; Alegría's effective contribution is that of polemicist and writer. She skillfully joins the private to the public, the intimate to the external, by grafting her own story to the historical testimony of many other "agents of change." A woman without a country, she can still sing in exile. To be authentically Claribel, she must sing in defense of herself and her people.

4

Manlio Argueta

Conscience, Oral Traditions, and the
Feminization of the Salvadoran Struggle

El Salvador's Manlio Argueta, a member of the activist Círculo Literario Universitario formed in 1956 by Roque Dalton and Otto René Castillo, combines political ethics and cultural aesthetics in novels that highlight the growing revolutionary awareness among the Salvadoran oppressed. Despite the success of his novels, he still considers himself primarily a lyricist.

Born in the provincial city of San Miguel in 1936, Argueta began his literary career as a poet at a very young age, much like Claribel Alegría, writing poetry secretly because his friends and local acquaintances would have ridiculed him had they known of his pursuits. University studies took him to San Salvador, where he encountered a much more favorable reception. It was there that Argueta began his longtime association with poets of the same "generation"—Dalton, Castillo, Roberto Cea, Roberto Armijo, and some forty others mainly from the law school where they were all students. Many of these writers gradually turned to narrative in order to interpret the complex reality of the country. Commenting on this choice, Argueta has observed that "upon reaching maturity we began to write novels" (1986b, 24). Poetry no longer sufficed: "Poetry is jealous, fragile, and limited, and not particularly suited to what we need to say related to violence" (interview 1992b).

Of his relation to other well-known members of the Literary Circle, Argueta finds he shares with Cea a love for imagery and formal beauty. Neruda and Vallejo inspired them. In contrast, Dalton, influenced by French writers Michaud, St. Jean-Perse, and Prévert, pursued the poetic idea in a more avant-garde, surrealistic, and intellectual poetry. Furthermore,

Dalton was more engaged politically and ideologically in the popular struggle than either Argueta or Cea. All of them, however, have written poetry of denunciation and have concerned themselves primarily with the problem of the nation—the desire to recover lost history, to define what it means to be Salvadoran, and to "feel Salvadoran through literature" (interview 1995b).

In collaboration with a number of writers, Argueta published an anthology of poetry, *De aquí en adelante,* in 1970; his own collection, *Las bellas armas reales,* appeared in 1975. He also wrote the poems that accompany Adam Kufeld's book of photography *El Salvador* (1990). Lengthy lyrical passages continue to punctuate his novels as well.

Argueta began to write the poem about San Salvador that became his first novel, *El valle de las hamacas* (1970), without having had sufficient training in the techniques of writing narrative. But he felt even less confident about his poetic skills when he learned that, at about the same time, Ernesto Cardenal had published a similar project, *El estrecho dudoso,* a history of Nicaragua in poetry: "I thought I could never surpass this poem. Cardenal frustrated me" (interview 1995b). Argueta justified his switch from poetry to prose saying that the novel as a form offered more possibilities for an epic but at the same time demanded more discipline, time, reflection, and preparation. What he lacked in formal training he tried to acquire by imitating canonical novelists such as Dos Passos, Fuentes, Cortázar, and Vargas Llosa. *El valle* was the first in a series of works that he has claimed is one long novel about El Salvador (1994, 33). Following *El valle,* Argueta published *Caperucita en la zona roja* (1977), *Un día en la vida* (1980), *Cuzcatlán donde bate la mar del sur* (1986), and most recently *Milagro de la paz* (1995).

Further explaining the change of genres, Argueta reports that "he began to conceive of his artistic work as a labor linked to the people and opposed to the repression" (Z. N. Martínez 41). He and other members of the Circle believe that the writer has a responsibility to transform society "in a combative literature of engagement with his people, especially against the oligarchy and against militarism" (1986b, 24). Argueta characterizes his novels as "testimonial." Testimonial discourse, combined with artistic inventiveness, serves him to document the struggle of the subaltern in the Salvadoran community, particularly its women and peasants, who are coming to terms with their own oppression in order to overcome it. Both groups figure prominently in the two novels that will occupy most of my attention in this chapter.

For Argueta, testimony offers a discourse "approaching a literary genre" that gathers together threads of a rich oral tradition and rescues voices that have been silenced and lost in order to give them resonance and relevance (interview 1992b). Through the experiences of persecution, imprisonment, and exile—which he and his colleagues have all endured—Argueta rescues his own voice as well as that of other marginalized Salvadorans: "[Persecution] gave us a handle. . . . Our country began to please us as a source of inspiration. We began to abandon . . . that aesthetic intellectual tendency of seeking our inspiration in European culture or in the cultures of the developed world. We looked for it in our own reality . . . and we find ourselves within the national problem" (1986b, 24). Argueta maintains that testimony has put Central America on the map; it has been Central America's contribution to the world (1986b, 24–25). Although this claim may be overstated, in view of the many testimonies arising from Third World conditions in other continents, Argueta is justified in calling attention to testimony as the most important development in Central American narrative in recent years.[1]

Deprived of a recognized cultural tradition by oligarchs and militarists and by European universalist literary tastes, El Salvador can now reclaim its literary classics, its "father" Salarrué and its "mother" Claudia Lars, states Argueta (1986b, 25). In *El valle de las hamacas,* he writes that it is time that El Salvador wake up, "y si nadie se atreve cuándo comenzará esta mierda a caminar como gente civilizada como país a nivel de siglo veinte alguien debería responsabilizarse de algo no podemos estar sumidos en la ignominia incultura cinismo cobardía . . . te duermes no sean cobardes" (75) (and if nobody dares when will this bullshit begin to walk like civilized people like a country in the twentieth century somebody should be responsible for something we can't be submerged in ignominy lack of culture cynicism cowardice . . . you're sleeping don't be cowards) (my translation). El Salvador's true wealth has been ignored; in its place squalor and violence have found a home. Little wonder that Central America is "una mierda" (bullshit) and its people "invisible" (*El valle* 31), that it is a collection of backwaters and banana republics, and that El Salvador itself is a "país polvoriento" (dusty country) (*Caperucita* 187–88) and "el culo del mundo" (the asshole of the world) (*El valle* 84). The self-deprecation underscores a collective inferiority complex that Argueta means to overturn with heavy doses of an ugly present reality, with references to history, and with calls to action. After all, he protests, "we are not a no man's land" (*Tragaluz* 25). Testimony is his instrument to create awareness—*una conciencia*—among the people that they live with injustice, an awareness that will stir them to change.

Art is present in testimony, according to Argueta, in the popular language and folkloric traditions incorporated in the text. One of his friends
told him that the best chapter in *El valle* is the description of the assault on
the university by the national police. Argueta refused to accept any credit
for that passage, saying he took it verbatim from the court testimony of one
of the victims of brutality. For him, the beauty of the text is its simplicity, a
quality he did not appreciate until after his first two novels were written
(interview 1992b). In these early texts, Argueta works straight testimony
into complex, Boom-style elaborations of fiction and succeeds in produc-
ing critically acclaimed literature.[2] However, as he appropriates the discourse of the peasant in his third and fourth novels, he simplifies his
textual strategies. The reader cannot help but note their lyrical quality. For
Osses, "it is a question of the poet writing a novel" (142). Argueta attributes
his musical, rhythmic use of language to the influence of Julio Cortázar
(Osses 144).

Argueta currently feels the need to continue writing simply so that
ordinary people, not just the specialists, will read him. During a visit to El
Salvador, where he was preparing to return after twenty years of exile in
Costa Rica, Argueta happily noticed that his novels *Un día en la vida* and
Cuzcatlán were being read over the radio to people who could not read.
While he realizes that his novels have "conscientized" foreigners to politi-
cal and spiritual solidarity with the people of El Salvador, he maintains that
reaching a foreign market was never his primary purpose.

Underscoring his mission to the people, Argueta summarizes his most
recent literary project: because over one-fifth of El Salvador's children
currently reside outside their country (in Australia, the United States,
Canada, Europe, and other parts of Latin America), he has published a
bilingual edition of one of his country's oldest folktales, the cadejo, entitled "Los perros mágicos de los volcanes" or "Magic Dogs of the Volcanoes."[3] He hopes the story helps the children recover the mentality, the
mythic world, and the cultural identity of their country of origin—in short,
a Salvadoran consciousness. He is presently working on children's versions
of two additional tales, "La Siguanaba" and "Chinchintora la culebra"
(Chinchintora the snake). Other than these stories, Argueta's primary focus
remains the novel. Also in progress is *La noche de los niños* (The night of the
children), a novel written from the perspective of children but not for
children. He recognizes his debt to Salarrué, whose *Cuentos de cipotes,* he
believes, is the crown jewel of Salvadoran literature. The "master" influenced his own taste for popular speech patterns and language (interview
1992b). The mythic folktale and the realistic testimony share a common

feature important to Argueta's work: they hold the popular voice that he wishes to recover.

Argueta's first novel, *El valle de las hamacas,* written in 1968 and published two years later, is important to my study in that it represents the first Boom-style novel of El Salvador and at the same time incorporates testimonial discourse to show growing awareness and discontent among the urban petite bourgeoisie. Passages depicting guerrilla activity alternate abruptly with descriptions of student life, the brutal assault on the university, political theory, personal remembrances of times past, and scenes of torture by government agents. Typical of new narrative, *El valle* moves quickly, chaotically, and sometimes incoherently from one level of discourse to another. Kathryn Kelly observes that the abrupt jumps and interruptions in the text "present a reality more true-to-life than a simple description and narration of the details of modern Salvadoran life" (99). Argueta's message is that hope for El Salvador's future rests with its youth—not one solitary hero but many.

In addition to the aforementioned verbatim court testimony of the assault on the university, Argueta weaves several other threads of documentary information into *El valle.* He includes an actual speech by an arrogant presidential candidate and a letter from the conquistador Pedro de Alvarado to the king about the great difficulty he encountered subduing the uncooperative natives in what now is El Salvador. Argueta explains his purpose for including the latter document: "This is to show that there are certain popular roots in the famous violence about which imperialism and the bourgeoisie speak; it is that the people have to defend themselves. . . . This is a way of awakening in El Salvador an interest in our own true history (Osses 145). Understanding the resistance and rebellion in their past may motivate today's oppressed Salvadorans to live up to their historic reputation. Remembering will renew their energy and hope.

Like *El valle,* Argueta's second novel, *Caperucita en la zona roja* (1977), grows out of a petit bourgeois experience in the city. *Caperucita* continues the denunciation of abusive authority and the appeal to popular conscience begun in *El valle,* again very much within the nueva narrativa mold. Popular expressions and pronunciations and an absence of punctuation shape the language experience of this text if not its communicative ability. Noting its difficulty, Argueta has encouraged his readers to approach it as a series of fragments rather than a novelistic whole (Osses 139).

Argueta widens his cast of characters in *Caperucita* to include women, peasants, and religious. Hormiga/Caperucita and Alfonso are lovers in the guerrilla underground who are fighting the "wolves" of repression, police brutality, and even petty jealousy. Of particular interest to me is Argueta's development of female roles that will become even more important in his later novels. Jack Zipes considers Argueta's Caperucita much more "gutsy" and astute than the passive character of the Grimm fairy tale, much more like the Little Red Riding Hood of the oral tradition: "[This one is] forthright, brave and shrewd. She knows how to use her wits to escape preying beasts" (quoted in Kelly 103). Women began to assume more visible, more responsible roles in the consciousness-raising and liberation movements of the 1970s and 1980s. One of the most famous passages of the text is the hymn to the woman-mother, a parody of the Ave María, of which the following is a fragment: "Mamá querida, Oración por todos. Mamá llena eres de gracia. . . . Mamá puta. . . . Mamá cortadora de café. . . . Mamá virgen maría madre de dios. . . . Mamá descalza. . . . Mamá hombre, abuela, abuelo, mamá mamá. Tu madre. Buenos días, madre" (60) (Mommy dearest, we pray for all. Mommy full of grace. . . . Mommy whore. . . . Mommy coffee cutter. . . . Mommy virgin mary mother of god. . . . barefoot Mommy. . . . Mommy man, grandmother, grandfather, mommy mommy. Your mother. Good morning, mother). Through the revolutionary process women discovered their own vitality and their own voice.

Un día en la vida (1980)

The majority of narrative voices belong to peasant women in Argueta's third and perhaps best-known novel.[4] Here women define their role within the Salvadoran struggle to an even greater extent than in *Caperucita*. Argueta has transcribed direct testimony by women who have lived the history they relate to him. Local Salvadoran expressions and lyricism fill their testimony. "The person who writes testimony," explains Argueta to Zulma Martínez, "is clearly conscious that he or she is transforming reality" (54).

    La conciencia, or the conscientization of the people, is one of the salient motifs of *Un día*. This novel develops the theme of conscientization through reflections by the peasantry, through testimony about events—triumphs and tragedies—in which the people have participated, and through examples of the growing solidarity that the Salvadoran Church has established with the poor as an expression of its theology of liberation. The awareness of oppression extends for the first time in Argueta's work to members of the National Guard; peasants realize that the guardsmen come from the same stock as they and that they too are victims, they too are

Other. Argueta explains that the peasants are finally breaking an internalized discourse of resignation and submission (Z. N. Martínez 45).

Un día offers a more hopeful vision than either *El valle* or *Caperucita* because it documents an epoch of immense change and possibility in El Salvador. It follows the explosion of activity by popular organizations and resistance groups in the 1970s, the increased importance of women in the struggle, and the activism of the Catholic Church and Archbishop Oscar Romero (archbishop from February 5, 1977, until his assassination on March 24, 1980). Furthermore, the success of a parallel liberation movement in neighboring Nicaragua could not but help increase the mood of expectancy and impending triumph in El Salvador in the late seventies so palpable in *Un día*.

Argueta links political liberation to linguistic liberation as he continues to experiment with language in the novel. He has deliberately chosen Salvadoran words and expressions from the countryside, defending his decision as both moral and practical: "How could it be that we were defending the people and, at the same time, we were ashamed of the way the people talked? We began to get rid of this embarrassment little by little, and suddenly we discovered that using local language, the language of the people, was also a form of rebellion" (Z. N. Martínez 48). If he claims to portray Salvadoran reality, he believes that his medium had better be authentically Salvadoran.

Argueta finds great beauty in the oral traditions of the peasants, from their magical folktales to their poetic musings on the natural wonders around them, all of which he incorporates into the text. A woman tells of her first experience with the voice of conscience, which happened to take the form of the Good Cadejo or magic dog to save her from a rattlesnake. She also recalls her husband's uproarious vision and version of the Siguanaba, a witch disguised as a beautiful seductress known to lure lone male travelers to the river's edge as if inviting them to make love. At the last minute, she reveals long claw-like fingernails, a face as pale as death, eyes shining like a cat's, huge teeth, and withered breasts, terrorizing her hapless victim until he defecates all over his clothes.

Powerful metaphors and imagery reveal the heightened visual and auditory sensibilities of the peasant to nature: "El cielo se coloradea como la sangre de un pájaro muerto. . . . El cielo es una chiva guatemalteca de colores" (6) (The sky turns the color of the blood of a dead bird. . . . The sky is a Guatemalan weave of many colors) (1992a, 4–5);[5] and "las chicharras chillan porque el sol es fuerte. Es una manera de protestar por el verano. Se oye el concierto por todo el monte. La música de las chicharras. Como timbre de camioneta: ring-ring. Por todos lados" (96) (the cicadas buzz because the sun is strong. It's a way to protest the summer. Their concert is heard all over the hills. The music of the cicadas. Like the horn of a pickup truck: chiquirun-chiquirin, ting-a-ling. Everywhere) (121). The language of *Un día* is direct, colorful, and earthy.

The novel gives an hour-by-hour account of a day in the life of a peasant woman, Guadalupe Fuentes, who lives in the town of Kilómetro in the northern province of Chalatenango. The title of the novel leads us to believe that this is just like any day in the life of a Salvadoran. This "slice of life" seems common or even banal in its ordinariness until we learn that this is the day Guadalupe is asked to identify José, her dying husband, who has been tortured and dragged to her with his one eye hanging out of its socket. This, then, is not just any day. It is as if Lupe has lived an eternity in a single day, remarks Kelly (114). But on second thought we realize that this experience is common, albeit horrific, in the El Salvador of the seventies and eighties. Between the cock's opening crow at five-thirty in the morning and José's appearance before Lupe at two in the afternoon, the reader travels with her through her memories as she reconstructs her family's, and by extension her country's, history.

Other narrative voices round out episodes in which they have directly participated and which are unknown or only partially known to Lupe. Text printed in italics relates events of Salvadoran history while text in regular type narrates the plot of the novel. Lupe's children and grandchildren participate in various phases of the revolution—attending union meetings, traveling to the capital to plead the peasants' cause with government officials, occupying the cathedral, suffering disappearance and death, searching prisons for loved ones. Interwoven with the various discourses of memory is Lupe's own account of her daily routine of mere survival.

Facing the guardsmen and her brutalized José, Lupe summons strength from a well of dignity and courage to deny knowing the man, to refuse to display her grief, and thus to deny the Guard the pleasure of her defeat. Her reaction reveals a conscious effort to resist playing into the hands that have historically oppressed her and her people.

Lupe repeatedly emphasizes the need for awareness and education in the peasant community. She will sacrifice in order to send her children to school, but her dream goes beyond the individualistic, bourgeois ambition of improving the lot of one's family and of seeing one's children do better than their parents. She explains the meaning of conscience: "La conciencia

. . . es sacrificarse por los explotados. . . . La conciencia son todas las acciones que hacemos en provecho de los demás sin andar buscando el interés personal" (135–36) (Conscience is to sacrifice oneself for those who are exploited. . . . Conscience is all the things we do for the benefit of others without seeking our own interest) (172–73). For her, a new conscience means changing old habits of thinking. Whereas she used to believe that it was "natural" for peasants to be poor and that she should just thank God for the little she had—her good health, corn, salt, and beans—she now knows that farmworkers suffer poverty because of exploitation (135). Every child has the right to medicine, food, and schooling (27). Therefore, children must go to school to have their eyes opened to injustice and to learn their basic rights.

Learning to think critically, Lupe finds, provides a foundation for effective community action. Complaining gains nothing, but unless matters are clear one has no other option. Once the peasants have clarified and understood injustice, they can "unlearn" submission and raise their heads high, looking the boss straight in the eye (27–28). With a new confidence, they have organized "la federación cristiana y la unión de trabajadores campesinos" (the Christian federation and the union of farm workers),[6] which has enjoyed some success in obtaining good loans. The members have taken their participation and responsibility seriously to the point that many of them have given up drunkenness and crapshooting (153)! José has set an example of solidarity and sacrifice for others within the peasants' federation, for which he is dearly loved (136).

The same spirit that has won the respect of his fellow workers has earned him the hatred of the landowners and the authorities. Realizing that the peasants are on to something and now threaten the age-old system of exploitation that has benefited a few at the expense of the many, the National Guard has targeted José and like-minded leaders of the cooperatives, forcing them to flee their homes and sleep in the hills.

The threat against the men of the rural community recalls for Lupe a story she once heard from her own mother, Rubenia Fuentes. This testimony adds to Lupe's awareness of the magnitude and longevity of their suffering. It also serves to incorporate textually the memory of the Matanza of 1932, an event in the nation's history that has largely been preserved through oral accounts such as Rubenia's as retold by Lupe. Lupe recounts what she has heard many times:

En esa época se hablaba mucho del comunismo y las autoridades andaban furiosas. "La indiada se había levantado y eso no lo iban a perdonar aunque se acabara toda la gente de por aquí." Me decía mi mamá. Fue despuesito del treinta y dos. "No te imaginás lo terrible que fueron esos días, ni siquiera se podía tener un santo de estampa porque ya creían que la oración que tiene escrita por detrás eran consignas del comunismo y ahí nos tenías vos quemando la virgen del Refugio, el Santo Niño de Atocha, y hasta el Salvador del Mundo." Y yo le digo que ha de haber sido una cosa terrible. "Es que debías tener cuidado hasta para suspirar, no fueran a creer que estabas lamentando a un muerto y con eso había presunción que tenías un pariente comunista muerto, más de cuarenta mil cristianos murieron en ese tiempo." (50–51)

[Back then there was so much talk of communism and the authorities were furious. "The Indians had rebelled, and they weren't going to forgive that even if it meant wiping out our entire population here." That's what my mother used to tell me. It was a little after 1932. "You can't imagine how terrible those days were. One couldn't even own a stamp with a saint on it because they believed that the prayers printed on the back were Communist slogans, and we had to burn the Virgin of Refuge, the Holy Child of Atocha, and even the Savior of the World." And I tell you things were bad. "You even had to be careful how you breathed so they wouldn't think you were grieving for a death and therefore presume that you had a dead Communist relative. More than forty thousand people died in those days."] (61–62)

Lupe shudders when Rubenia describes how all the male workers of the coffee plantations were rounded up and shot for being suspected Communist sympathizers. Her mother heaves a sigh of relief that her man did not work on the plantation; in fact, she feels fortunate that they lived in poverty far from the agitation on the coast: "Para nosotros la pobreza es una bendición" (51) (For us poverty is a blessing) (62). Lupe stares at her in wide-eyed amazement. Later in her life, Lupe will realize that such an attitude only perpetuates their servitude.

Awareness shakes Lupe out of her resignation. She and her family learn that awareness or conscience shows strength of character (92). It is a voice from within, severe, sometimes punishing, a voice that in the long run is a favor (15). She remembers José's words: "Dios es la conciencia. Y la conciencia somos nosotros, los olvidados ahora, los pobres" (163) (God is conscience. And conscience is we, the ones forgotten now, the poor) (211). La conciencia is all they have; but it is a powerful weapon that gives hope, courage, and direction.

The idea of God as la conciencia reveals a radical change in religious thinking in El Salvador and many other parts of Latin America. Indeed, a primary focus of the "New Church," which Argueta discusses in *Un día*, has been the conscientization of the oppressed, the preferential option for the poor. This new theology of liberation was first articulated in 1968 by the Latin American Council of Bishops in Medellín, Colombia, to apply Vatican II and the new understanding of the social gospel to the Church in their continent. In 1979 the bishops met again in Puebla, Mexico, to refine this theology.[7] Liberation theology grows out of the experience of suffering in Latin America; its point of departure is the daily reality of millions of the continent's exploited. In other words, this theology comes from below, from the Third World, rather than from Rome or the First World. Like testimony and resistance literature, liberation theology has as its goal the mental, physical, and spiritual decolonization of the Third World (Sobrino 180).

One of the first thinkers to develop liberation theology, the Peruvian Gustavo Gutiérrez, writes that "in order for this liberation to be authentic and complete, it has to be undertaken by the oppressed people themselves and so must stem from the values proper to these people" (91). Liberation theology entails theory and doctrine as well as praxis. The Church must stand in solidarity with the poor even if such action leads to martyrdom. From the Old Testament Exodus to Jesus's fulfillment of the prophecy that he will come to "set at liberty those who are oppressed," the dominant theme of biblical history is liberation, according to Gutiérrez and like-minded theologians. But awareness must precede liberation: "The participation of the oppressed presupposes an awareness on their part of their unjust situation. 'Justice, and therefore peace,' say the Latin American bishops, 'conquer by means of a dynamic action of awakening (*concientización*) and organization of the popular sectors which are capable of pressing public officials who are often impotent in their social projects without popular support'" (Gutiérrez 114).

Leonardo Boff, bishop of Petropolis, Brazil, explains that the theory is to be applied in base Christian communities, which educate and promote awareness, solidarity, and action in "one of the most original expressions of faith lived by the people of Latin America" (46). The conscientizing function of the Church is necessarily a politicizing function (Gutiérrez 269), one that evokes rebuff and retaliation from institutional powers who see their hegemony threatened. According to its practitioners, liberation theology represents an authentic, informed response by Others to their situation of exploitation.

When I asked Argueta about the future of liberation theology in El Salvador, considering the demise of leftist discourse on the world scene, he responded by emphasizing the basic role the Church continues to play in his country: "There have been so many martyred priests. This has created an entire tradition among the people who greatly admire their priests. The Church has played a historic role, and liberation theology is not a fashion or a fad. It will not be forgotten" (interview 1992b).

Activist priests and base Christian communities bring the gospel of liberation to Lupe's family in *Un día*. Lupe draws a contrast: the Old Church produced fear and suspicion in the peasants and promised them respite in heaven from this "vale of tears" if only they accepted their fate here with resignation; the priests of the New Church arrive dressed ready to work alongside the poor and to share their suffering. Formerly, when the peasants would complain to the priests that their children were dying of worms, they were told not to worry about worldly things: this was "la justicia de Dios" (19) (God's will). No longer do the parishioners equate goodness with resignation (44). Lupe credits her new awareness to the change in the priests' methods and message. Now speaking in the vernacular, the priests opened her eyes: "Nada más entendíamos eso de dominus obispos, que por cierto siempre hacíamos bromas diciendo dominusvobispu, el culo te pellizcu" (20) (We no longer had to hear about *Dominus obispos,* which we used to make fun of, saying *"Dominus obispu,* I'll kick the ass in you") (23). The people gain access to the word/Word.

Furthermore, the priests help Lupe and the other peasants form cooperatives so that they can better help themselves. Argueta explains that the formation of cooperatives in the sixties and seventies permitted peasants to recover the organizational skills they had lost following the Matanza of 1932: "Certainly, the present [mobilization] does not come from out of the blue: it grows out of a complete awareness in the countryside which the previous repression intended to wipe out" (Z. N. Martínez 47). It was the priests who helped create that awareness.

Neutrality is impossible for the Church. When one critic blames the clergy for abandoning the traditional Church, Lupe reminds him that Christianity instructs them to do good deeds for the poor (30). Either a priest is part of the traditional "santa trinidad" (holy trinity)—the old alliance between Church, landowners, and military—or he must forsake it.

The new theology espoused by the priests signifies betrayal to their former allies. The "voice of the voiceless," Archbishop Romero serves as an example of the new priesthood in *Un día* as he supports the peasants who occupy the cathedral in public protest.

In a brief digression, I would point out an interesting piece of information that Argueta recently shared about the apparent redemption of Oscar Romero. In 1958 Argueta returned to San Miguel and formed an activist literary group, Enero, of professor friends and young poets. Enero was shortlived; its members were expelled from the area for their "subversive" activity when a young churchman denounced them. In an apparent reference to Romero, Argueta relates that the accuser "was a young member of the Church who, years later, when the war began in 1980, would become a notable eccesiastical figure and one of the most outstanding historical personages of my country, admired by almost all Salvadorans, and who was assassinated in an attempt to silence his voice" (1994, 31). The reverence and admiration for the saintly Romero that Argueta portrays in his novels may derive from his own experience of watching the remarkable transformation of a cautious conservative to an outspoken defender of the poor.

One could deconstruct the role of the priests, even as Argueta represents them within the "New Church," arguing that they still occupy a position of authority and that liberation is still an elitist or "top down" operation—first the priests and other intellectuals must instruct and conscientize the poor, who only then can act on their own. Even though they live with the poor, the priests enjoy the weight of a powerful institution behind them, in contrast to the truly poor who belong to no power structure at all. The idea of conscientization may also be related to the positivist notion of educating people in order to improve their lot. The activist priests would most likely counter these arguments saying that, by becoming poor like their parishioners, they have adopted their Otherness and to some extent have equalized the relationship. The spark for liberation must begin somewhere. Apologists for liberation theology might also say that the Catholic Church was responsible for the "perversion" of the gospel in the first place; now they need to undo the damage some of their forefathers caused. One could also argue that conscientization goes beyond positivism. Instead of being educated to the standards of the establishment, the poor are being educated to take matters into their own hands and establish their own agenda. Needless to say, the issue remains problematic, especially as Protestant evangelicalism now claims more and more to be the "popular church."

Indeed, Argueta includes religious fundamentalism as another counterdiscourse to liberation theology in *Un día*. The pentecostal and independent sects made great headway in Central America during the period documented by the novel, preaching personal salvation or damnation and punishment. In the text, these voices claim that the gringo advisers and their Salvadoran sympathizers possess the true religion as "soldados de dios, los salvadores de este país maldito y con amor al comunismo. . . . Todas estas miasmas van a terminar cuando seamos todos en cristo, abracemos a cristo, derrotemos a los curas comunistas" (102) (soldiers of God, the saviors of this damned country that loves communism so much. . . . All those perversions are going to end when we are all united in Christ, when we all embrace Christ, and destroy the Communist priests) (129–30). Argueta clearly disapproves. This imported discourse of fundamentalist Christianity imposes another religious and political neocolonialism on El Salvador, precisely the outcome that liberation theology says it opposes.

It is interesting to note that evangelicals and Pentecostals continue converting hundreds of thousands, if not millions, of Latin Americans to this day, especially among the poor. It looks as if this movement may have more grassroots, popular support than liberation theology; in other words, Pentecostal discourse may be more appealing to, and representative of, the Other's experience than previously thought (Berryman 1994).[8]

The liberation of the Other—of the peasant and particularly of the woman—is the desired effect of the theological discourse and testimonial function in *Un día*. The genesis of *Un día* helps to explain the strength of the feminine perspective for which the novel is known. Argueta explains his creative process as one that began with a letter and several tape recordings of testimonies by two different women; he drew on these to create a fiction. The challenge came in retelling the stories from a woman's point of view. Argueta began by transcribing the testimonies directly but then needed to call upon all the resources of storytelling and imagination as he elaborated fact and fiction in a sort of literary transvestism: "To a certain extent, I became the woman in order to reproduce this strength of hers" (interview 1992b).

Argueta's fictional elaboration includes the proliferation of female voices in *Un día*, in part because these very voices are multiplying in El Salvador's current history. Women are not waiting to be granted rights anymore; on the contrary, they are demanding them out of necessity. They, too, shall be subjects of history. Lupe's story actually spans four generations of women beginning with her mother Rubenia and continuing with her own daughter María Pía and her granddaughter Adolfina. Adolfina's friend María Romelia is also included as a narrative voice. One generation's resignation is transformed to awareness in the next and then to defiant activism in the third.

Traditional mores consider the woman to be an extension of male property. It is no surprise to Lupe that her parents exclude her from the discussion regarding her own marriage to José (7). But both she and José mature together. As José flees to the mountains to hide from pursuing authorities, Lupe proves wary yet hospitable, offering a drink to abusive members of the Guard because "water shouldn't be denied to anybody" (69); adept at salvaging a little humor from the direst of situations—she conceals a laugh when her dog lifts his leg to urinate on a guardsman; shrewd and intelligent, independent and resourceful—"por mí no necesito hombre en mi cama" (85) (As for me, I don't need a man in my bed) (104).

Her most difficult moment comes when she must identify the dying prisoner, the moment she summons her greatest strength. Despite her sickening visceral reaction, she must lie to her interrogators: "Estos vampiros hijos de cien mil putas, asesinos de mierda. Entonces dije que no. Tenía que ser un no sin temblor de voz, sin el menor titubeo" (149) (These vampires, sons of a hundred thousand whores, killers of the dirtiest stripe. Then I said no. It had to be a no without any quavering of my voice, without the least trace of hesitation) (191).

Anguish at the disappearance and death of loved ones causes Lupe and, by extension, many Salvadoran women to become old at an early age (88). In this sense, Argueta's novel is a tribute to the women of El Salvador who must endure seemingly unbearable pain. People may gossip about Lupe's hardness of heart. How could she deny first her son, Justino, and then her husband, José? Her neighbors realize that "es una manera de darse valor para el resto de vida que queda" (87) (it's a way of gaining courage to live what remains of life) (108). Barbara Harlow sees Lupe's denial as an act of affirmation: "It affirms both the continued existence of the resistance movement and its solidarity and it affirms the new bonds of affiliation which are evolving between men and women as a vital part of that movement" (102).

Lupe's strength is passed on to her granddaughter Adolfina, "una cipota chispa," an intelligent child despite her lack of schooling. At the age of fourteen, she has already joined the guerrilla and has directed several operations. Adolfina tells of the occupation of the cathedral in which she plays a key role. She represents the future generation of El Salvador, the hope of the country, the full realization of the new womanhood.

While Argueta's focus in *Un día* is the woman and peasant as Other, he begins to consider the Otherness of members of the Guard. He will develop this theme further in *Cuzcatlán*. In their growing awareness of their exploitation, the peasants realize that the guardsmen come from the same peasant background as they do and that they, too, are victims (99). Unfortunately, these victims can still victimize their neighbors. Several entire chapters, entitled only "Ellos" (Them) to highlight the polarized nature of the community, are narrated from their point of view. Their open disdain for peasant women, whom they call "whores," their arrogant abuse of authority and lack of humor, their anticommunist rhetoric, and their hatred of priests and blind worship of gringo advisors make them thoroughly despicable characters.

The contradictions and gross misinterpretations of their political ideology appear laughable until the reader remembers how much power they wield over the lives of their compatriots. A member of the elite special forces boasts of his importance to the future of the fatherland, the Western world, and civilization in general: "Aunque le parezca exagerado, pues el mundo occidental está en peligro y nosotros sabemos que el peor peligro que tiene el mundo occidental es eso que le llaman 'pueblo.'. . . '¿Quién es el peor enemigo de la democracia?' Y respondemos todos: 'El pueblo'" (75) (This might seem like an exaggeration, but the Western world is in danger and we know that the worst danger to the Western world is what they call 'the people.'. . . 'Who is our worst enemy?' And we shout, 'The people!') (92). The grossest irony of all is that these men could come from the families of Lupe and José's close friends and neighbors.

Several critics have found fault with this Manichean, social-realist view of Salvadoran life. I would have to agree to the extent that the novels are first and foremost political and the characters barely nuanced. The texts achieve a degree of aesthetic success more as expressions of lyricism than as novels. Argueta responds by calling attention to the magnitude of the polarization in Salvadoran society, the assassination of priests, and the violation of nuns: "Life is black and white. There are no prosecutors, no prisoners, no courts of law in El Salvador. There is only assassination. . . . The novel is a way to recover strength and to get rid of anger. It is a catharsis" (interview 1992b). The fact that Argueta may idealize his peasants and vilify the Guard does not bother Fernando Alegría. In his opinion, the subtleties of a polished narration are not to be expected here: "His artistry is different: to create life from the earth, to exalt it for a moment with the light of an anonymous heroism, to give it to the four winds. Let it be" (417). Alegría's critique excuses the reduction of the novelistic world to good and evil and defends it as raw or momentary beauty. Perhaps this art is more typical in times of political emergency but not exclusive to it, nor is it the only kind of art produced under such circumstances.

In *Un día de la vida* Argueta's characters deal with the most basic elements of life: solidarity, beauty, work, justice, and survival itself. Lupe's awareness of oppression leads her to struggle to give meaning to that survival. Mere survival will not be sufficient for her children; life must offer more. Liberation of the peasant and of the woman will grow out of a new consciousness and a sustained struggle. For now, the struggle justifies itself.

Perhaps some day liberation of the Guard and subsequent demilitarization will free the rest of the country from terrorism. It is significant that Lupe does not end her testimony with her denial of José at two o'clock in the afternoon. She goes on for several more hours remembering him fondly, finding inspiration in his life of engagement and purpose, and nurturing the hope that his spirit will not die: "por ahí vamos caminando. José Guardado nos acompaña" (154) (we're getting there. José Guardado accompanies us) (197).

As the Guard hunts down Adolfina, Lupe cries defiantly that her granddaughter is alive and well beyond their reach: "Ella vive por todos nosotros, ella respira por nosotros, ella nace mientras nosotros agonizamos, posiblemente ella también nos salvará" (151) (She lives for all of us, she breathes for us, she is being born while we are in our death throes; it is also possible that she will save us) (151). La conciencia has been passed on to Adolfina and the future.

Cuzcatlán donde bate la mar del sur (1986)

The reader may consider Argueta's fourth novel a continuation of the saga begun in *Un día*. Argueta acknowledges the series-like quality of the two books, although he believes that he has achieved an independent novel (interview 1992b).

While the action remains in the countryside with the peasants, the focus shifts to Pedro Martínez, the National Guard corporal from *Un día* who interrogates Lupe and who drags the dying José to her for identification. Like Lupe's family and like Ticha, the young woman guerrilla commander who narrates the most recent episodes in *Cuzcatlán*, Pedro has roots in the country. Emphasizing the close relationship between the members of the Guard and the peasantry, Argueta reveals toward the end of the plot—some critics may call it irony, others a contrived peripeteia or anagnorisis—that indeed Pedro is Ticha's uncle who had been conscripted twenty-five years before into military service and had lost all connection to his family. The themes of roots and generational heritage, the lost glory of the mythic Cuzcatlán, the continued importance of women to the narration and plot, the discourse of liberation in the Church, and the motif of reflection and dreaming all develop la conciencia of the Other that has characterized most of Argueta's work.

A simple and direct lyricism and the incorporation of testimonial voices and oral history within *Cuzcatlán* maintain the easy access established for the reader in *Un día*. Narrative polyphony and ruptures of time and space place *Cuzcatlán* well within the currents of the new novel, enough to "democratize" the text but not enough to divert attention to textual gymnastics and away from the referent of Salvadoran reality.

Six generations of one peasant family—that of Ticha, the nom de guerre of Lucía Martínez—provide the framework for the plot of *Cuzcatlán*. Fifteen different episodes narrated by various family members (and some narrated in the third person) tell the story that begins with Ticha's great-great-grandfather Macario and continues to include her young children. The order is not at all chronological but begins and ends with 1981. (There is a definite pattern, starting in the present and then going back to the earliest date of 1936, returning to the present, and then reaching back into the past although not quite so far. Each return to the past gets closer to the present.) Interspersed are also Mayan myths and stories of the Conquest.

The story of the Martínez family is the allegory of the nation. The very ordinariness of the family name supports this idea: Martínez is one of the commonest surnames in El Salvador (271–72). The Cuzcatlán of the novel's title is the indigenous word for the pre-Columbian territory forming present-day El Salvador, meaning land of riches, fruits, jewels, and rivers (99). Twice in the text we read the Mayan myth of creation—first through the thoughts of Ticha's grandmother, later through those of Ticha herself. The repeated narration of their origins and their Golden Age defines who they are and fortifies their resolve to reverse their present Otherness and to recover their past autonomy and happiness. The god Gucumatz created sturdy but soulful "hombres de maíz"—men of corn—who were masters of the land, cultivating it and sharing its harvest equally. In those days all people were poets, "hechos para amar" (276) (made to love). Before the cataclysmic events of 1492, this advanced civilization created a perfect calendar, one that calculated the movement of the stars and dates of eclipses.

But the Conquest metaphorically and literally turned the world and time upside down, "como si el tiempo hubiera sido destruido y todo estuviera retrocediendo. Hecho mierda todo" (24) (as if time had been destroyed and everything was going backwards. Everything had become bullshit) (translations of *Cuzcatlán* are mine). An unidentified but sympathetic narrator sarcastically notes that the conquistadors appropriately changed the name of the country to one that more accurately reflects the tribulations of the country—El Salvador (169). Misery, massacres, famine, rebellions, and one natural disaster after another replaced the wealth and tranquility of Cuzcatlán as the new colonial power introduced "progress" to the New World. The production of indigo dye left the natives "amarillentos . . . tuberculosos, cancerosos" (98) (yellow . . . tuberculous, cancerous) and decimated their population while enriching the landowners who lived in the city far from their fields. The Martínez family of *Cuzcatlán* is a remnant of the indigenous peoples, descendants of the "salvadoreños medio muertos, medio vivos" (half-dead, half-alive—an intertextual tribute to Argueta's friend and colleague, Roque Dalton, from whose poem "Todos" this line is borrowed), who for centuries suffered exploitation in dye factories and sweatshops (98). But they survived because they were men made of corn and water, the species that does not perish (86).

As in *El valle,* they find solace in the fact that there is a tradition of fierce indigenous resistance that dates from the Conquest. Argueta again uses part of a letter from Pedro de Alvarado, this one addressed to Hernán Cortés and dated July 27, 1524, in which he expresses awe at the native forces. This letter is also the source for the title of the novel. The tradition of resistance is traced through another retelling of the 1932 Matanza, which Ticha's great-grandfather Emiliano narrates as part of the national epic (43); it culminates in the current, and hopefully final, insurrection in which Ticha is fighting.[9]

The reader learns that the family originally occupied land south of Lake Apastepeque. But when floods came, the government and wealthy landowners wanted to plant rice; they forced the peasants to relocate to the other side of the lake, on mountain slopes where the land was poor. In addition to farming, the family has always made stones out of *metate* (lava rock) for grinding corn and has sold them to neighboring peasants. This tradition is continued by Emiliano, who is later killed by his own grandson and Ticha's uncle, the corporal Pedro Martínez, during an army counterinsurgency campaign in the area. In the opening pages of the novel, Ticha is on her way to a secret camp to interrogate Pedro, who recently fell into guerrilla hands and is now a prisoner of war. The novel ends on a hopeful note with Ticha's confrontation of Pedro and his subsequent pardon by a guerrilla tribunal. The conclusion may be Argueta's proposal for an amnesty and general reconciliation to end the Salvadoran conflict.

On the first page of the novel, Ticha expresses one of the text's major themes, her favorite distraction: "reflexionar. O soñar, como se dice" (9) (reflecting. Or dreaming, as we say). At times she feels that all of life is a dream, but she enjoys the opportunity of thinking about her experiences after she has lived them because, as she explains, it is a way of living twice (16). Perhaps in thinking about them, she can make sense of them or at least dream dreams of a better life. She envisions the benefits of good health care and of schools that will bring people out of darkness. In his old age, Emiliano realizes what devastation hunger and disease inflict upon the poor because people do not open their eyes (222).

In *Cuzcatlán* Argueta uses the sea as a metaphor for the vastness of the mysterious unknown, the dream of freedom and knowledge. All Salvadorans hope to look at the sea one day before they die (42). Aware that their land has been denied them, they turn to the sea as a symbol of their liberation. Ironically, the native Salvadorans were conquered by ships that came from the sea. Thus, the sea as metaphor is complex. Part of their awareness consists in understanding how the Conquest of five hundred years ago still goes on. Another part of it embodies the hope that someday they will escape the confines of their isolation and deprivation to discover a world beyond: "Quizás por eso los padres y los padres de los padres de los padres llevaban a sus hijos a conocer el mar, como un acercamiento intuitivo a otras naciones" (42) (Perhaps for this reason our fathers and the fathers of the fathers of their fathers used to carry their children to meet the sea, like an intuitive approach to other nations). They assume that there is a reality much larger than their own.

La conciencia involves an intergenerational communication especially through bloodlines. Retelling the stories of the family's past fortifies their will to survive; beyond mere survival, generational memory inspires them to resist oppression and to claim a full life as their birthright. "La sabiduría," Emiliano believes, is inherited; "se transmite por la sangre. . . . Los abuelos se lo heredan a los nietos, y éstos a sus hijos, en una cadena luminosa como el Camino de Santiago en el cielo. 'No seremos esclavos de nadie'" (39) (Wisdom . . . is transmitted through bloodlines. . . . Grandparents pass it on to their grandchildren who give it to their children in a luminous chain like the Santiago Road in the sky. "We will not be slaves to anyone").

Honoring the past, they also anticipate a future in which their children, guns in hand, will pursue and drive out the executioners. This future is being realized as the war is now being waged by Ticha and her young friends. Her choice of pseudonyms—that of her grandmother—reveals strong ties to the past, the belief that family is "something sacred" (183), and the awareness of how she fits spiritually and politically into that family.

Symbolic of the family's strength and survival is the lava rock, el metate, a central metaphor of the text. Emphasizing its importance on the opening page of the novel, Ticha explains that generations of her family have earned a living making these stones to grind corn (9). Corn, which represents life, is sacred to the peasants as their basic diet. Their vocation has allowed the family to avoid the destructive indigo dye industry and, in this way, has given them life as well. Carving the stones is "un oficio sagrado" (118) (a sacred job). Like the family, the rocks are "eternal" (180). The family takes pride in its high-quality product, quite unlike modern industrial society's throwaway goods with their built-in obsolescence. However, their durability does present a problem; because the grinding stones never wear out, the family has to search far and wide for new clients, a job Ticha's father, Jacinto, fills as a salesman. Ticha believes that at times "somos más duros que las piedras de moler que hacían mis abuelos. Entre más golpes nos dan, más fuertes somos" (260) (we are stronger than the grinding stones my grandparents used to make. The more beatings they give us, the stronger we are). She taps into this moral force to build a better society.

Although *Cuzcatlán* is a novel about resistance and insurrection against an oppressive order, very rarely does a dictator, a wealthy landowner, or any other such figure appear except as an abstraction. The textual distance parallels what Argueta sees as a "technification of the dictatorship," a concept key to the awareness of what has caused the proliferation of atrocities. He elaborates: "There is a technical, scientific office behind the repressive actions" (Z. N. Martínez 44). Since 1932, the National Guard has assumed an increasingly important role as what Althusser calls the primary repressive state apparatus. Considerable resources have been spent in military training of recruits made up mostly of peasants. Jacinto observes that basically the training teaches the soldiers to kill their own or at least keep them in their place (190). The captain reminds Pedro that all peasants are subversives and that the "real Christians" are the soldiers who defend law and order (235).

The same discourse claims that the country is overpopulated. Ticha calls the military approach an extermination plan (14), a project the captain reiterates in a passage of free indirect style: "La solución era fácil: exterminar de una vez para siempre a los pobres" (240) (The solution was simple: exterminate the poor for once and for all). He complains of "esa mierda de derechos humanos" (this human rights crap) from the gringos that forces the Salvadoran army to certify improvements in its human rights record in order to qualify for more U.S. aid (236). With imported technology, Jacinto notices a concerted effort now not only to subdue the peasantry but to destroy its way of life completely by uprooting the characteristics of an ancient culture of "poets and warriors" (273).[10] Unnecessary insults, disappearances, and scorched-earth practices by the military are destroying the soul and the morale of the peasants.

Through interior monologue and free indirect style, we travel inside Pedro's mind to learn that he takes pride in a military education that has saved him from the shame of poverty. He has worked hard for minimum promotions; now he enjoys his newly acquired status and the power to determine life or death for his enemies. The authorities have exploited his humble origins, playing on his inferiority complex: "Por desgracia soy de la raza maldita" (238) (What a shame I'm from the cursed race).

Furthermore, he misinterprets his ancestors' teachings by explaining away his mean-spirited nature as the violence in his blood (237–38) and by defending the law of the jungle and the supremacy of the strong individual at the expense of the weak (247). He ignores their traditions of love and solidarity. Obviously, Pedro has missed part of his family's story, the legacy that spurs Ticha and the others to acts of justice. He unwittingly puts his finger on the problem when he says to himself: "'El día que me salga una lágrima, habré terminado como hombre y como soldado'" (247) (The day I shed a tear, I'm done for as a man and a soldier). At the end of the novel, a guerrilla commando fills in some of the gaps of Pedro's family history and accuses him of a list of crimes that include many of the abuses committed against Lupe's family in *Un día*. Then, in the future tense, Ticha, still riding on the microbus that forms the frame of the novel, describes her confrontation with Pedro. Her strong resemblance to her grandmother Beatriz-Ticha, Pedro's mother, whom he has not seen in many years, moves him to tears. Recognizing that he is also part of the family (275), Ticha intervenes on his behalf to ensure leniency. She wants him to have to live with his conscience and with the knowledge that, in the family spirit of "compañerismo eterno" (285) (eternal friendship), she has shown him undeserved mercy.

Argueta's choice of the name Pedro for this character is significant. He shares the name of the conquistador of Cuzcatlán along with some of his warlike tendencies. The name Pedro derives from the same Latin root (petra) as *piedra* (stone), the metaphor in the text referring to the family's occupation and their eternal strength. Pedro prides himself in the strength of his military position but is obviously working toward ends opposing the values of his family. Like the biblical Peter, the "rock" on which the Church was to be founded, this one has betrayed those closest to him. One possible reading might consider that the positive note on which the novel ends suggests that even the most despicable can be redeemed.

Another hopeful sign for the future is the representation of women in the novel. Much (but not all) of the character of the Martínez family comes from its generations of strong women, who, of necessity, mature quickly. While other children of the world play, the Martínez women work, "enfrentándose a los huracanes, a las tormentas, a los caporales, a las autoridades" (267) (confronting hurricanes, storms, bosses, the authorities).

As we have already seen, the women of *Cuzcatlán* in many ways embody the same growing awareness and activism as their counterparts in *Un día.* Other women stand out in *Cuzcatlán,* most notably Lastenia, the archetypal woman who represents a tradition of popular wisdom and service. She is all things: the midwife, tortilla maker, official prayer giver, nurse, reading tutor, and religion teacher, the "shoulder to cry on" of the peasant village. In a hymn to *la tortillera* reminiscent of his tribute to *la madre* in *Caperucita,* Argueta writes that all Salvadoran women are self-sufficient and can make their own tortillas. However, there is always a village tortillera to help in time of crisis: "La tortillera es la reserva para que a nadie le falte la tortilla. . . . La tortillera del poblado hace el pan de Dios. . . . [E]s como el cadejo blanco. . . . [E]s la mamá de todos los salvadoreños. Desde hace siglos es así. Es la Virgen María de los pobres" (120) (The tortillera is the reserve so that nobody lacks for food. . . . The tortillera of the village makes the bread of God. . . . [S]he's like the white cadejo. . . . [S]he is the mother of all Salvadorans. For centuries it's been like this. She is the Virgin Mary of the poor). A counterweight to the macho culture of death and destruction in the military, woman is the giver and sustainer of life in *Cuzcatlán.*

One can problematize this representation of woman and wonder whether the hymn may be a literary overcompensation that brings us full circle to place her on the traditional pedestal, once again canonizing the suffering virgin and saintly mother. One might also find some wishful thinking on the part of the author/narrators, who hope that the conscientization and struggle finally lead to the full emancipation of women. We need only consider recent remarks by Nicaraguan feminist Gioconda Belli regarding the neighboring Sandinista project as "continued machismo" (see Chapter 6). Her hopes and enthusiasm of the early days of the revolution turned quickly to cynicism as she saw female aspirations to true leadership thwarted. While the conditions of the two countries differ somewhat, in questions of sexism there is considerable common ground. Argueta's women characters may not yet be the full counterpart to Cabezas's "new man."

In another carryover from *Un día*, the discourse of liberation theology in *Cuzcatlán* fulfills the same function of contrasting the old catechism of fear and irrelevance with the new gospel of hope and justice. Just as the old Church in this text is linked to imperialism and greed, the new one sides with the poor and preaches justice for the oppressed. Enemies see the work of subversion: "Los curas hijos de puta han convertido la Biblia en un libro comunista" (231) (The priests sons of bitches have converted the Bible into a communist book). The downtrodden now delight in the promise of the kingdom of God on earth as it is in heaven. No longer will they have to wait stoically for their final reward in the next life.

In an ironic and humorous passage, Emiliano mourns the death of his wife, Catalina, but deliberately ignores the teachings on eternal life by the parish priest, who visits him just once every three years. Instead, Emiliano prefers to think of Catalina as nearby in the earth, a part of nature: "Que Cata no se vaya al cielo," he utters in an unorthodox prayer: "Que no se fuera al cielo, porque al cielo se irían los dueños de la tierra, sus capataces, sus patrones, porque eran ellos los más cercanos a los emisarios de Dios en la tierra. No le gustaba la idea que su Cata se fuera a encontrar eternamente al lado de quienes habían sido sus verdugos, sus guardianes de presa" (31) (Don't let Cata to go to heaven because heaven is where the landowners, their foremen, and their patrons have all gone because they were closer to the emissaries of God on earth. He didn't like the idea of Cata going to be eternally at the side of the people who had been her jailors and executioners). Emiliano wants nothing to do with the Church of the rich and powerful. Later generations of his family will discover a popular Church that ministers to their needs, opens their eyes, and empowers them to take control of their own lives.

Cuzcatlán, like *Un día*, announces a future of hope for the Other. Ticha has joined the struggle because she believes that, together with other newly conscientized activists, she can overcome the victimization of her people. The message they must keep on repeating is one of optimism, "para que no se nos olvide" (so we don't forget). It also involves keeping alive the traditions and testimonies of her family and its generations of resistance. Someday even men like Pedro will lay down their weapons. The nation's collective memory of the material and spiritual riches of Cuzcatlán will help recover that lost ideal.

All of Argueta's novels document Salvadoran life at and from the margin. From pre-Columbian times to the current civil war, from city life with its urban guerrillas and student activists to the countryside and its peasant farmers, industrious women, and patrols of peasants-turned-guardsmen, Argueta's texts read like an epic of Salvadoran history and contemporary reality. As is often the case in other postmodern fiction, there are no individual heroes in Argueta's novels. Marginalized Salvadorans work in solidarity to achieve their collective liberation. At the same time that Argueta is combining testimonial function with art and fiction, he is struggling to define his own role as a committed writer in society. He finds that the nueva narrativa strategies he favors in his earlier novels do not serve him nearly as well as a more direct, simple, and lyrical style to communicate the nation's conciencia. Like his compatriot Claribel Alegría, he indicts the evil of society through the insights of an active imagination. His work differs in that his characters are less subtle, less existentially and culturally conflicted, and, in the case of his women protagonists, more idealized than hers. Nevertheless, literature for Argueta is both an artistic and an ethical practice that creatively conscientizes and interpellates Others to their reality and energizes them to change it.

Argueta's most recent work has taken a new direction since the crisis of the seventies and eighties has largely passed. Warring factions have indeed laid aside their arms. Instead of the discourses of testimonio and epic history, Argueta has turned to a more introspective, psychological narrative in his latest novel, *Milagro de la paz* (1994). He continues to experiment with narrative structure, alternating from the first- to the third-person point of view for the same narrator. At times the narrator is fully conscious, at others she is dreaming. The dreams often turn into nightmares.

Argueta's protagonists—again several generations of women—face the future fearing the unknown; they are isolated, poor, and unprotected. The women of *Milagro* are obsessed with fears especially during the night, when they think they hear "los perros coyotes," "los seres desconocidos," "los asesinos," and "los hombres que se disfrazan de animales" (coyote dogs, unknown beings, assassins, and men disguised as animals). Their terror acquires human proportions "como si . . . estuviera dentro de la casa" (87) (as if it occupied the house). This theme affords Argueta the possibility of a more "poetic evocation" where he can ask questions about sacrifice, insecurity, and death (interview 1995b). However, he has not completely forsaken the political sphere in *Milagro;* the women of the novel—in a kind of refrain—constantly note the ominous presence of the military, who occupy the town ostensibly to "mantener la paz" (maintain the peace). But one suspects that the troops contribute more to a general uneasiness than to any tranquility or security.

The United Nations–brokered peace accords have given Argueta genuine hope that the polarized sectors of his country can achieve some measure of reconciliation. To be sure, deep wounds remain to be healed, especially among Salvadoran children. His current writing projects reflect a cautious optimism and relief at the luxury of being able to direct his gaze inward. Back in El Salvador after twenty-one years of exile (he returned in early 1993), he now heads the Librería Universitaria. He is also directing his present energies toward healing rifts in the literary community that were exacerbated by the war. Gradually, he reports, "se va abriendo puertas" (doors are opening) between the classical poets of the art-for-art school, such as David Escobar Galindo, and Argueta's own politicized, conscientized Círculo Literario (interview 1995b). The fact that the education budget is larger than military expenditures today in El Salvador is cause for celebration for a writer who has understood his work as having both an aesthetic dimension and an ethical responsibility.

5

The Word According to Arturo Arias

Guatemalan Arturo Arias (b. 1950) writes the voice of the subaltern into Boom-style texts as he creates counterhistories. Arias himself does not call his novels testimonial. Whereas he admits both to writing about a reality that is his own and, to a certain extent, to documenting history, he states as his primary purpose the "creation of a work of art with all the rules and regulations of the craft of fiction and literature" (interview). Arias is afraid that most Central American narrative literature tends to be categorized as social realism with "the art wrestled out of it." He resists this homogenization and stereotyping. Instead, he goes to the opposite extreme: his characterization of testimony as art's Other recalls Beverley's observation that testimony is "subversively anti- or extra-literary" (Sklodowska 1990–91, 105). While I appreciate the theoretical distinction that Beverley draws (having made a similar case myself in Chapter 1), I find helpful Sklodowska's argument of testimony's "conquest of the literary" (112). Testimony is not necessarily the antinovel.

With this qualification in mind, we can better approach Arias's work. Signifier competes with signified for the reader's attention; belles lettres sensibilities exist side by side with political denunciation. Guatemalan Max Araujo, recalling Prada Oropeza's observation, notes this combination when he affirms that "[a]lmost all Guatemalan literature has been testimonial, no matter how fantastic it may seem. Guatemalan writers are always portraying national realities in a conscious or unconscious way" (quoted in Zimmerman 1995a, 258). Zimmerman concurs that testimony as a discourse will continue to document regional interests as writers attempt, at the same time, to appeal to universal tastes: "Indeed, given the continuing national fascination, most Guatemalan works, in their particular configurations in relation to a global postmodern ethos, will probably be instances of a mode involving variant syntheses of fantasy and testimonio" (1995a, 259). We are reminded of Angel Rama's writers of transculturation (see Chapter 2).

I find testimonial function throughout Arias's novels. Its importance and effect are, of course, a matter of degree. One cannot be sure where fiction stops and nonfiction begins. Sklodowska has observed the contradictory nature of the genre of the novel—a contradiction appropriate to Arias's work: "The novel claims to be something it isn't, disguising its own fictionality with discourses considered to be non-fictitious"; letters, memoirs, documents, manuscripts found by chance, autobiography, legal testimony, diaries, newspaper articles, sociological treatises, and history serve to validate the novel's supposed realism or mimesis (1990–91, 107). Language—the spoken and written word, *la palabra*—is Arias's tool in the service of memory and imagination. La palabra issues from one who has voice or from one who has claimed voice in the struggles of history.

Even Arias argues that one cannot separate language and art from ideology: "The word is . . . essentially, an ideological sign; it is a sign of how one understands, defines, and names the world, his world" (1992a, 42). The act of speaking or writing about a historical drama that is unfolding at the same time as the speaking or writing has its own contradictions, according to Arias: "[Such] texts are constructed as metaphors where the historical drama takes the form of the drama of the writing. It's impossible to speak, it's impossible not to speak. The historical process of writing, the historical process of reading, and the historical process of social transformation all go together and are entangled in one another" (1990d, 9). In this way the form can be as revolutionary as the historical situation of enunciation. Thus, la palabra has both a historical and a literary dimension. Arias clearly delights in verbal acrobatics, name distortions, and outrageous banter—all aspects of his concept of art. His linguistic playfulness and literary irony situate him well within the tradition of irreverent and jocular Guatemalan writers that started with the first Guatemalan novelist and humorist, Irisarri. Arias's palabra entertains, but it also documents and denounces.

Arias's literary career began with the publication of a collection of short stories, *En la ciudad y en la montaña* (1975), followed by his first novel, *Después de las bombas* (1979). In 1981 he received the Casa de las Américas prize in the essay genre for his doctoral dissertation on the sociology of literature, *Ideologías, literatura, y sociedad durante la revolución guatemalteca 1944–1954* (1979). In the mid-1980s he collaborated with director Gregory Nava on the screenplay of the movie *El Norte,* writing the dialogue for the Guatemalan protagonists Enrique and Rosa. Other novels followed: *Itzam Na* (1981), for which Arias won the Casa de las Américas prize for best novel; *Jaguar en llamas* (1989); and his most recently published work, *Los caminos de Paxil* (1990), which was also adapted as an opera libretto. He is working on the manuscripts for two more novels, *Cascabel* and *Sopa de caracol.* Arias is the only writer of the four whom I study in depth in this book who has not published poetry.

In this chapter, I will examine testimonial function and the appropriation of la palabra by the Other in *Después de las bombas* and *Los caminos de Paxil,* noting the change especially in the narrative voice. In the early novel, the "I" represents a politically alienated middle-class youth; more recently, the "I" is a Mayan Indian, a voice emanating from circumstances vastly different from Arias's own and a voice rarely so directly represented in Guatemalan literature.

Después de las bombas

The cover of the English translation of *Después de las bombas* highlights the creative mixture of art and testimony in this novel, calling it "a lyrical documentation characterized by zany humor and harsh insights in the repression of Guatemala." Arias's point of departure is 1954, when we saw the overthrow of the reformist Arbenz government by the Guatemalan military with CIA sponsorship. The year 1954 separates the "before," the ten-year period of democracy and openness under Arévalo and Arbenz, from the "after," when the bombs fell and military dictatorship returned to Guatemala.

Arias's first novel and bildungsroman, *Después de las bombas* documents his earliest and most vivid personal memories, which are of the bombing and his coming to terms with his past as a writer. Applying new narrative techniques—such as free indirect style, stream-of-consciousness narration, ruptures in time and space, and interior monologue—Arias's narrator recounts the experiences of Máximo Sánchez from infancy to manhood.

Let us follow the text closely in order to understand how Arias develops a testimonial discourse within his particular style. Born into a petit bourgeois family, Max barely knows his alcoholic father. A scrupulously honest man, the father works in a minor post for the Arbenz government and disappears during the 1954 bombing. Max's mother spends her days exclusively with and for her infant son in a never-ending, self-abnegating cycle of "carruajito / bebé / ronchas . . . carruajito / bebé / ronchas" (7) (Carriage. Infant. Hives.)[1] Max's skin is a perpetual eruption of oozing hives; his bottle and pacifier rarely leave his mouth. Several years after the bombing, the young Max meets a strange old man who tells him the legend of the Indian resistance leader Tecún Umán, the hero and martyr of the battle against the conquistador Pedro de Alvarado. Alxit, Tecún Umán's lover who commits suicide rather than submit to Spanish torture and violation, lies buried at the María Tecún mountain. Max enjoys the story of indigenous lore although he does not yet fully understand it. His passion in life is soccer, his strength his mother, his mission the quest for his father. Because school is always canceled for one reason or another, Max eventually receives his diploma without ever having attended a class. Book burnings, election frauds, afternoons at the races in which the losing jockeys are executed (reminiscent of the Mayan practice of sacrificing the losing team in the traditional ball game), duels between rival officers, road blocks and machine guns, meddling U.S. ambassadors, "technical advisers bearing gifts"— all form the political landscape and backdrop for Max's adventures.

His first love, Karen Johnson, the daughter of the U.S. ambassador, awakens his adolescent sexual desires with her teasing exhibitionism, although we suspect Max of possessing a few "hang-ups" as he continues to suck his pacifier and gaze at her from afar. Political oppression intensifies, whores and soccer players go on strike, public executions commence at the National Stadium, while dissidents chant a subverted form of the republic's motto: "¡Adiós, Patria y Libertad!" (Goodby, Fatherland and Liberty!). Max and Karen themselves are sexually violated and grotesquely tortured by an armed patrol. Traumatized, she leaves the country while he falls victim to fears and nightmares.

After several years Max begins to write secretly in order to get hold of himself and still attempt to deal with the loss of his father. He eventually falls in love with Amarena, daughter of the pastor of the Union Church. She and a wise man, Chingolo, become Max's spiritual advisors. Following the assassination of the U.S. ambassador and the subsequent murder of a CIA agent, Max steps up his political involvement. When an impromptu speech he makes at the funeral turns into a defiant call to arms and an orgiastic free-for-all, Amarena—with whom he has recently consummated his love—helps disguise him to spirit him out of the country. Max has reached manhood and finally discards his pacifier. His allergy has cleared.

As he leaves in exile, Max detours for a brief pilgrimage to the María Tecún shrine.

A comment regarding the autobiographical-testimonial nature of several elements of the plot is in order here, especially since this novel is the closest of all to Arias's own experience. Although admitting to an occasional exaggeration of "real-life events" for the benefit of fiction, Arias incorporates segments of his early life in the text. For example, he remembers the "total hysteria" of his own mother during the 1954 bombing of Guatemala City. Like Max's mother, she put him under a huge desk for his protection. The memory is vivid also because his mother had to cancel his fourth birthday party on June 22, two days after the bombing began—Arias still recalls his resentment.

While his own father never disappeared as Max's did, he did pay the social, economic, and political consequences of working for the Arbenz government. He lost his job in the Supreme Court offices and, as a pariah, could not find another one for a long time. The family suffered economically and psychologically. As a typical middle-class liberal, Arias's father found the 1954 invasion and subsequent military regime "morally and ethically intolerable" and taught Arturo and his sister to hate the armed forces. Arias's hatred also stems from an incident that happened to him and a date when he was sixteen years old. The rape episode with Max's first love, Karen, is a retelling of this incident, albeit exaggerated. Arias recalls that his father loaned him the keys to the family car and that, shy and nervous, he picked up his first date. The two were stopped at a roadblock by police who searched the car for weapons and subversive literature, using the occasion as an excuse to rough him up and fondle his date. The experience left him with a feeling of total impotence and fright. This attitude amidst the all-pervasive climate of violence that existed at the time in Guatemala permeates *Después de las bombas*.

Arias's doctoral dissertation, which he published in 1979 under the title *Ideologías, literatura y sociedad durante la revolución guatemalteca 1944–1954*— also the year of publication of *Después de las bombas*—may also shed some light on the historical context of the novel. As a defining moment in his own young life and in the life of the nation, the 1954 coup was obviously uppermost in Arias's mind during the 1970s. In his dissertation Arias examines the somewhat contradictory ideology of one of the revolution's foremost writers, Mario Monteforte Toledo. According to Arias, Monteforte correctly identified the national problem of the Indian and the land in his masterpiece, *Entre la piedra y la cruz,* but failed to propose a radical socioeconomic restructuring to correct it. Instead, Monteforte finds the solution in education and liberal reform.

When I asked Arias whether *Después de las bombas* was a reworking of the ideology of Monteforte, he denied that to be the case. *Después de las bombas,* he explained, was actually finished in 1975, although Joaquín Mortiz did not publish it until 1979. *Ideologías* was written afterward— between 1976 and 1978 in Paris, at the "peak of his radicalism"—in exasperation when General Lucas García seized power in Guatemala and initiated massive campaigns of oppression, and in hope when the Sandinistas' prospects of winning looked promising in Nicaragua. Monteforte captured Arias's interest for two reasons: he was not Asturias (Arias wanted to show that Guatemala could produce other fine writers); but along with Asturias, Monteforte was trying to deal with the issue of Mayan culture. In *Después de las bombas,* Arias is already beginning to consider the significance of Guatemala's Other, a theme he will develop successively with each novel until the indigenous subject actually becomes the narrator in *Los caminos de Paxil.*

Después de las bombas is a counterhistory that denounces what was and yearns for what should have been. Natural disasters of mythic proportions alternate with excruciating regularity to create an eternal cycle of death, as regular and recurring as Katún 8 Ahau of the Mayan calendar (12). There are volcanic eruptions and earthquakes that recall early twentieth-century Latin American tales of man against nature; there are violent upheavals in government as well—"otra dictadura, otra revolución" (12) (another dictatorship, another revolution). Max's mother narrates her family's agony as it picks up stakes following the explosion of the Santa María volcano and moves to the capital: "Lo poco que lograron rescatar, lo tiraron dentro de una carreta de bueyes. Y a turnarse para jalar, jalar, jalar los 200 kilómetros hacia la capital" (12) (The little they managed to save was thrown onto an ox cart. Then it was a matter of taking turns pulling, pulling, pulling the 200 kilometers to the city) (13). With Sisyphean effort they arrive in the capital and build a new house, only to see it "caerse, aquella famosa nochebuena de 1917 en que dios sacudió la tierra para despertar al pueblo. Era la hora de marchar contra Estrada Cabrera" (12) (collapse on that famous Christmas Eve of 1917 when God shook the earth to arouse the people. It was time to march against Estrada Cabrera) (13). The sorry state of Guatemalan history is only complicated by its insignificance on the world scene. The national joke has it that Winston Churchill, upon learning that Guatemala had declared war against the Germans in World War II, ran to his atlas to find out where this new ally was located (16). Like the "pulgarcito" El Salvador, Guatemala wallows in a misery made worse by isolation and anonymity.

The title of the novel establishes a temporal opposition: if the text declares as its point of departure the time "after the bombs" (actually the text begins "during the bombs"), the reader may ask what things were like "before the bombs." The ten-year period immediately preceding the 1954 coup becomes a mythical paradise before the Fall: "Todo había sido antes de las bombas, siempre antes de las bombas. Cuando había escuelas y leche y sueños" (61) (Everything had been before the bombs, always before the bombs. When there were schools, and milk, and dreams) (69). It was a time of golden afternoons and cloudless skies, of reconciliation and demilitari-zation—all of which Arias's narrator describes in a chapter appropriately entitled "Amanecer" (Dawn). They burned uniforms and weapons instead of books. The time before the bombs was also the time of the Father. People like Max's father ruled the country and "el sol brilló" (122) (the sun shone). After the bombs, the Father disappeared. Cast out of Eden, the Father's children wander directionless, much like Max kicking cans instead of soccer balls down the street.

Arias juxtaposes myth and history in his narration of the time before the bombs. Both friends and relatives give Max vivid testimony of the events leading first to the 1944 revolution and overthrow of the dictator Ubico and later to the period of reform under Arévalo and Arbenz. Gaping holes exist in the nation's historical awareness. Some incredulous listeners ask the narrator: "¿Hubo revolución? ¿En este país? ¿Cuándo?" (121) (There was a revolution? In this country? When?). He documents for them the abuses of the Ubico years and the hopes of the 1944 revolution. Appar-ently, as Ubico drove his Harley-Davidson through the city streets, he would literally and metaphorically run people down, spreading panic and misery in his wake. Fed up, the people created their own solution, taking to the streets and fomenting revolution. For the narrator, textual strategy accompanies the historical reality. Only words can reconstruct forgotten time to "comunicar la gran mentira que había sido todo después de las bombas" (123) (communicate the big lie that everything had been after the bombs) (140). To reawaken the nation's historical conscience, he will commit the past to writing.

Max's mother helps him to fill in the details so important to an under-standing of the past. She paints a picture of a self-reliant, willful people who rise up to take control of their own destiny. They have not always been kicked and silenced by the boot of the general. She herself participated in the struggle for liberation. Moreover, she met Max's father while fighting in the streets. Before June of 1944, "ella vio al país arder de punta a punta, los cuerpos carbonizados echados como basura en fosas comunes" (132) (she saw the country burning from end to end, the charred bodies thrown like garbage into mass graves) (151). Sewage ran down the streets, and the smell was so bad they had to wear clothespins on their noses. Watches and calendars were forbidden in an effort to ignore time, to deny history. Time, in effect, stood still; stagnation led to deterioration, compounding the feeling of historical impotence on the part of the people.

But in June 1944, the metaphoric volcano "empezó a llover ceniza" (134) (began raining ashes). Like the volcano, the people awakened; they ran to their closets and began to clean the cobwebs off their guns. His mother recalls mass demonstrations, exploding tear gas canisters, clattering machine guns, smashing bullets, martyred friends, a fleeing dictator, and finally students dancing in the streets proclaiming "que el siglo veinte por fin llegaba" (139) (that the twentieth century had finally arrived) (158). The people had reclaimed their place in history. All nature, too, rejoiced in the triumph, adds Max's mother. The sun came out, and like the biblical floodwaters receding after the deluge, "la superficie pantanosa de la tierra se empezó a secar y hubo tierra firme en que pararse. Y todos los generales y coroneles se volvieron piedra" (137) (the swampy surface of the earth began to dry and there was solid ground on which to stand. And all the generals and colonels turned to stone) (157). A new beginning, a new Eden had come to Guatemala.

Imbedded within Max's mother's testimony is the story of his grandmother and even that of his great-grandmother. Here we find Max tracing his political lineage through his mother's family (a practice not uncommon to the Mayan culture, where the women are the conservators of culture). His mother tells him: "Mi mamá, tu abuelita, nos había contado repetidamente cómo el terremoto del 17 había llamado al pueblo a sacar a Cabrera. Ella contaba esa historia con frecuencia, en el secreto de la noche" (134) (My mother, your grandmother, had told us over and over again how the earthquake of '17 had roused the people to throw out Cabrera. She often told the story in the secrecy of the night) (153), afraid that Ubico's spies would hear her. The popular struggle had to be remembered and passed on by word of mouth. Despite the dangers, the family maintained a tradition of resistance.

In another episode, his mother tells him that when it appeared that the

Ubico government was about to fall in 1944, her mother—his grand-mother—sent her out to look for white and yellow corn, the sacred grain of the Mayans. The family had a tradition of grinding the corn to make *atole* for the people who had taken to the streets: "Y mi mamá, tu abuelita, y yo levantamos la enorme olla de atol de elote y la pusimos en la carretilla de la cabra, hijo, y salimos a la calle. Era una olla enorme de barro que tu bisabuela había hecho para celebrar la llegada de Barrios en el 1871" (142) (And my mother, your grandmother, and I lifted the huge crock of *atole* and put it on the goat cart, son, and went out in the street. It was a huge clay crock your great-grandmother had made to celebrate Barrios's arrival in 1871) (162).[2] Likewise, the family carbine that served her brother in 1944 is the same weapon that her grandfather had used in the streets in 1920 and that her great-grandfather had carried against the city in 1871 (138). It seems that Max's genetic inheritance mandates a continued resistance.

Max recounts this already-layered testimony to his lover, Amarena, to explain his complex identity, his search for his father—the side of his family he does not know—and his desire to define his own existence and purpose in life. His story is far from straightforward, however; Arias weaves Max's voice together with the voice of his mother, his grandmother, his mother's brother and her friends, the old man, his peers, student fighters and the multitudes in the streets, and of Amarena as she responds and questions him. Narrative voice alternates rapidly and abruptly between first and third person with no warning, forcing the reader to pay close attention. This multidiscursive, polyphonic structure augments the chaos of already turbulent times. It sets the stage for many players of whom Max is only one, and not a very extraordinary one at that. The authorial subject has been decentered.

In contrast to the hope embodied in myth and history before the bombs, June 1954 marks a return to the despair inflicted by tyrants like Ubico and Estrada Cabrera, a sorry saga that began at Conquest. Max admits that the country's problems go all the way back to 1520 and that the cyclical nature of evil and oppression will continue until it is completely uprooted. It all began with the Spanish treachery against Tecún Umán. Ever since that time, "seguimos matando solamente al caballo" (132) (we keep on killing only the horse) (151). The rider—the perpetrator—is allowed to go free. All Guatemalans share this tragic history.

Now that the bombs have begun falling, the cycle will be repeated. The generals are back, church bells invade the air,[3] officials burn books, and people disappear (123). The rain falls in torrents and roaring waters cover everything, again an illusion to the mythical flood that drowned the wicked. "After the bombs" also signifies a return to bodies strewn on the streets and pools of blood Max has to jump over (65). Max is numbed to the death around him. He has lost all track of time and no longer remembers if or when the bombs actually stopped falling: "Tenía ya días de no verlas. Tal vez meses. No sabían si eran años. ¿Importaría?" (23) (He hadn't seen any for days now. Maybe months. Maybe even years. Did it make any difference?) (24–25). Insensitive and passive, Max and his fellow countrymen have forgotten what "normal" is. In this state they present a minimal threat to the authorities, who would like to keep it that way.

After the bombs, Max's identity crisis comes to a head. Obsessed by not knowing his father's whereabouts, intrigued by the old man's story of Tecún Umán, Max feels that somehow the two are related and he begins his search. It is in part an oedipal search that culminates in his achieving manhood and liberation. Early in the search he develops a fascination with words—las palabras—storytelling, literature, books, and oral and written history. Words hold the key to the success of his efforts. After the old man tells him his story, Max wants to know what it means and whether it will help him find his father. The old man's answer is enigmatic: "Tal vez sí, tal vez no" (41) (Maybe yes, maybe no) (45). The story means whatever one wants. He is not about to spoon-feed Max; instead, he urges him to enjoy it simply as a story (41). Max will decipher it in time, but he should look for literary truth, not necessarily a scientific or empirical one. In stories, "la verdad no siempre es una verdad que vos podás mirar, tocar. Pero recordá. Es una verdad de todos modos, tan grande, si no más grande, que cualquier otra verdad" (41) (the truth isn't always a truth that you can see and touch. But remember. It's a truth, anyway, as great, if not greater, than any other truth) (45). Metaphor, not reason, will seduce Max. Let the foreigners— Russians, gringos, and Europeans—wallow in their reason (108). As an old truism observes, there is sometimes more truth to fiction than to fact.

Words—the raw material for narration—will enable Max to reconstruct his own past and that of his country. Words are sacred and powerful, a way of making things his (182). By writing books Max will discover that he can return history and the power of the word to the people: "Mantener aquel glorioso pasado vivo y dinámico. . . . Devolverle las palabras al pueblo, llenar los espacios en blanco" (123) (To keep that glorious past alive and vigorous. . . . To return words to the people, to fill in the blank spaces, the blanks) (140). Although they are often unspoken for many years, words are immortal and invulnerable to bullets (189). Max comes to the realization over the course of the text that through las palabras he can fulfill testimonial function by giving voice to the voiceless.

Max thirsts for words from his mother in order to understand his own origins, to glean any tidbit of information about his father. At times his mother becomes the synedochic "boca abierta, una enorme caverna" (22) (mouth open, a huge cavern) (24). Sometimes she appears as if she is without shape or image,"como si no fuera nada más que la encarnación de las palabras mismas, sonidos escapándose de un par de labios flotantes" (132) (as though she were nothing but the incarnation of the words themselves, sounds coming from between a pair of floating lips) (150). Because she possesses the Word, she is the family archive of history and culture. But she can never give Max enough of her verbal breast milk before she breaks down in sobs. He remains fixated in the oral stage; perhaps his pacifier symbolically meets that need until it is fulfilled later in another way.

The time finally comes for Max to act. For him action entails picking up a pen rather than a gun. He starts writing secretly at night. To her horror, his mother suspects he is masturbating, implying perhaps at a symbolic level the "sterility" of literature in the public opinion; his pen has become a substitute phallus. He has second thoughts at first, unsure of his ability to develop interesting plots and characters, to refrain from arrogance and sentimentalism, or to manipulate the language: "¿Que qué hacía escribiendo tonterías de todas maneras? Que debería irse a la montaña y luchar como un hombre" (150) (What the hell was he doing writing rubbish, anyway? He ought to go to the mountains and fight like a man) (170–71).

He faces the old "armas o letras" dilemma of the writer in the revolution. Arias explains that during the 1970s the writer had to justify his or her choice of weapons—the pen or the gun. In a situation so highly polarized, the only area of agreement was that each side had to shoot the other. Thus the dominant discourse was that of the gun. The writer lacked respect. At the time, Arias found it difficult to explain the role of culture in framing the consciousness of a people and in framing the issues and debates taking place. Now, he believes, things have changed. In the 1990s there is a different perception of the role of culture in the Central American revolution (interview).

However, Max makes his choice based on personal need and desire. He is determined to bring his father back to life with words. Moreover, he adds: "Construiré una catedral de palabras. Crearé al país con mis palabras. En mis palabras encontraré al universo y entenderé el eterno presente a través de mis palabras. En mis palabras encontraré, acabaré, me volveré las palabras mismas, seré palabras, palabras, palabras, encarnaré palabras, palabras, palabras (147) (I will build a cathedral of words. I'll create a country with my words. In my words I'll find the universe and I'll understand the eternal present through my words. In my words, I will find, I will end, I will become the words themselves, become words, words, words, I will incarnate words, words, words) (167). When he begins to write seriously, he buys himself a parrot. Arias explains that the parrot symbolizes sheer verbosity; it speaks with no purpose, no understanding, and no concern about communication (interview). A parrot is just words—signifiers—while Max is more concerned with shaping his words into weapons, the signified. The two come together in literature and serve him equally in the act of writing.

Metaphor, symbol, wordplay, and hyperbole are central to Arias's art. The soccer metaphor and motif run throughout the text. One passage is pure sportscaster discourse—an exciting play-by-play description of a neighborhood match (78). We learn early in the novel that Max is a talented soccer player with a strong leg. His mother encourages him to stick with the sport since these days being a soccer player is about his only hope (61). A career like his father's in politics would be suicide, she counsels; soccer is safe. When he is not playing soccer with his friends, Max prefers to kick stones or tin cans around in the street, aiming straight for the sewer and missing every time. At one point when his friends invite him to join in the game, he hesitates, torn between his love for the game and his desire to search for his father and discover the pleasure, meaning, and power of words. One might ask whether it is engagement or escape that tempts Max more. But then, which pastime—soccer or writing—offers the engagement and which one offers the escape? In time we learn that it is writing that offers him both. On his way to the airport to flee the country, Max finally kicks a can into the sewer: "La lata se resbaló por el asfalto cayendo directamente dentro de la negra abertura. Por fin. Anotado" (193) (The can slid along the pavement straight into the black opening. Finally. Goal) (217). He triumphs.

Max has symbolically reached his goal of discovering his father in himself, of becoming a man. He understands his father's struggle and sacrifice: "Hubiera muerto antes de someterse al dominio extranjero. Morir para que yo pudiera vivir. Y ahora puedo tratar de contar el cuento que todos están tratando de olvidar" (146) (He would have died before giving in to foreign domination. To die so that I could live. And now I can try to tell the story that everybody is trying to forget) (166). This moment of self-actualization occurs at the same time he succeeds in making love to Amarena. Using the same metaphor, one might say that Max "scores" here as well. He has grown up. And he understands his responsibility to craft the words to tell the story of his father and the people.

The other powerful metaphor-motif is the contrast between light and dark. Light shines during the ten-year period of the revolution; the bombs usher in the time of darkness. History seems doomed to follow the cycles of day and night. Indeed "the sun had shone" from 1944 to 1954; but the long night of Ubico had preceded that day. Cowering, the people feared they would never see "el amanecer"—the dawn. Now they cower again as the bombs drive them back under their beds and dressers. Arias links the metaphor of darkness with the truncated Word, the abyss of the wordless mouth. When Max first tries to find out why the bombs have fallen, "Todos pretendían no oírlo o que no sabían. Como si hubieran roto toda conexión con ese tiempo mítico anterior a las bombas quedándoles sólo ese ombligo negro que era la boca abierta sin dientes, sin palabras" (49) (Everybody pretended they didn't hear him or that they didn't know. As though they had broken off all connections with that mythical time before the bombs, leaving them only with that black umbilicus, an open, toothless, wordless mouth) (56). An open mouth full of words and full of teeth belongs to the pre-bomb period of light. Moreover, the liberated word—the vehicle for history and truth—not only feeds on light but sheds light as well.

Arias as a writer revels in wordplay. He emphasizes the ludic quality of his work and explains that he arrived at his concept of the "carnivalesque" in the 1970s before he actually became aware that Bakhtin had studied it. Bakhtin examined the history and function of laughter in his *Rabelais and His World*. In observations that we can directly apply to Arias's work, he highlights laughter's emergence from folk culture, the place of vulgar and popular language in "great literature," laughter's tendency to break down the walls between official and nonofficial literature, and laughter's universal and liberating character: "True ambivalent and universal laughter does not deny seriousness but purifies and completes it. Laughter purifies from dogmatism, from the intolerant and the petrified; it liberates from fanaticism and pedantry, from fear and intimidation, from didacticism, naiveté and illusion, from the single meaning, the single level, from sentimentality" (122–23).

Laughter is particularly suited to postmodernism in its deconstruction of power. For example, Arias has changed the names of Guatemala's most infamous leaders to outrageous, sometimes hilarious, derivations of the originals, such as Colonel Castle Cannons, General Peralta Absurdo, General "Spider" Arana Sobrio, General Shell Genial Longitud, and General Idigyorass.[4] Street names are picturesque and telling; rapid enumeration adds to their absurdity: "El Callejón de los Cojos, la Avenida de la Desventura, el Paseo del Macho de Pelo en Pecho, Callejón de los Desalojados, Plaza del Maíz Molido, y Callecita de los Meados de Gato" (127); (Alley of the Lame, the Avenue of Misfortune, the Boulevard of Hairy-Chested Machos, the Alley of the Dispossessed, Ground Corn Square, and Cat Piss Lane) (145), to name a few. A certain Mr. Foster Sucks helps direct U.S. covert operations in Guatemala, and the Organization of American Colonies is about as effective as its name implies.

The carnivalesque atmosphere reinforces the irreverence and satire: the archbishop sells balloons to the children while the soldiers armed with machine guns tell their parents for whom to vote; Catholic priests' daughters are hard to get to know; but Mormons are worse than Catholics; democracy is alive and well in Guatemala, where the United States is defending freedom's frontiers; the assassination of five candidates causes a delay in the elections, but calm is restored when the public learns that all the military candidates miraculously survive; the people are the law as in any true democracy, "cualquier gobierno del pueblo, por el pueblo, para el pueblo, a pesar del pueblo" (57) (any government of the people, by the people, for the people, in spite of the people) (64). The U.S. culture invasion descends on the Guatemalan middle class, which voraciously imports No Nonsense pantyhose, Gillette razors, Kentucky Fried Chicken, TV programs in color from San Antonio, and Eveready batteries. With every crisis the Guatemalan schools close, but the children are all given credit for a missed year of work, "reconocimiento por su inocencia" (48) (in recognition of their blamelessness) (55). "They canceled school for the coming year" becomes a familiar refrain. After years of cancellations, Max's class finally graduates by government decree. No wonder his compatriots have trouble with basic skills! A philistine general murmurs to his lover "como siempre le había caído mal la literatura porque era tan difícil entender qué diablos quería decir" (165) (that he never liked literature because it was always so difficult to understand what the hell it meant) (187). When the crazy people from the asylum are let loose in the city park, one has to ask, "Who is really crazy here?"

The carnival atmosphere culminates in the final chapter, "La ensalada de los flamas"[5] (The salad of the flames): polyphonic cacophony, accelerating rhythms, words erupting like machine gun fire—pandemonium reigns as Max launches into his narration-turned-denunciation. People react slowly at first, then finally explode: "Qué buen escándalo. Se formaban grupos de gente discutiendo lo que acababan de escuchar" (167–68) (Wonderful pandemonium! Groups of people arguing about what they had just heard) (190). For the first time since the bombs began to fall, people are arguing in free-wheeling intercourse. The chaos grows.

Before Max flees for his life—he has managed to offend everyone with his words—Amarena throws a masquerade ball in his honor at the Union Church. Whores dressed up like Carmelite nuns and soccer players disguised as whores, all prancing "like exorcists" (187) in a wild frenzy, spill out of the church, "bailando, bailando furiosamente para aniquilar el presente, bailando alto, gritando, brincando, sudando, bailando para borrar las pesadillas de las noches tristes, agarrándose las manos para enfrentarse al futuro" (185) (dancing, dancing wildly to wipe away the present, jumping up high, yelling, leaping, sweating, dancing to wipe away the bad dreams of sad nights, holding hands to face the future) (209). Leaping and twisting their way down the Avenue of Liberation past crowds of silent bystanders, they bid Max a jubilant farewell at the airport.

Never far from the levity, however, lurks a sinister, grotesque side to the humor. Between laughs, the reader shudders as the child Max picks up a beautiful gold ring, "precioso a pesar del dedo que tenía dentro" (31) (beautiful even with the finger inside it) (33); or as mutilated bodies float down the river past Max and Karen; or as the police flay their political enemies; or, in an act reminiscent of the rites of ancient sacrifice, the chief executioner tears the still-beating heart from his victim, lifting it to the roar of the bloodthirsty throngs. The obscenities, grotesqueness, and *malas palabras*, added to the structural and textual violence of nueva narrativa, recreate the historical nightmare.

In *Después de las bombas*, Arias spins a tale from fragments of personal memory, oral histories, and his own creative imaginings to produce a narrative of resistance. To this end, his characters are allegorical and symbolic representations of a national reality rather than flesh and blood, psychologically wrought renditions of real people. Arias's Other in *Después de las bombas* includes a whole cast of politically and socially alienated characters. Max's perspective is the artist's on the road from political persecution to liberation. Just as important as the portrayal of symbolic characters is Arias's love of words and word play, metaphor, colloquialisms, hyperbole, satire, outrageous language, the shocking image, exuberant humor, and the carnivalesque. Indeed, he succeeds in entertaining his readers and in making them laugh; but it is an uneasy laughter because the reader knows that just beneath the surface of hilarity and playfulness is the ugly and intolerable reality of Guatemala.

Between *Después de las bombas* and *Los caminos de Paxil,* Arias's two novels *Itzam Na* and *Jaguar en llamas* merit brief attention as they relate to our theme of testimony, the Other, and artistic invention. In *Itzam Na* the narrator Pispi Sigaña reconstructs the life of his dead girlfriend, La Gran Puta, as he goes through her personal papers, letters, and journal. Narrative voice alternates between Pispi's somewhat hallucinatory, stream-of-consciousness chronicle of Guatemala's version of the hippie and drug culture of its upper-middle-class youth, La Gran Puta's rambling diary entries recounting her incestuous fantasies and her bisexual promiscuity, and letters her sympathetic Uncle Milo wrote to her documenting family as well as national history during the Estrada Cabrera years. Arias admits that about 90 percent of those letters are actual letters his own uncle had written to him (interview). The narrator even includes newspaper clippings of letters to the editor written by the warring "Greenback" and "Scheissmark" families, symbolic and satiric representatives of Guatemala's elites tied either economically to the United States or ethnically to Germany.

Lost in a haze of marijuana and incense, addicted to self-destructive behavior, and challenged by a popular revolt, Guatemala's spoiled youth mark the decline and defeat of the selfish ruling class. Arias compares these youth to García Márquez's children with pig tails who represent the end of the line in *One Hundred Years of Solitude,* and he likens this demise to that of Itzam Na, the god of the classical Mayan nobility overthrown in the eighth century by a peasant insurrection which then established the cult of the young god of corn (interview). The narrator's audience, including the reader, are presumably members of the popular revolt who are attempting to reconstruct and interpret their history.

Arias chooses insolent nicknames for the young gang of social dropouts—"La Gran Puta," "La Pervertida," "Amor de mis Amores," "El Gran Chingón," "El Niño Dios" (the Great Whore, the Pervert, Love of My Loves, the Great Fuck Up, the Child God)—and parodies the drug culture's values and discourse: "Sólo era encender el purito y se aclaraba la nublasón, desaparecían los grises y los negros y el mundo se comensaba a poner celestito, amariíto, rojito y visto como a través diuna bola de cristal" (26) (All you had to do was light up your joint and the clouds cleared up, the grays and blacks disappeared, and the world began to get so way out man, so yellow man, so red man, just like looking through a crystal ball). (Translations for *Itzam Na* and the rest of the texts by Arias are mine.) These techniques, together with his use of neologisms, Americanisms, profanities and obscenities, attest to a continued fascination with la palabra and its value in the postmodern representation of pop culture.

The social problem, however, is not lost amid the humor and wordplay. In their self-preoccupation, La Gran Puta and her friends misrepresent the indigenous Mayan culture of their country: They idealize the natural, simple native—*el buen salvaje*—who lives harmoniously with the good vibrations of the earth, but they fail to note his suffering.

The narrators of *Jaguar en llamas* do sympathize with the Indians' plight and do come to their defense. Marginalized themselves, the narrators are the expelled Sephardic Jews, Moors (one Cide H. MontRosat is decidedly "quijotesque"), and gypsies of fifteenth-century Spain who come to the New World, side with the Indians, and write a vast counterhistory of the Spanish Conquest, colonization, and subsequent neocolonialism under "monstruamericano" imperialism emanating from "Washandwearington." In the early years, the Jew Ajoblanco loses his magic sword, La Ceremoniosa. To complicate matters, his female companion of Moorish descent, Trotaprisiones, is kidnapped. The text narrates the journeys of Ajoblanco and his friends and their search for both sword and damsel in distress.

Various participants and observers, some purporting to be more factual than others, join in heteroglossia. Footnotes by supposed historians and anthropologists and excerpts from the mythopoeic *El juego de pelota* by Othón René Castilla y Aragón,[6] all force the reader to play detective. What really happened to La Ceremoniosa and to Trotaprisiones? The journey is transformed on a symbolic level to a quest for the unifying principle of existence—the "materia prima," the wisdom of the ages, the Arabic "jawhar." "Jawhar" is the homophone of the Mayan "jaguar" or the "jaguar en llamas." According to legend, the flaming jaguar contains the divine spark, the elixir that transforms and unifies everything (304). The point is that true victory necessitates unification; in this case, the ladino and the Indian would have to live in solidarity to best resist all imperialisms. Some of the narrators realize the dangers of arrogantly trying to speak on behalf of the natives: "Mi temor es que los indios no pueden reconocerse en mis palabras, no tanto en cuanto a dificultades de comprensión de esta lengua escrita, que no es la mía tampoco, sino de que no se identificasen en lo que de ellos digo" (110) (My fear is that the Indians won't recognize themselves in my words, not so much because they can't understand the written language, which isn't my native language either, but because they won't be able to identify themselves with what I say about them). He fears doing Spivak's epistemic violence to them, that is, misrepresenting them and failing to note their differences (their heterogeneity) as he speaks on their behalf. Would it not be better if the natives spoke for themselves?

In this vein, the travelers organize a theater troupe that tours various prisons where Indians are incarcerated. The appeal of the plays lies in their open endings. The actors begin the drama and then let the prisoners create their own endings. In this way, everyone contributes by telling personal stories as well as stories of the community. They become protagonists of their own works (105). The natives appropriate la palabra to tell their side of the story.

Storytelling is the theme of the text. Symbolic representation through language is the only way to understand oneself and the community and to claim autonomy. We learn that Ajoblanco loves to read the poetry of Castilla y Aragón "porque en ella la realidad aparecía como un conjunto de símbolos, una cosa era siempre imagen de otra, y el único acceso a las cosas eran las palabras" (174) (because reality appeared as a group of symbols, one thing was always the image of something else, and the only access to things was through words). Language mediates reality, and words furnish the raw material by which the writer and ultimately the reader access that reality.

Los caminos de Paxil

The natives do speak for themselves—inasmuch as is possible in a text whose author is still a well-educated member of the ladino middle class—in Arias's most recent novel, *Los caminos de Paxil*.[7] The narrator throughout is an Indian. Arias has stated that this narrative marks the first time he has written from the point of view of a Mayan: *Los caminos* is an "exercise of the imagination . . . an imagined discourse" (interview). Arias developed his interest in Guatemala's indigenous peoples while he was working in Mexico at the National School of History and Anthropology during the 1980s. He had immediate access to information about the Indians since so many were fleeing Guatemala into Mexico at the peak of the oppression against them. Indian leaders such as Rigoberta Menchú, Domingo Hernández Ixcoy (who eventually wrote the Quiché dialogue in *El Norte*), and Francisca Alvarez actually lived with Arias in Mexico for many months. After considerable research, Arias began writing anthropology in order to deal with ethnic issues (although he insists he is not an anthropologist). The close contact with native Guatemalan voices gave him the confidence to adopt their perspective in *Los caminos de Paxil*.

The reader needs to remember, however, that what emerges from the text is the Indian filtered through Arias's lens, no matter how well intentioned the effort. Such treatment borders on the paternalistic—as does all testimony produced in collaboration with an agent—and brings to mind Martin Lienhard's concept of "ethno-fiction" in which the "non-ethnic, in trying to create a poly-ethnic nation, reduces the Indian to a mythic, rather than historical figure" (567). The process removes an element of immediacy or even reality (documentary reality, that is) regarding the actual Indian question. On the other hand, we can counter these criticisms by also remembering that the objective of a fiction writer is to imagine the Other and to create a work of art beyond journalistic or ethnographic description. The loss of immediacy is not regarded in my mind as a "defect" as much as it is indicative of another narrative strategy and purpose. If one is looking for testimony in the strict sense, one should look elsewhere. This novel, like many others we have examined, exposes the tensions between fiction and testimony.

Another problem is the somewhat simplistic, un-nuanced presentation of the characters. As Dante Liano has noted, the Mayan protagonists are all good, the non-Mayans generally not (71). Perhaps Arias refrains from taking a more critical stance toward the indigenous communities precisely because he is an outsider in solidarity with them. I would also suspect that, as part of his project to include the Mayans in the national space, Arias might feel that any negativism on his part would further alienate them just at the time he is working to do the opposite. Could this project also be the reason Arias has adopted a more serious and respectful, less carnivalesque, tone to narrate *Los caminos*? He has moved away from the jokes and hilarious obscenities that, as Ileana Rodríguez explains, "establish distances and avoid the appropriation of indigenous history by ladinos, as Lienhard says Asturias does, and certainly Monteforte Toledo, and even Cardoza y Aragón" (1994a, 100). The distance now absent, the indigenous protagonists are in danger of being appropriated by the narrator.

With these tensions in mind, let us turn to the text. The first-person narrator works his way through *Los caminos*, although his voice is punctuated frequently and abruptly by dialogues involving other voices, other characters. In this sense the text is polyphonic and the reader must pay close attention in order to follow the narrative thread. The narrator's is not necessarily an authorial voice. Only occasionally does he have characteristics of the omniscient narrator. We are not even sure who he is much of the time as he slips invisibly in and out of the scene he is witnessing and recounting. He blends easily with the natural world around him. It is unclear whether other characters are ever aware of his presence. Rarely does he mention that he speaks directly to anyone else. He introduces himself in the first line: "Mi nombre es Patrocinio Saki C'oxol. Llegué a la tierra durante un eclipse de sol, bajando a una de las cuatro montañas sagradas que rodean mi pueblo de origen. Los sacerdotes celebraron mi llegada con fuegos artificiales, incienso y oraciones" (7) (My name is Patrocinio Saki C'oxol. I came to the earth during a solar eclipse, coming down from one of the four sacred mountains which surround my native village. The priests celebrated my arrival with fireworks, incense and prayers). Is he a heavenly being? Is he a *nahual*—the shadow or spirit often residing in an animal that accompanies the human on earth? (He even claims to understand the language of the birds.) Or is he merely confused or trying to confuse us? Arias may be playing with or actually deconstructing the European construct of the omniscient narrator. Perhaps he is even offering his reader the "indigenous version" of that narrator.

Eclipses mark important events, such as the birth of the narrator and bizarre phenomena related to his own life and to his people. He describes what happens on the night of an eclipse of the moon when he goes out for a walk (102). A woman gives birth to a lizard because she dares look at the eclipse. The head of a serpent appears within the corona of the eclipse. Shortly after, the natives behead their gringo oppressor, Halach Uinic Emerson (who also appears in *Itzam Na* as the representative of the invading gringo culture), and then celebrate with fireworks, dancing, and a religious procession, knowing full well that a deluge of violence will follow when the enemy seeks revenge.

The prodigious events raise many questions surrounding Patrocinio's identity. He takes leave of the reader on the last page of the novel, announcing his intention to return to the mountain. The moon and the sun "serán los símbolos de jade que colgarán siempre a mi lado. Los planetas y las constelaciones serán joyas brillando en torno a mí" (136) (will be the symbols of jade that will always hang at my side. The planets and the constellations will be the brilliant jewels around me). His mysterious nature only intensifies the elements of myth and magic that fill the text.

Like Arias, the narrator places memory in the service of art: "Anduve por la selva como sonámbulo, tratando de evocar los geranios de abril, y de recordar que, como dijo mi abuelo, la felicidad consiste en haber visto y poder recordar, y que las imágenes de la memoria se adaptan a la fantasía, de manera que nunca aparecen empolvadas sino siempre con brillantes colores, como cuando acaba de llover y todo está reluciente" (128) (I went through the jungle like a sleepwalker trying to evoke April's geraniums, remembering that, as my grandfather said, happiness consists in having seen and being able to remember and that the images of memory adapt to fantasy, in such a way that they never seem dusty but always brilliantly colored, like after the rain when everything sparkles). Fiction adds "brilliance" to the historical truth. Patrocinio the storyteller weaves ancient Mayan myths and legends throughout his documentary, inserting tales of the "tronchadores"—half men, half animals; "el indio haragán"—the lazy Indian; the origin of the marimba, instrument of the gods; and others. His texts resemble the famous Guatemalan tapestries. In describing them he not so subtly condemns the deforestation necessary for the production of writing paper: "A los indios de Guatemala no les gusta ver a los árboles convertidos en papel. Los tejidos son sus libros y cada quien escribe el suyo propio" (45) (The Indians of Guatemala don't like to see trees converted to paper. The weavings are their books and everybody writes his own). The Indian voice speaks in metaphor and symbol to discern the truth of his existence and to relate it to others. This multidiscursive strategy juxtaposes the discourse of myth to that of rational history. It recreates a different way of interpreting the world through a "tipo de lógica, tan diferente de la occidental en la que parecen creer que la distancia más corta entre dos puntos es una línea recta" (71) (a type of logic very different from Western logic which believes that the shortest distance between two points is a straight line), a logic that represents the Indian, not the Western, understanding of reality. Indigenous cosmology perceives time from a mythical rather than a historical, linear perspective (Cornejo Polar, 75).

At times the narrative resembles a popular, oral history. Repetition, the accumulation of details, and a rhythmic cadence recreate the conditions of oral storytelling so that the reader feels as if he has become a listener. For example, Patrocinio describes his descent to the village: "Caminé ese día y la noche de ese día y el alba del día siguiente y ese otro día y esa otra noche, durante nueve días y nueve noches, hasta llegar a un poblado donde parecía no haber nadie" (8) (I walked that day and that night and the dawn of the next and the next and that night, for nine days and nine nights until I arrived at a village where it appeared there wasn't anybody). Like the Peruvian Arguedas, Arias also incorporates passages of pure Indian idiom;

occasionally, Spanish alternates with Quiché. Using his own language and his traditions of oral history, the Other attempts to speak on his own terms and in his own territory.

The basic narrative line of *Los caminos de Paxil,* in contrast to the epic scope of *Jaguar en llamas,* deals with the specific struggles of the indigenous communities to organize themselves to fight the landgrabs in Guatemala by foreign oil companies in the 1970s. Not only are foreigners robbing them of their land, they are also destroying their natural habitat and culture with their imported "progress" and "civilization" based on power and greed. Oil drilling pollutes the earth so that corn will no longer grow: "A nosotros, el petróleo no nos sirve" (17) (Oil is of no use to us). The Quiché realize they face several options: they may resort to violence, or they may rely more creatively on "magia y seducción"—magic and seduction, a common refrain throughout the text. Emerson arrives in their region to take charge of the oil-company operations. To the Indians, he appears to be a monster who is part vulture, crocodile, lizard, serpent, and deer. Equally bestial, army colonel Lobos y Moras, who has horns on his head and wings on his legs, is waiting for the end of the world—the Indians' world—to descend to earth and eat up all of humanity (12).

Other equally traitorous Guatemalans include Emerson's ladino stooge and "dueño del cerro" (king of the hill), the Tigre de Ixcán; and the depraved Sebastián Guzmán, who was a "principal de principales," (24) an actual historical personage.[8] Justín, the only sympathetic gringo in the novel, tries to understand the indigenous people and to stand in solidarity with them. His skin symbolically darkens as he identifies more closely with them: "Ahora que me uno a los que observan el sol con ojos de oprimido, normal es que asuma su color discriminado" (133) (Now that I am linked to those who observe the sun with eyes of the oppressed, it's normal that I take on their color of discrimination).

The women of the Indian community are more complex and better defined than their men. According to the *Popol Vuh,* the Quiché people were created by a "Creator/Former" who is both mother and father of life; they are also the descendants of both the "Gran Abuela" Ixmucané and the "Gran Abuelo" Ixpiyacoc (24). Editor Adrián Recinos observes that when persons of both sexes are named in the *Popol Vuh,* the women are "gallantly" named before the men (157). Perhaps the gesture is gallant, but perhaps it is more than that. Arias has commented that women have always held a place of high regard within both the Mayan economy and body politic; gender discrimination grows as one moves out of the indigenous community into the ladino capitalist economy (Davis and Rivera 35). Rigoberta Menchú would concur. Indian men who have successfully integrated into the ladino world have also learned ladino gender prejudices (Maxwell).

In *Los caminos de Paxil,* the high priestess of the Quiché community, Ixchel, commands the respect of women and men alike. The archetypal Indian woman, Ixchel "es la luna que cuelga desnuda en el firmamento, la primera mujer, envuelta en humo verde. . . . Ixchel era nuestra fuerza, nuestro amor" (36) (is the moon who hangs nude in the firmament, the first woman, enveloped in green smoke. . . . Ixchel was our strength, our love). She is the axis around which the drama unfolds. Patron of the ball game and the underworld, weaver of fine tapestries, governess of the night and of the moon, woman always in motion but also in control, wise but impatient counselor, healer—Ixchel defies the prophets of doom and dreams of overcoming the enemy by unorthodox means. She frequently metamorphoses into a quetzal to hide from danger.

To win back the land, Ixchel proposes a strategy of magic and seduction rather than the traditional, simplistic, male-generated solution of force and violence: "No quiero masacres, nada de muertes, todo por magia y seducción. Pero eso sí, que no quede duda, esas tierras a nosotros volverán" (49) (I don't want massacres or deaths; just everything through magic and seduction. But let there be no doubt, those lands will be returned to us). War is not the answer; female-generated compassion and tenderness alone can overcome man's exploitation of man (60). Ixchel convinces Justín to deceive Emerson into thinking that there is no oil on these lands. Emerson discovers the treachery and sentences her to torture and death. However, her resurrection, which attains mythic proportions, vindicates her death and her people: "Después de que el polvo de las cenizas de Ixchel se fue para el este en el río Motagua, los peces juntaron todos los pedazos y los pegaron de nuevo con sus escamas de plata. Entonces, tomando cada uno en su boca la cola de otro, se convirtieron en una red para que Ixchel pudiera subir al cielo y alcanzar el sol. Pero el calor era tal, que no pudo alcanzarlo. Entonces, los peces dejaron a Ixchel en el cielo donde, como la luna, aun busca darle alcance al sol. Los peces se convirtieron en la Via Láctea" (131) (After the dust from Ixchel's ashes went off to the east in the Motagua River, the fish joined all the pieces and stuck them together again with their silver scales. Then, each one taking in its mouth the tail of the other, they made themselves into a net so that Ixchel could go up to heaven and reach the sun. But the heat was such that she could not reach it. Then the fish left Ixchel in the heavens where, as the moon, she still tries to reach the sun. The fish changed into the Milky Way.) She appears ever after in the final metamorphosis as the sacred moon of corn.

The other major female figure in the text, Ik'Chawa, is the beautiful young daughter of thunder and rain, fragile and simple, as impulsive as Ixchel is astute, the obsessive defender of the earth and of the cornfield (18). Justín finds himself symbolically torn between these two women who together represent the full spectrum of indigenous womanhood.

The Indian men who remain faithful to the community have run out of their own ideas and must turn to the women for answers. Kukulcán, traditional warlord of the Quiché, realizes that even a child knows more about the mysteries of the human heart than he does: "Esa ignorancia, esa ceguera, me llevó de joven a creer que podía hacer cualquier cosa. . . . Pero con el pasar del tiempo, conforme mi sabiduría se ensanchaba y mi verdadero poder crecía, iba descubriendo cada vez más limitaciones" (60) (That ignorance, that blindness, made me believe ever since my youth that I could do anything. . . . But with the passing of time, as my wisdom grew and my real power increased, I kept on discovering my limitations). He learns to appreciate Ixchel's approach. Likewise, the two young warriors, Rabinal Achí and Quiché Achí, whom we see always "peleando entre ellos"—fighting with each other (another refrain common to the text)—finally announce a truce to their hostilities. In one of the last scenes of the novel we see all of them with Kukulcán surrounded by butterflies and carrying guns (132). Aware that for the time being they will have to let the aggressor choose the weapon, more importantly they are united in defense of their community against that aggressor.

The new age has finally arrived with the death and resurrection of Ixchel. Heaven and earth have been moved to the end of the *katún* (age or epoch) of the Flor de Mayo as showers of blossoms "[hace] de toda la población indígena una sola voluntad" (131) (make the entire indigenous population of one mind). Justín is united with Ik'Chawa. Here we note that Arias more than once resolves textual conflicts by the symbolic union of a gringo with a Guatemalan (for example, Max with Karen and then Amarena in *Después de las bombas;* here, Justín and Ik'Chawa), perhaps envisioning the ultimate reconciliation of the two worlds.[9] The entire Indian community comes together in common purpose. Together, they look forward to the fulfillment of time, to the return of the Golden Age: "Volveremos a Paxil, . . . tierra de abundancia, lugar del maíz amarillo y el maíz blanco originales, tierra bañada por el espíritu de Ixchel" (134) (We will return to

Paxil . . . land of abundance, land of the first yellow corn and white corn, land bathed by the spirit of Ixchel).

Like the mythical Salvadoran Cuzcatlán, Paxil is the cornucopia and promised land of the Guatemalan Quiché. All roads lead to Paxil, sacred *milpa* (cornfield), source of life. Unity is the first step: "Y al hacerlo, asustábamos al sueño de los egoístas, porque para nosotros, la felicidad de cada uno presuponía la felicidad de todos. No podía ser de otra manera" (135) (And in doing so, we surprised the dreams of the egotists, because for us the happiness of each one presupposed the happiness of all). In contrast to the selfishness of its oppressors, the reconciled Indian community looks to the welfare of all as the source of each one's happiness. No one will be left out; there will be no more Others in the utopia of Paxil.

In *Los caminos de Paxil,* a more thoughtful, lyrical Arias emerges. He is less given to the irreverent linguistic revelry and excess, youthful insolence, and grotesque humor characteristic of *Después de las bombas.* Despite the evolution, Arias still remains true to his Guatemalan heritage, just as fascinated by the power of words and language as he ever was, albeit in a different way. His early novels grow out of his own experience as a politically alienated youth, nostalgic for the spirit of freedom and openness that flickered so briefly during the revolution of 1944–54, a revolution he experienced only vicariously through the memory and words of his parents. *Los caminos* reveals a passion for discovering his country's indigenous roots and a search for a nonrationalist, mythopoeic understanding of its reality. The dispossessed—women, disgruntled youths, rebellious Indians—find a voice in Arias's texts. The testimony they give becomes more potent as it is shaped by art, metaphor, and imagination.

Arias's as yet unpublished recent work, *Cascabel* and *Sopa de caracol,* speaks to the tensions still present within Guatemalan politics of the 1990s (during the Serrano and León Carpio years) and within its community of letrados from the middle sectors. As Zimmerman explains, Guatemalan writing is divided between "uncommitted and committed, innovative and conventional, testimonial and imaginative narrative fiction" (1995a, I:220). Some of the writers who remained in Guatemala during the crises of the past decades understandably resent former colleagues like Arias and Morales who left the country to work and write abroad. "How can they still maintain close contact with the Guatemalan reality which they claim to represent?" ask their critics. (Writers in exile often defend distance as an advantage, one that permits them to see the "big picture" and put events into perspective.) Even among those who work in the United States—Arias,

Morales, Perera, and Goldman—differences are pronounced and rivalries exist. For example, Perera and Goldman, who write in English, enjoy a greater market for their books than do either Morales or Arias. Morales continues to publish testimonies as "testinovelas" while Arias pursues his fascination with testimonio wrapped in experimentation, Boom-style narratives, Bakhtinian carnival atmosphere, and polyphony in the tradition of the great vanguardist experimenters, Asturias and Cardoza. But this very European cosmopolitanism and insistence on artistic freedom has indeed driven a wedge that separates Guatemalan writers today.

6

The Indian Princess
and the High-Heeled Warrior

Gioconda Belli's Revolting Women

Nicaraguan writer Gioconda Belli's first novel, *La mujer habitada* (1988), dramatizes the simultaneous struggle for national liberation and women's emancipation in her country at a particular moment of increased Sandinista successes against the Somoza regime in the early 1970s. Not only does Belli examine her protagonist's growing awareness of patriarchal oppression or "machismo," but she also links feminine consciousness with the earth and nature and with rebellious indigenous roots. As a contemporary testimonial novel, *La mujer habitada* is a hybrid text embracing postmodern tendencies and characteristics of nueva narrativa, *telenovela* (see Craft 1996b), and nineteenth-century realistic, romantic, and historical novels. This text forms part of the general current of Third World resistance literature.

Both women and the indigenous peoples of Mesoamerica are Other, although the native tribes referred to in the text are predominantly those of the ancient past rather than the present. Some might argue that nature, too, is constituted in *La mujer habitada* as Other and even as a speaking subject. Such an ecofeminist reading would find a holistic relationship between woman, Indian, and nature that joins mind, soul, intuition, and body and refutes a hierarchical, rationalist male-dominated discourse. Others would regard the presence of nature as simply a trope for Woman. Sometimes magical, lyrical, sentimental, and erotic, and sometimes testimonial, *La mujer habitada,* like other feminist texts, illuminates the female experience, as described by Cheri Register, in order to determine how to transform the world (quoted in Shea 53). I will follow Shea's distinction, which she bases on Register's work, between a feminine work and a feminist one; that is, "the former interprets and describes, while the latter transforms and advocates change in the existing culture" (58).

Although one could say that Belli actually writes *La mujer habitada* from a position of relative power herself, enjoying the fruits of the Sandinista triumph of 1979 and laboring in the projects of the young revolutionary government, one still feels a spirit of defiance in the text, a surge of pride in a victory that will not be surrendered easily to the threat of counterrevolution. Neither Belli nor her compatriots are "home free"; and certainly her struggle against machismo goes on.

In order better to appreciate Belli's writing, we need to understand some of the circumstances surrounding the production and publication of her work. We find that her "position of relative power" predates the Sandinista victory. Born in 1948 to an upper-middle-class Managua family, Belli received instruction in the Catholic faith and attended schools in Nicaragua and Spain. She studied advertising in Philadelphia and then returned home to work in that field. She was radicalized by the political activism and gains of the FSLN against the dictatorship of Anastasio Somoza Debayle in the early 1970s. Following her participation in the Sandinista assault on the Castillo home in 1974 (the historical referent for *La mujer habitada* which will be discussed later), she fled into exile in Costa Rica. Upon the success of the 1979 insurrection, she rejoined her compañeros in Nicaragua to work for the consolidation of the revolution in various capacities: in journalism, the Ministry of Planning, AMNLAE (the Nicaraguan Women's Association), and broadcasting.

Belli began her publishing career in 1974 with a book of poetry, *Sobre la grama*, and continued to write verse, winning the Casa de las Américas prize for *Línea de fuego* in 1978. Themes and strategies of the latter collection reappear and are reworked in *La mujer habitada*. Half of *Línea de fuego*, explains Electa Arenal, consists of sensual love poems that affirm the sexuality of the poetic "I" and celebrate the male lover as muse, mediator (to the revolutionary struggle), and martyr. The other half presents a participatory "I": "She is a woman of action and sorrow, a mother wrenched from her children to fulfill a larger mothering role in clandestine activity and exile. The poems illustrate the marches, hunger strikes, and mourning rituals devised as tactics of motherly militancy by Latin American women" (24). (Arenal's comments recall Sommer's "incompatible codes" [1988, 130].) Other important collections of poetry include *Truenos y arco iris* (1982), *Amor insurrecto* (1984), *De la costilla de Eva* (1987, translated as *From Eve's Rib*), and *Nicaragua under Fire* (1989). Belli recalls that her first poems, best known for their erotic themes, scandalized her friends and family as well as Nicaraguan society (interview).

She reports that she did not belong to any literary circle in her country, although a number of other young bourgeois women had begun writing political and feminist poetry at about the same time. Best known are "The Six"—Michele Najlis (in the feminist vanguard during the 1960s, experimenting with form and political themes), Belli, Yolanda Blanco, Vidaluz Meneses, Rosario Murillo, and Daisy Zamora. Murillo, wife of former president Daniel Ortega, became president of the ASTC (the Sandinista Association of Cultural Workers) after 1979, at which time Zamora assumed the responsibilities of director of the Literature Section of the Ministry of Culture and later became its vice-minister. Greg Dawes finds that Belli's poetry shares Najlis's militancy (116); he thinks that, when compared to that of Daisy Zamora, Belli's work presents a less concrete, and therefore less forceful, critique of gender roles in Nicaragua (154). However, just because Belli's work may be "less concrete" and more magical, lyrical, and mythological, does not make it any less forceful, in my opinion. We will return to a discussion of the relationship of these women to the entire revolutionary cultural project at the end of this chapter.

Love, sexuality, politics, and revolution are themes of Belli's poetry just as they continue to mark the narrative of *La mujer habitada,* in which she memorializes the heroic deeds of the women and men who gave their lives for the liberation of Nicaragua. In remarks made about her poetry, which are also applicable to her novel, Belli integrates the personal with the collective in explaining her creative process: "At first I had problems with the so-called political poems. They always came out of my own individual experiences, and I considered that to be a limitation. But when one lives collective experiences as an individual—although the form appears to be personal, or one speaks in the first person—the truth is that one expresses feelings or ideas which have the force of many experiences born from collective practice and struggle. And that's what gives them a political value" (M. Randall 149). The realization of the collective value of the personal—the metonymic and even allegorical nature of narrated individual experience—leads to the development of a testimonial discourse in her first novel.

Her second and most recent novel, *Sofía de los presagios* (1990), turns away from testimony and political history while amplifying the feminist voice. I will discuss this novel briefly when I consider the current directions Belli's work is taking. My focus in this chapter is Belli's rendering of marginalized subjects, especially women, in *La mujer habitada.*

A third-person narration in free indirect style tells the story of Lavinia, the young protagonist of *La mujer habitada*. Back from Europe, where she has studied architecture and traveled extensively, Lavinia cannot find much excitement in the frivolous social world of her aristocratic family in Faguas (a fictitious name for Nicaragua). Nevertheless, full of enthusiasm for the challenge of her profession, Lavinia embarks on her new career. Belli explains that she chose the field of architecture for Lavinia because this profession is "less mathematical and more artistic and oriented toward people and the environment" than many other traditionally male-dominated professions (interview). Timothy A. B. Richards comments that Lavinia's chosen profession is appropriate and metaphoric on both a personal and social level since "the themes of construction and destruction are understandably recurrent in resistance literature" (210).

The challenges she faces go beyond her profession to questions of gender, sexuality, class, and politics. Already alienated from her parents, she flouts custom and sets up housekeeping on her own. In the man's world of the architectural firm, Lavinia stands out as an exceptional woman. She falls in love with a fellow architect, Felipe, who tries to keep secret from her his "other life" as an activist in the Movimiento, the National Liberation Movement. His other world intrudes into hers as one evening in desperation he leads Sebastián, a comrade wounded in a gun battle with the Guardia Nacional, to her house to recover. Terrified yet intrigued, Lavinia is gradually drawn into the activities of the Movimiento.

From that moment on, she divides her life into two periods, "antes y después de tu balazo" (111) (before and after your gunshot wound). Felipe sends Lavinia to contact a nurse friend, Flor, also a Movimiento member, to treat the infection spreading in Sebastián's wounded arm. A strong friendship develops between Flor and Lavinia, and it is Flor who administers to Lavinia the oath of commitment to the organization. Lavinia then undergoes a "crash course" in guerrilla warfare.

At the same time, Lavinia is asked by her architectural firm to design plans for the new mansion of General Vela, a favorite of the "Gran General" (presumably Anastasio Somoza Debayle). At first repelled by this assignment, especially on the heels of her conversion to the cause of revolution, she finally accepts it and becomes the Movimiento's conduit of information about Vela's habits and his family. Lavinia must also maintain her social contacts as a cover, much to her displeasure; feeling the weight of her birth and class, she wants badly to become "one of them" and to be accepted fully by the Movimiento.

Through bits of information gleaned from Flor and Felipe, Lavinia learns that the Movimiento's activities are escalating: "Queremos generalizar la lucha" (262) (We want the struggle to spread). It is planning a major action, Operation Eureka, somewhere soon in the capital. We learn, along with Lavinia at the last moment, that the target of the action will be Vela's new mansion; it is to occur on the evening of a lavish housewarming party to which all his influential and wealthy associates are invited. In a preparatory action the day before Operation Eureka, Felipe is gravely wounded; he manages to make his way to Lavinia's house, begging her before he dies to take his place in the commando unit. She joins Flor, Sebastián, and the other guerrillas in a successful operation in which they take hostages; they demand and obtain the release of political prisoners, access to news media, and a large sum of money. In a final hail of bullets, Lavinia dies heroically as she kills General Vela.

The historical referent for Operation Eureka, which in the novel takes place on December 20, 1973, is the assault on the José María Castillo home by the Juan José Quezada Commando of the FSLN on December 27, 1974. Castillo served Somoza as consul to the United States; that evening he gave a party in honor of the North American ambassador.[1] Following a series of discouraging defeats to the insurgents, this successful Sandinista action added to their credibility, gained national and international attention, and swelled their ranks.

Among faithful historical details, including information about political parties, rivalries, and assassinations, Belli incorporates several interesting anachronisms. The mention of the Patty Hearst kidnapping, which did not occur until February 1974, and the Aldo Moro kidnapping in Italy in March 1978 remind us that we are still in the world of fiction. When asked about them, Belli explained that, indeed, she had taken liberties with historical fact in the interest of fiction: these events were part of the sensational news of the era and help recreate its atmosphere (interview).

Well drawn as a character and incorporating many of the characteristics and feelings of the author herself, Lavinia represents both an autobiographical, historical figure and an allegorical one—much as Jameson and Sommer have theorized. Lavinia's experience is not exactly unique or atypical (in that many other youth from middle-class and professional families were being converted to the revolutionary cause at the same time), and she would like to believe that she is developing a "collective identity" representative of what many women experience. Belli explains that both Lavinia and Flor incorporate many of the author's own sentiments at the time but that the succession of events in their lives in no way reflects her own life or that of any particular female participant in the struggle (interview). Lavinia and Flor are more or less composites of various women who joined together to fight the Somoza dictatorship. Ileana Rodríguez points out, nevertheless, that Lavinia's status, like Belli's, as a "porcelain woman" or as Rubén Darío's *princesa*[2] burdens her with a nexus of predictable social relations, preformed stereotypes, and the luxury of being able to travel, receive an education, and break out of traditional mores—options not available to most women (1994b, 179–80). She is not Everywoman.

At the same time that we follow Lavinia's adventures, we read a parallel tale of indigenous resistance. The Indian princess Itzá, whose spirit now inhabits the orange tree in Lavinia's patio where she is buried, narrates in the first person a segment of each chapter in which she describes the fight she and her warrior-lover Yarince waged together against the Spanish conquistadors five hundred years earlier. Itzá dies bravely at the hands of the invaders. As the grieving Yarince draws strength from his lover's death to face the Spanish and to die heroically, likewise Felipe's death inspires Lavinia to fight to the end as a hero.

The tree symbol is an intriguing one, especially since it serves as the link between Lavinia, Itzá, and the indigenous past. Citing Merlin Stone's research, Kathleen N. March notes that "when God was a woman . . . the tree was not a phallic symbol but a female one, representing the communication of heaven with earth" (252). Itzá explains that her *savia* (sap) will make the orange blossoms turn to fruit so that Lavinia will soon be able to drink the juice from her tree. Like an expectant mother, Itzá feels "los embriones recubrirse de la carne amarilla de las naranjas. Sé que debo darme prisa. Ella y yo nos encontraremos pronto. Llegará el tiempo de los frutos, de la maduración. Me pregunto si sentiré dolor cuando los corte" (28) (the embryos covering themselves with the yellow flesh of the oranges. I know I have to hurry. She and I will meet soon. The time of fruits, of maturation is coming). Like blood and semen, other vital bodily fluids, her savia sustains life. As it mingles with Lavinia's blood, Itzá's sap carries the memory of her indigenous roots and her fighting spirit. She will ground Lavinia literally and metaphorically in her natural and historical past, connecting her with the "umbilical cord" of roots and earth (207).

While she cannot control Lavinia's life, Itzá can transmit certain images of her past. "Sé que habito su sangre como la del árbol" (93) (I know I inhabit her blood like that of the tree), Itzá states explaining the title of the novel. She goes on to describe their relationship and her responsibility in Lavinia's increased awareness and activism. Although she denies that she and Lavinia are one being or that she possesses her like a demonic figure, somehow Itzá feels responsible for her creation. Itzá's is a voice from the past: "hemos convivido en la sangre y el lenguaje de mi historia, que es también suya, ha empezado a cantar en sus venas (121–22) (but we have cohabited the blood, and the language of my history which is also hers has begun to sing in her veins). Itzá delights in knowing she inhabits the earth, the tree, and Lavinia's body in a godlike ubiquitousness: "Todo aquello era yo. Prolongaciones interminables del ser" (44) (All that was I. Interminable prolongations of being). Lavinia peels her, liberating her "cuidadosas lágrimas" (careful tears) from inside the world of the fruit and brings her to her lips so that the concentric circles of existence are once again joined (44–45). Creation, being, life, and purpose flow through Itzá in animistic relation to Lavinia and surrounding nature. No being is forever condemned to death: "La vida brota de la muerte como la pequeña planta del grano de maíz, que se descompone en el seno de la tierra y nace para alimentarnos" (301) (Life springs forth from death like the little plant from a seed of corn, which decomposes in the bosom of the earth and is reborn to feed us). Everything changes, but nothing dies. Life is a never-ending renaissance.

Man and woman, writes Eduardo Galeano citing a Makiritare Indian myth in the novel's epigraph, "will never stop being born because death is a lie." Following suit, Belli dedicates her novel to Nicaraguan resistance fighter Nora Astorga, "quien seguirá naciendo" (who will keep on being born). Belli has explained that Astorga, a prominent Sandinista fighter and a childhood friend of hers, was dying of cancer when she wrote *La mujer habitada*. Belli wished to immortalize Nora's spirit of resistance in the novel and to emphasize the continuity of the rebellion. Unfortunately, Nora was able to read only a fragment of the novel before her death (interview). The point the text makes is that la savia, the sap and substance of life, unites all of creation just as it unites the participants of today's struggle—those who would honor and protect the dignity of others—with those of the past and of the future.

Within the imagery of animism and resurrection, the reader finds that Belli's novel posits the interrelatedness of human and natural being. In a theory that may interest the North American reader, Patrick D. Murphy has applied a Bakhtinian ecofeminist dialogics to the understanding of nature as a speaking subject. Speaking subjects can be more than just humans, maintains Murphy; they can be "constituted by a speaker/author who is not the speaking subject but a renderer of the other as speaking subject" because the self is multiple" (45–46). Murphy believes that one should not confuse the nature of the romantics, which only serves to fortify their own speaking subject status, with the nature that acts as an authentic character; instead, "an ecofeminist dialogics requires this effort to render the other, primarily constituted by androcentrism as women and nature . . . as speaking subjects within patriarchy in order to subvert that patriarchy not only by decentering it but also by proposing other centers" (49). In an ecofeminist dialogics, women and nature find their voices and occupy a place at one of the centers rather than at the margins.

Doris Sommer quoting Rigoberta Menchú affirms the closeness of woman to the earth: "The relationship between the mother and the earth is like the relationship between husband and wife. There is a constant dialogue between the earth and the woman. This feeling is born in women because of the responsibilities they have, which men do not have" (1988, 128). This dialogue and interconnectedness is an intriguing approach to *La mujer habitada*. Is nature as a speaking subject really distinct from other speaking subjects in the text, or is it the traditional metaphor used for woman's body and her nurturing qualities?

The tree/Itzá provides the text's most visible example. At times Lavinia wishes to be "vegetal" (72); she recognizes that the orange tree in her garden is a vibrant being and talks to it frequently as if it were a pet (44). We readers know by the printed words we see that the tree/Itzá responds as a speaking subject in each chapter. Lavinia, however, *feels* the tree's response. After a falling-out with Felipe, Lavinia asks the tree for advice. It answers her in the comforting voice of her favorite aunt, Inés, now dead (245). The reader may suspect, however, that the voice of the tree is merely a ventriloquism or a Lavinia in stereophonic sound—that is, her own voice rather than an autonomous natural voice or that of her dead aunt. She hears what she wants to hear.

The narrator relates Lavinia's ability to communicate with all of nature and her confidence in her own perceptions: "Confiaba en sus presentimientos, en su capacidad de leer posibilidades en el peso de la atmósfera, la manera de moverse de las flores, la dirección del viento" (154) (She trusted her feelings, her ability to read possibilities in the pressure of the atmosphere, the way in which the flowers moved, the direction of the wind). It appears that feeling and intuition, which are often considered part of a female epistemology, provide as valid a way for arriving at truth as does empirical observation, a traditionally masculine approach. (We will discuss intuition later as a form of feminist discourse.)

A preponderance of feminine imagery to describe the land in *La mujer habitada* further illustrates the bond between the female body and nature. (This is nothing new. Mother Earth has traditionally borne feminine epithets, a fact that ecofeminists use to explain the ease with which a patriarchal society has abused her body.) Josephine Donovan points to "evidence—provided by contemporary theorists—that women's epistemology remains more integrated with the environment than men's (perhaps because of their base in use-value production)" (88). Itzá laughs at the great discovery of the Spaniards that the earth is round like an orange, like her (37). The motherland is a body of lakes and volcanoes (338), a woman to be possessed; and Faguas is "la sensualidad. Cuerpo abierto, ancho, sinuoso, pechos desordenados de mujer hechos de tierra, desparramados sobre el paisaje. Amenazadores. Hermosos" (14) (sensuality. A body open, wide, sinuous, licentious breasts of a woman made of earth, scattered across the countryside. Threatening. Beautiful). The earth like a fertile woman gives birth to new life, to the future. Symbolically, the orange tree blooms for the first time on Lavinia's first day of work. Lavinia repeatedly refers to Flor, Felipe, and Sebastián as "árboles serenos" (serene trees), attributing to the guerrilla fighters, many of whom are men, qualities related to nature. They earn the metaphor because they defend and protect the land with a nurturing attitude more often associated with women. In contrast, a rich industrialist who profits from deforestation belongs to the male-dominated discourse of capitalism. He is, fittingly, a friend of the general and attends his party the night of the guerrilla assault. The eco-feminist discourse of the text divides the world into two camps: the nurturers and the violators.

Like her poetry, Belli's *La mujer habitada* is a text highly charged with sensuality and eroticism. Lavinia's aroused and alert body is "su antena del universo" (28) (her antenna to the universe). Again the narrator affirms the relation to the natural world. When she and Felipe make love, "tenían ese algo de animales olfateándose, las emanaciones del instinto, la atracción eléctrica, inconfundible" (33) (they had something of the animal in them, smelling each other, the emanations of instinct, electric attraction, unmistakable). Discussing the eroticism of the text, March suggests that "writing the Body Erotic . . . is a pleasurable game, resonant of remotest antiquity, when a greater portion of human activity was devoted to the sensual and the instinctual, rather than to the calculated productivity of work" (249). In this way, Felipe and Lavinia's shared eroticism links them to Yarince and Itzá.

While finding great pleasure in Felipe's embrace, Lavinia bemoans the inequality of their relationship. "Where there is strong eroticism, there is power," writes Mariana Valverde in *Sex, Power, and Pleasure;* "the point is that we have to change gender relations (and race and class relations as well) so that one person's power is not another's humiliation" (cited in March 252). Lavinia feels like a trapped Penelope when, after entering the Movimiento, she finds that Felipe wants her to remain his "oasis," his refuge and source of sustenance, a flowering "copa de polen" (cup of pollen) from which he can drink to renew himself. She finds that her only access to true vitality is an inward experience through her body, but she longs for something more than just sensual pleasure, as seductive as it is.

Lavinia's trajectory in the novel is toward outside fulfillment; she is a changed woman compared to the speaker in Belli's early poems. In both cases, she is sexually liberated and exuberant. From the woman largely preoccupied with her own sensuality and satisfaction in her guerrilla lover's arms, she becomes the guerrilla herself. The passion continues but she refuses to experience the action any longer through her lover's eyes. She has become a revolutionary subject in her own right.

While I note this general trend, I must add that it is not always consistent. Dawes, Kaminsky, and Rodríguez all note Lavinia's ambivalence. Occasionally, she still subordinates herself to her lover (after all, she only takes up the gun when Felipe, on his deathbed, anoints her). And we are reminded of poems in *Línea del fuego,* "A Sergio" (Ramírez); "Al Comandante Marcos" (perhaps the "real-life Felipe"—Sandinista theorist Eduardo Contreras Escobar, who died fighting in Managua in 1976); and "Ché" (Guevara), in which she writes: "¿Si el poeta eres tú, / qué puedo yo decirte comandante? / . . . Qué hermoso sos, comandante, / un hombre con cara de futuro, / un hombre grande, lleno de alegría y victoria" (40) (If the poet is you, / what can I possibly say to you comandante? / . . . How handsome you are, comandante,/ a man with the face of the future, / a big man, full of happiness and victory). The speaker is awestruck in the presence of the heroic and dashingly romantic fighter.

To return to the eroticism of the novel, an atmosphere of sensuality is heightened as the narrator extends the flower metaphor to a variety of situations and characters. The very name of Lavinia's compañera, Flor, equates this mature, self-actuated woman with nature in full bloom. Flor's garden of abundance and variety radiates warmth and grace (78); Sara, Lavinia's best friend from childhood, carefully tends a garden of beautiful flowers surrounding a malinche tree that blooms bright red once a year (38). In contrast, General Vela's wife and sister buy imported lotus flowers from Miami to decorate their new home for its inauguration; they will appropriately complement the "mucha conversación intrascendente" (the inconsequential conversation) of the evening (192). General Vela himself commits the final affront to nature, the extreme example of macho alienation from the Earth Mother, with "adornos de flores plásticas" (241) (plastic flowers) on the tables of his office. Beyond the fact that flowers and gardening have been a traditional domain of the woman, Ileana Rodríguez explains how in this novel, as in many others written by women, the *garden* together with the *house* and *nation*—perhaps she should have added the *womb,* creative matrix of all human life—"constitute some of the terms a disenfranchised majority employ to enter the ongoing struggle and to signal the appropriation by women of ever-larger social spaces in the organization and reorganization of privatized spaces and in the territorial administration of the globe" (1994b, 19). Women, thoroughly familiar with the space of the garden, see it as reflective of taste, character, and hard work; they know that "in the garden" literal and metaphorical seeds are planted and cultivated that, with careful tending, will produce sturdy plants. (Consistent with Rodríguez's architectural metaphors and descriptions of spaces occupied by women, I see the title of the novel itself, *La mujer habitada,* as a reference to a body inhabited or occupied—by spirit, by myth, by memory, by sensuality. Again, it is an intimate space from which female consciousness develops outward.)

Other sensual images abound in the novel. Aromas and fragrances appeal to the heightened olfactory senses. The aroma of orange blossoms frequently intoxicates Lavinia; she notes the odor of semen, of anger and sweat, of a new automobile, and the stench of poverty and disease, of dirty rags and stuffiness, of an abortion poorly performed. Lavinia can even smell danger (51). A sign of her growing awareness and her changing sympathies, the "zona campesina" (peasant areas in the countryside) "olía bien, a limpio, a vacas lejanas, a caballos" (221) (smelled good, clean, like distant cows, like horses).

In such a representation of female sensuality and eroticism, Gail M. Schwab sees a more decentered, polyphonic perspective on the world than one would find in a monologic, phallic-centered patriarchal discourse. "The morphology of the female body, which has erogenous zones all over, anywhere from head to foot, and where eroticism is not centered, focalized in a single organ," she explains, "becomes a metaphor through which to grasp a textuality which is diverse, plural, circular, centrifugal—in fact, multi-voiced and dialogic" (65).

One particular trope, striking in its frequency in Belli's text and consonant with the theory of the decentering quality of feminine discourse, is the synecdoche of body parts used to represent the whole person. Each one elicits a strong emotion from Lavinia. When Felipe unexpectedly enters Lavinia's house with the wounded Sebastián, the narrator describes how Lavinia fixes her attention first on the blood pouring from the mangled arm: "Vio la piel del brazo un poco arriba del codo; el boquete redondo, la piel en carne viva, la sangre manando roja, intensa, indetenible" (52) (She saw the skin of his arm a little above the elbow; the round hole, the raw flesh, the flowing red blood, intense, unstoppable). Lavinia contemplates the arm, feeling simultaneously a rising terror in her own body, then moves her gaze to his features, his strong traits, his olive skin, his paleness, and his pursed lips (52). Not until several paragraphs later does she seem to acknowledge an entire human being by giving a more complete description. Even the wounded Sebastián observes Felipe operating on his arm "como si no se tratara de su brazo" (53) (as if it weren't a question of his arm), as if it were detached or belonged to someone else.

In a later episode, Lavinia sits in a waiting room at the public hospital while doctors work to save the life of her maid, Lucrecia, the victim of a bungled abortion. Feeling conspicuous and uncomfortable, Lavinia lets her eyes drop to the filthy floor where she studies the feet of other people who are waiting: feet of an older woman with varicose veins; toes protruding from holes cut out of shoes to make them fit; broken, violet, grotesque toenails; younger feet in once-white sandals; chipped purple nail polish on rough, dark toes; worn-out soles of a man's shoes; short, ripped socks with worn-out elastic. As she studies the feet, she suddenly becomes self-conscious of her own: "Sus pies finos, blancos, asomando por la sandalia de tacón, la sandalia marrón suave, cuero italiano, las uñas rojas. Eran lindos sus pies. Aristocráticos. Cerró de nuevo los ojos" (146) (Her fine, white feet peeking out of her high-heeled sandals, soft maroon sandals, Italian leather, red toenails. Her feet were pretty. Aristocratic. She closed her eyes once more). Her feet scream out her status. Guilt ridden, the "porcelain" Lavinia fears that people outside her own class will never accept her.

Yet another synecdoche, this time Vela's hands, evokes a wave of nausea in Lavinia. Invited to dinner at the Vela home, Lavinia later recalls the "manos regordetas, de dedos cortos y nudillos gruesos del general" (214) (the plump hands with short fingers and thick knuckles of the general); she tries in vain to tear her eyes away from the fingers, which are deliberately deboning a juicy piece of chicken. Shuddering at the sight of the hands of a torturer, her imagination runs wild as she pictures him doing the same to a prisoner.

Her fixation on various body parts, the sensuality and eroticism of the text, the metaphors of the natural material elements of the earth, and the attempt to render nature as a speaking subject all contribute to construct a female, natural subject. By contrast, the Spanish conquistadors of Faguas's past—and, by extension, the neocolonial powers of the present and their local cronies, like the "Gran General" and Vela—represent the very antithesis of this discourse. The tree/Itzá recounts the majority of historical passages of the novel, in which she shows that Captain Alvarado and his invading Spaniards, who "tenían miedo de nuestros árboles y animales" (42) (were afraid of our trees and our animals), are out of touch with nature. Their anti- or unnatural "dios extraño" (strange god) prohibits the pleasures of love that the natives used to enjoy "como animales sanos, sin cotonas, ni inhibiciones" (35) (like healthy animals, without garments or inhibitions); sex has become a perversion and rape its violent and ugly consequence. Not only are the Spaniards unnatural, they violate the land much as they violate the indigenous people they find: "Descargaban el estruendo de sus bastones, alarmando a las loras, desatando las bandadas de pájaros, haciendo gritar a los monos que pasaban sobre nuestras cabezas en manadas, cargando las monas los monitos pequeños que, desde entonces, se quedaron con la cara asustada" (42) (They discharged the clamor of their truncheons, alarming the parrots, letting loose the flocks of birds, making the monkeys which were passing over our heads in droves scream, the female monkeys carrying their babies which, from then on, were left with frightened faces). Greedy, dishonest, and treacherous, the Spaniards profane the honorable rules of war, which the gods established from the beginning of time in order to protect nature and the defenseless and in order to allow the enemy sufficient time to prepare its defenses and equalize arms (313).

Part of the Spanish project involved erasing indigenous culture and history. The conquerors burned their temples and their sacred codices: "Una red de agujeros era nuestra herencia" (116) (Our history was a network of holes). The phallocentric subject increases his own self-esteem as he perceives absence or lack on the part of his Other. An absent history invites the imposition of a false substitute, such as Spain's arrogant assertion that it had "descubierto un nuevo mundo" (discovered a new world); the tree/Itzá protests that "nuestro mundo no era nuevo para nosotros" (our world was not new for us) and that many advanced civilizations lived and flourished in this part of the world long before the Conquest (86). Itzá finds it ironic that the Spaniards set out to civilize them and free them from their barbarism. Instead, "con barbarie nos dominaron, nos despoblaron"

(87) (with barbarity they dominated us and decimated our population). She exposes their hypocrisy; her outrage will drive her campaign of subversion.

Belli explores a variety of ways in which women express themselves. Like Lavinia and Flor, some rebel at the limitation of being forced to know life only inwardly. They believe in "la necesidad de darle trascendencia al paso por el mundo; 'dejar huella'" (317) (the necessity of giving transcendence to their passage through this world; "to leave tracks"). Others do not rebel for reasons sometimes beyond their control. The first quality to recognize is the multiplicity of female voices—Spivak's heterogeneity or Diane Price Herndl's "heteroglossia" (9). No one voice can claim to speak for all; rather, as Bauer and McKinstry argue, using the theories of feminist dialogics, one can recognize "competing voices without making any single voice normative" (6), and one can make a case for "critical subjectivity that shows gender, classes, and races in dialogue rather than in opposition" (3). It seems to me that this type of feminism—and we can extend this approach to any activism such as antiracism or anticlassism—avoids an adversarial "winner-take-all" model and advocates negotiation, compromise, and common space to accommodate different interests. (I would qualify their use of the word *competing* because it is misleading. Competition implies a winner and a loser.) In summary, to paraphrase Mary O'Connor, the goal is not to portray all women as equal and identical but to show their uniqueness and connectedness (213). And the only way to show someone's uniqueness and connectedness is not by her absence as a banished, humiliated loser but by her presence in the text and "at the table" where the rest listen and dialogue.

Returning to the novel, in addition to Itzá, Flor, and Lavinia, we meet Lavinia's maid, Lucrecia, who chooses an abortion because her man abandons her and she cannot afford to stop working to care for a child. Nor does she have the wherewithal to provide for the child's necessities: "No quería un hijo para tener que dejarlo solo, mal cuidado, mal comido. Lo había pensado bien" (144) (She didn't want a child and then have to leave him alone, poorly cared for, with little food. She had thought about it a lot). Indirect free style, as written here, is one of the narrative strategies that come closest to probing and expressing the mind of the various characters. We understand that Lucrecia sees her only salvation in returning to school.

Among other women of the novel, the prostitutes whom Felipe meets contradict his stereotype of "mujeres tristes y ajadas en los prostíbulos" (sad and withered women in the houses of prostitution); they seem to enjoy an "ancient power" they wield over men, and one in particular,

Terencia, says with a beautiful smile that "en ese negocio había que tener sentido del humor" (111) (in this business you have to have a sense of humor).

Busybody Mercedes, the office secretary, confides to Lavinia that she feels trapped in her relationship with a married man who has been promising her for two years that he will leave his wife. She wants to believe her lover but learns the wife is pregnant again, thus putting into question his actual resolve. Lavinia advises her: "Vos sos una mujer joven, Mercedes, sos guapa, inteligente. Te merecés algo mejor que estar de segundona" (197) (You're a young woman, Mercedes, you're pretty and intelligent. You deserve better than playing second fiddle). All men are the same, rationalizes Mercedes. Anyway, she feels, now that she is a "used" woman, no decent man will want her. She lacks the will or the energy to change her situation or to rebel against the double standard. Lavinia ponders Mercedes's problem: "Era casi una maldición, pensó, aferrarse así al amor. Y tan femenino" (198) (It was almost a curse to cling so much to love. And so feminine). While for men it is easy to compartmentalize their intimate lives in order to avoid "contaminating" the rest of their dealings, for women a love affair becomes the "axis" of existence. Any deviation is catastrophic (198).

One last example of the variety of female voices within *La mujer habitada* is Lavinia's childhood friend Sara, who enjoys the "cotidianeidad" (everyday quality) and domesticity of her life as a comfortable bourgeois housewife. For her it is all so "natural" (20). Nevertheless, Sara observes that in her world men like her husband Adrián are "intrusos" or "interrupciones," (intruders or interruptions); it feels strange sharing bed, bath, and shower with someone who comes in at night and leaves in the morning (150). The irony of men believing that this world, in which they couldn't be less important, exists for them is not lost on Sara. But when Sara exclaims that women are truly "el poder detrás del trono" (the power behind the throne), Lavinia retorts that "eso es un invento de los hombres" (151) (this is a man's invention). Sara dismisses Lavinia's refutation, preferring to cling to her own worldview and letting Lavinia have hers.

Ileana Rodríguez finds certain women characters of the novel emblematic of specific ethnic groups and classes. Itzá, of course, represents the indigenous woman; Aunt Inés, the white or "porcelain" middle-class woman; and Flor, the mestiza. Sara and Lavinia, both "porcelain women," are two sides to the same coin, one being traditional and the other a contemporary revolutionary and a figure of transition (1994b, 177–78). For the purposes of her discussion, Rodríguez puts the rest of the women of the text into the service sector and notes that they are all women of color. Basically, the pluralism of major and minor female voices in the novel "argue[s] in favor of a postmodernity . . . and of a development encompassing an ample spectrum of the social body" (178). This is *mestizaje*. The major voices, like Lavinia, recognize that they will have to take a leadership role in promoting democratic representation. Nowhere, to my knowledge, does Belli suggest that Lavinia should step aside to allow the "service-sector" women to take over in a classic Marxist revolution and dictatorship of the proletariat. Hers is more a project of shared space. Lavinia replaces Felipe when he dies; it seems logical to assume that someone of similar class and stature will take Lavinia's place after her death.

While the text does not espouse a traditional Marxist meta-narrative, we wonder to what extent it is truly decentered and democratic. Lavinia expresses her opinions, tries to influence her friends' behavior, and generally finds herself in solidarity with other women; but she certainly does not claim to speak for them all, nor does the narrator give her the final word on womanhood. To the degree that the text incorporates a variety of female voices, it is dialogic. However, Lavinia's voice is the loudest of the novel. While I would not call the text "totalizing," I do find that it tends to privilege her experience and perspective. After all, it is Lavinia who dies the hero's death during the final assault. By her own words she partially deconstructs her notions of strength in the collective and in solidarity with her sisters. Exhilarated by the possibilities of independence, she seeks authenticity: "'Estoy sola y nadie puede decirme certeramente si mis acciones son un error o un acierto.' Era lo tremendo de conducir la propia vida, pensó" (155) (I'm alone and no one can tell me for sure if my actions are an error or a lucky guess. That was what was so wonderful about leading her own life, she thought). This voice is more of an "I" than a "we."

Faguas society considers Lavinia a "liberated woman," for better or worse. Whether she is or not, the issue bothers her throughout the novel. Independence has brought confusion and ambivalence, and she finds herself "en terreno de nadie" (96) (in a no [wo]man's land) regarding her role as lover, professional, daughter, friend, guerrilla fighter. She is hired by the architectural firm originally because the manager believes she will be able to deal effectively with women clients since "women understand each other" (15). That is, she is hired because she is Other. Does the fact that she is the only woman in the office with a "substantive" position just prove that she is the exception to the general rule of female inferiority? She struggles with her identity, wondering if she must act manly—avoid smiling or gracefulness (240)—to survive in a man's world. Or she wonders whether there is another way. At times, she resorts to her feminine wiles to tease, to seek revenge, to control: "Exhibirse ahora sería un placer. . . . Exhibirse ahora que nadie podía tocarla, penetrar su intimidad, amenazarla con matrimonios perpetuos, servidumbres disfrazadas de éxito. . . . Era un placer casi maquiavélico" (179) (Being an exhibitionist now would be a pleasure. . . . To exhibit herself now that nobody could touch her, penetrate her intimacy, threaten her with eternal marriages, slaveries disguised as success. . . . It was an almost Machiavellian pleasure). Like Itzá, Lavinia knows she is as strong as a man but feels invisible when men talk of serious issues and ignore her (74). As a fledgling activist, she perceives the contradiction between Felipe's "hermoso discurso" (lovely discourse) of the revolutionary new man and new woman and his refusal to invite her to join him in "la transformación del mundo" (129) (the transformation of the world). She ultimately earns the respect of her coworkers at the job site and compañeros on the front line. Significantly, the image of her Madzen assault rifle as a "cuerpo de mujer, de una novia negra y sólida" (315) (body of a woman, of a black and solid sweetheart), transforms the traditionally masculine metaphor of the gun as extension of the phallus into a feminine symbol.

Throughout the novel imagery of birds and flying highlights Lavinia's desire for freedom and transcendence as a woman. Her name can be read metathetically as a variation of the word "liviana," which the tree/Itzá uses to describe women's wish to be lighter than air so that they might literally and metaphorically soar. Itzá muses: "Me puse a mecerme en el aire, a columpiarme sintiéndome liviana" (22) (I began to rock myself into the air, to swing feeling myself so light). Just as she has "inherited" the spirit of resistance from her indigenous past, Lavinia inherits the will to "ponerse las alas" (22) (put on wings) from her two favorite relatives, her grandfather and her aunt Inés. Lavinia lives out her aunt's dreams, which her epoch did not permit her to achieve (12). Her grandfather has given her a love for reading, fantasy, politics, and adventure. She dreams of her grandfather putting great wings of white feathers on her (50), and she dreams prophetically that she flies far away from Felipe (129). Itzá refers several times to Felipe and Yarince as "colibrís" (hummingbirds), describing their soaring spirits and lofty goals of freedom for their people. It is this side of Felipe that Lavinia loves and wants to emulate.

Ironically, birds also interest Vela's gentle young son, much to his father's displeasure and embarrassment. Vela instructs Lavinia to decorate his son's room with helicopters or warplanes in an attempt to channel this love of flying into a more "manly" interest. The son breaks free of his father's tyranny as he silently alerts Lavinia to his father's hiding place the night of the assault on the mansion. The greatest of ironies, however, is that Vela himself sports the nickname "el volador" (334) (the flyer)—not because of any pretensions to transcendence but because he flies about the country overseeing counterinsurgency dirty work and he delights in pushing suspected subversives out of airborne helicopters.[3] By perverting a lovely natural phenomenon into a machine of brutality and death, Vela's machismo offends nature and sickens Lavinia.

In this way, an integral part of the construction of a feminist discourse in *La mujer habitada* is the deconstruction of machismo. The comment by Sara's husband, Adrián—"Gracias a Dios que a mí no me tocó ser mujer" (186) (Thank God I'm not a woman)—poses the problem. An ambivalent Adrián seems to sympathize with the difficult social demands on a woman; nevertheless, his sympathy has its limits, and he is truly grateful for his superior station in life as a male. Like most men, with the possible exception of Sebastián, Lavinia finds both Adrián and Felipe patronizing. Extreme cases find such lascivious *gorilas* like Vela determined to possess whatever or whoever strikes their fancy: "Siempre logro lo que me propongo" (243) (I always get what I want). Likewise he insults women by saying to Lavinia that it is rare to find women who are not only beautiful but also intelligent (43).

High society's debutante ball is emblematic of male-controlled greed and commerce. Fathers present their eligible daughters to society "para que la husmearan animalitos de sacos y corbatas. Animalitos domésticos buscando quién les diera hijos robustos y frondosos, les hiciera la comida, les arreglara los cuartos" (16) (so that the little animals in coats and ties can smell them. Little domestic animals looking for someone who can give them robust and leafy children, make them dinner, clean up the bedrooms). Men exhibit them like fine china "en aquel mercado persa de casamientos con olor a subasta" (16) (in that Persian market of marriages with the smell of a public auction), and Lavinia, who has experienced this humiliation, hates their condescension and exploitation. Women are commodities to be acquired on the market.

To maintain her sanity, she must separate the two Felipes—the one she loves from the macho, "él que ella consideraba no hablaba por sí mismo, sino como encarnación de un antiguo discurso lamentable" (287) (the one she thought didn't speak for himself but as the incarnation of an ancient lamentable discourse)—hoping one day to liberate him from his sexism. Frustrated that she cannot "penetrate" his mind and his prejudices, she resents the fact that his penetration of her is merely physical, that he does not seem to care what she thinks. Lavinia's dual desires further underscore her ambivalence—the external female hope of changing the man she already loves.

The emancipation of women forms part of the Movimiento's agenda, but Lavinia questions its sincerity and commitment to such a distant ideal while Sebastián admits to its difficulty. He emphasizes the importance of continually trying to change present attitudes by changing praxis. It is difficult, he concedes: for example, as soon as men and women occupy the same safe house, the women assume the domestic chores without anybody telling them to, as if it is natural (164). The underlying message is that this division of labor is not natural but arbitrary, but it has such a long cultural tradition that people perceive it as natural. Lavinia, realistically, understands that women will enter history not because men want them there but out of necessity, "necesidad de los hombres que no se daban abasto para morir, para luchar, para trabajar" (297) (necessity of the men who cannot cope with dying, fighting, working). Felipe has to die before she can take his place (318). His spirit of justice and resistance now inhabits Lavinia: "Ella era Felipe. Felipe era ella" (315) (She was Felipe. Felipe was she). Gender equality is achieved only in death.

In a 1984 interview with Margaret Randall, Belli suggested that women had achieved a position of professional equality with men in the new Nicaragua but that they had not yet been accepted as both equals and women. More recently, Belli has stated that such comments were "benevolent" on her part (she was still euphoric with victory) and that, in fact, real equality was not achieved under the Sandinistas (interview). Women did enjoy some positions of middle-level responsibility, but a "glass ceiling" still prevented their reaching top posts. Machismo existed under the Sandinistas and continues under the UNO government where the "maternal"—as distinguished from the authoritative—Violeta Chamorro is president.[4]

To achieve equality, women like Lavinia, Flor, Lucrecia, and Itzá create subversive discourses, different languages from the ones shaped by men. Women use their bodies as signs. Itzá weeps as she remembers how she and other women protested subjugation by denying their strong maternal instinct and by refusing to bear children who would become street beggars or slaves to foreign masters. Lavinia, too, doubts she will have children, although that thought is not comforting (234). In the text, subversive women think, speak, and act with their bodies—unlike Sara, who insists on waiting for the laboratory report to confirm her pregnancy rather than trusting intuition and reading the signs from her body: "Es verdad que uno se da cuenta, pero vos sabés, el examen es el gran acontecimiento, ya cuando ves el 'positivo' en la hoja de papel. . . . No es lo mismo que intuirlo" (233) (It's true that one realizes it, but the test is the grand event, when you see the 'positive' on the sheet of paper. . . . It's not the same as sensing it). Lavinia, on the other hand, trusts her body more than words. In her bed "era misterioso aquello de poderse comunicar tan profundamente a nivel de la epidermis cuando frecuentemente se confundían en el terreno de las palabras. No le parecía lógico, pero así funcionaba" (236) (it was mysterious how they could communicate so profoundly on the level of the epidermis when frequently they would get confused in the field of words. It didn't seem logical, but that's the way it worked). In this venue she feels equal and confident.

Granted, the construction of a female subject who is in touch with her natural roots remains the primary interest of *La mujer habitada,* but one must also consider her in relation to the struggle for national liberation. The two are inseparable in the novel. In fact, the movement toward female emancipation often takes a back seat to the general revolution. To explain the results of such a double agenda, Amelia Mondragón writes that Lavinia has not achieved an "unfurling of feminine conscience" (which Mondragón defines using negative terms: alienation, difference, fragmentation, and dynamism). Her actions, Mondragón finds, fuse with the male-dominated, revolutionary discourse (1991). This sporadic fusion leads to Lavinia's ambivalence, as we have seen, regarding her own role and responsibility.

Class, as well as gender and race, defines alterity. Sebastián explains the goals of the Movimiento saying that they are fighting an unjust system and institutionalized violence. Only an effort by all the people will bring true change. Revolutionary discourse deconstructs the resignation and fatalism of the poor. Lavinia asks Lucrecia, "Vos crees que ser pobre o ser rico es un destino escrito por Dios, ¿verdad?" (168) (You think that being poor or rich is a destiny written by God, right?). The brand of religion that ensures inequality is man-made, says Lavinia. In no way is it natural, of God (168).

Sara, while not poor, echoes the helplessness that paralyzes most of the nation and plays into the hands of the Gran General and people like Vela. She says that one has to accept the way the world "is" (234). Disagreeing, Lavinia retorts: "El mundo no 'es' de ninguna manera, Sara. Ese es el problema. Somos nosotros quienes lo hacemos de un modo u otro" (234) (It's not that the world 'is' in any manner, Sara. That's the problem. We're the ones who make it one way or another). Lavinia is first conscientized by a group of shantytown dwellers who are about to be displaced by a commercial center her firm plans to construct. They protest the injustice but, aware of their powerlessness, add that "Nadie nos oye" (24) (Nobody hears us). Lavinia does hear them and here begins her politicization. She understands that one must do, not be, and that one has to enter history to change it.

The aristocrats of Faguas may criticize the Gran General's philistine tastes, coziness with foreign interests, and heavy-handed security tactics, but they are actually complicit with the status quo: "Critiquémoslo pero no lo cambiemos, era la consigna" (190) (Let us criticize but not change, that was their motto). The Velas and other nouveaux riches of the Gran General's party, the real locus of power, throw high society an occasional bone to keep it satisfied and quiet. Having all been taught to think of themselves as "el centro del mundo, el principio del universo" (193) (the center of the world, the origin of the universe), Faguas's elites turn inward in self-absorption and vanity, refusing to "mirar a su alrededor y descubrir lo 'otro' y a los 'demás' bajo distinta luz, sin la necesidad infantil de hacer girar el mundo a su alrededor" (193) (look around and discover the Other under a different light without the infantile need to make the world revolve around themselves). The few who manage to break free like Lavinia discover the emptiness of their abundance (317). The rest have failed to open their eyes to a reality all around them, thereby giving their blessing to the perpetuation of injustice. It is thus impossible, believes Lavinia, to be apolitical and neutral.

In revolutionary discourse, moral maturity is achieved when one begins to consider the needs of the Other in addition to, or instead of, one's own needs. Flor explains to Lavinia, at the beginning of her training: "Hoy empieza tu tiempo de sustituír el 'yo,' por el 'nosotros'" (120) (Today you will begin to replace the "I" with the "we"). She must learn to act as a disciplined member of a team (219). Lavinia finds in the "sincronía colectiva" (316) (synchronized collective) a love that alleviates her grief and loneliness and redeems her guilt.

Conscientized, ready to enter history to challenge oppression, Lavinia and the Movimiento claim the moral upper hand. Distantly sympathetic citizens of Faguas, like Adrián, consider the revolutionaries' idealism to be a "heroic suicide" or a madness worthy of Don Quijote, two images that appear more than once in the text. (Yarince's death is also termed a "heroic suicide.") Members of the Movimiento explain that they have chosen the path of violence only because nothing else has worked. As they plan the action at the Vela mansion, the commando unit exercises caution. The means by which they achieve their objective will convey a message as important as the objective itself. As they take hostages, they do so less brutally "recordando que ellos debían demostrar que eran diferentes. No eran esbirros, no eran guardias" (326) (remembering that they had to show that they were different. They were not henchmen, nor were they the Guard). They are revolutionaries, not assassins; they cannot afford a blood-bath (312).

Despite Lavinia's death at the end of the novel—another example of what some would call heroic suicide—*La mujer habitada* remains a story of hope, victory, and life. Tying the two narrative strands together, Itzá explains that she has completed a cycle with the death of Lavinia. Her destiny "de semilla germinada" (as a germinated seed) is to sow life, to realize the dreams of her ancestors. Although Lavinia is now earth and humus, her spirit still dances and her "cuerpo abona campos fecundos" (338) (body fertilizes fecund fields). The traditional image has been inverted: it is the woman who now fertilizes the field. Earlier, Flor had expressed a similar hope in the resurrection of her dead compañeros; she denies death, thinking "que el día del triunfo los encontraremos a todos, que allí nos daremos cuenta que no habían muerto, que estaban escondidos en alguna parte" (302) (that on the day of triumph we will find everyone, that then we will realize that they hadn't died, that they were hidden somewhere). Their spirit of resistance and sacrifice lives on, a triumph to which Belli's novel gives testimony.

Part of her literary achievement is the recording of a heroic struggle by the nation's oppressed; and part of it is the special attention given to the spirit of women who, by will and by necessity, join in the work of liberation. The women who especially make a difference are those who, in touch with nature, have an indigenous understanding of the cycles of life. Richards writes that in "correcting the dynamic of the Conquest, the Indian [that is, natural] configuration is reconstituted alongside the European; the cyclical coexists with the linear. In short, it offers a hybridized and syncretic vision that subverts [what Ashcroft calls] 'the apparently inescapable dialectic of history . . . in which division and categorization are . . . the bases of perception'" (213). Belli's is a distinctly feminist view of history: liberation and victory will result not with the reinstatement of a rationalist, monologic discourse but with the combination of the cyclical with the historical and linear, a dialogics with women and men working creatively together to produce a better world for all.

In a final hymn to this new spirit, Itzá sings of future possibilities:

> Nadie poseerá este cuerpo de lagos y volcanes . . .
> Ni ella y yo hemos muerto sin designio ni herencia.
> Volvimos a la tierra desde donde de nuevo viviremos.
> Poblaremos de frutos carnosos el aire de tiempos nuevos.
> Colibrí Yarince
> Colibrí Felipe
> danzarán sobre nuestras corolas
> nos fecundarán eternamente . . .
>   Los barcos de los conquistadores alejándose para siempre
> Serán nuestros el oro y las plumas
> el cacao y el mango
> la esencia de los sacuanjoches
> Nadie que ama muere jamás (338).

(No one will possess this body of lakes and volcanoes . . . Neither she nor I have died without purpose or inheritance / We return to the earth from which we will live again / We will populate with fleshy fruits the air of a new age / Hummingbird Yarince / Hummingbird Felipe / will dance on our corollas / will fertilize us eternally . . . The ships of the conquistadors leaving forever / the gold and the feathers will be ours / the cacao and the mango / the essence of sacuanjoches [Nicaragua's national flower] / No one who loves ever dies.) Women as Other, women as nature speak through Belli's text and announce a future of love and life if one lives in harmony with the earth and in solidarity with all creation.

Before leaving *La mujer habitada,* I want to bring to the reader's attention several other questions that emerge when considering this text. Some readers find it tendentious and similar to the Latin American social-realist novels of this century in its division of society into polarizing good and evil, "us against them" factions. Moreover, the "effect of the real," an important aspect of testimonial discourse, is clouded by the play of myth, fantasy, and lyricism, as I have mentioned.

In fact, this "magical clouding" is precisely the reason some critics have posited for Belli's novel falling *outside* a revolutionary aesthetic. Ileana Rodríguez judges Lavinia still to be a prisoner of romance (1994b, 180–81).

Kaminsky more directly identifies Lavinia's truncated revolutionary self: "Lavinia is not given access to the history that shapes her own participation in the struggle. Inhabited by the spirit of an indigenous woman who fought against the invading Spanish conquistadors but who has been forgotten by the official histories of the country (even in its oppositional form history appears to contain only male actors), Lavinia is largely impelled to act by a force she experiences only as the trace of subconscious activity—dreams, automatic drawing, irrational impulse" (53). Certainly love in this novel, as the mysterious chemistry that bonds two people, is not based on rationality either.

Dawes likewise denies Lavinia revolutionary subject status in a rationalist sense. Belli, he writes, tilts too much toward an "irrationalism that debilitates [her] revolutionary commitment and reduces her political stance to that of a utopian socialist" (137). Nor does she deal adequately with sociohistorical contradictions. Obviously, male-female "chemistry," magic, and intuition pull Belli away from the material and the rational. If this is a simple observation, I am certainly in agreement. If it is a judgment and disqualification, I am not. Dawes, especially, seems to equate "rational" with "worthy," and therefore "irrational" with "silly" and "less weighty." This dismissive gesture recalls other traditional male discourse. And, to my mind, this way of thinking is what feminism is trying to undercut—the privileging of the totally rational as the supreme epistemology. Furthermore, I take issue with the idea that somehow love as Belli interprets it cannot fit into a revolutionary aesthetic because of its irrational sentimentality. Why is it that Belli is by far the most popular female writer to come out of revolutionary Nicaragua? Perhaps the people know something the theorists do not.

As a feminist testimonial novel, *La mujer habitada* stands as a striking example of resistance literature, especially challenging long-held societal assumptions about gender and class. It occasionally shares postmodernism's tendency toward polyphony and a decentered "dialogics" as it chips away at a European and indigenous legacy of machismo. Belli's work also recalls the historical, realistic, and romantic novels of the nineteenth century with a mimetic representation of reality and the transcendent hero. One might ask whether Lavinia's sacrifice represents a beneficent "trickle down" paternalism rather than a postmodern project that begins at the bottom and works its way up. Her "otherness" is problematic. Has she really moved from the individual to the collective? We can answer this question by saying "yes, occasionally."

What emerges in the end is a hybrid novel that pays homage to Nicaragua's fighting women who, in touch with their natural and indigenous roots and in solidarity with their sisters, demand freedom from oppressive social values and access to power alongside their male counterparts.

Belli's most recent novel, *Sofía de los presagios* (1990), lacks a specific historico-political referent and the testimonial discourse of *La mujer habitada*. Referring to *Sofía*, Belli declares that there is a level of life beyond politics and history, a level that forms the novelistic universe in this narration (interview). More ludic and carnivalesque in the manner of Arias's *Después de las bombas*, *Sofía* does pursue the themes of eroticism, magic, illuminism, necromancy, feminism, and contemporary women's issues.

Rather than a mimetic description of reality, *Sofía* draws a mythical portrait of the female Other while still considering such contemporary feminine issues as the obsessions and fears of motherhood, the mystery and trauma of childbirth, the role and function of cosmetics, the possessiveness of husbands in a macho culture, and the double standards of sexual morality. Humorous, erotic, ironic, and satirical, *Sofía* presents a strong and independent female protagonist who scorns social conventions as she sets out to discover herself.

Sofía de los presagios signals the direction Gioconda Belli's work is currently taking. Written before the Sandinista electoral defeat to UNO in 1990, *Sofía* indicates the extent of Belli's disillusionment with the failures of Sandinismo with respect to women's issues. Perhaps she expected too much too fast, as Zimmerman has suggested, hoping to achieve a U.S.-style women's liberation in a country unprepared for such a feminism (1995b). And perhaps her enthusiastic eroticism grated on more sexually conservative alliance members, such as liberation theology proponents and more traditional-minded sectors. At any rate, her dissatisfaction had grown acute toward the end of the 1980s. She distanced herself from some of the FSLN leadership because of their refusal to espouse a more feminist agenda and moved to the United States.

As did most other major women writers of Nicaragua in the late 1980s, Belli also parted company with Rosario Murillo, president of the ASTC. Murillo, in what they saw as a power grab, moved to oppose cultural minister Ernesto Cardenal's program for the "massification" or democratization of art and to dissolve the Ministry of Culture. These maneuvers, according to Dawes, indicated a partial return to elitism and a basic dismissal by the FSLN leadership (including Murillo and Belli) of the needs and interests of the rank-and-file members (192–95). (Murillo and the Ortegas represented the insurrectionalist or *tercerista* faction. They came to power aligned with the GPP, or the Prolonged Popular War, which included Belli, and with the rank-and-file PT, or Proletarian Tendency, to form the Sandinista Front.) But Dawes may be missing a crucial split within the artistic community. Even though Belli may never have fully embraced the idea of the poetry workshops of Cardenal, she remained relatively silent about them. She did, however, denounce Murillo's takeover of the Culture Ministry and her arrogant and dogmatic management—ironically, in the name of the people—of that office. Among other problems, Murillo's moves were implicitly antifeminist. At a loss to theorize such behavior adequately, Zimmerman writes: "No justice can be done here to the bizarre story of absurd posturings and power plays which enabled a very unbalanced woman poet to walk over her rival feminist poets and ultimately marginalize a master-writer [Cardenal] whose literary and personal international standing seemed to have made him untouchable" (1995b, 4). Indeed, "Madame Mao Murillo," as Zimmerman has dubbed her, bore a major share of the blame for undermining the confidence of Nicaraguans in Sandinismo as well as for the disillusionment of former "fellow travelers" in the revolution, such as Belli.

Dawes sees the problem differently: Belli and the Sandinista leadership were never true socialists. He maintains that their own antirationalism and utopian socialism destroyed their movement. Perhaps, as Dawes suggests, Somoza never would have been toppled but for the agitation of the proletariat; but we might also ask whether change would have occurred without the entry of the petite bourgeoisie and bourgeoisie as well. It seems to me that all sectors were needed in the end. Certainly, it is far easier to form an alliance to oust a tyrant than it is to maintain the alliance for the purposes of governing afterward. (The UNO government learned that lesson, too.) That does not mean, however, that one need throw out the difficult alliance, install a dictatorship of the proletariat (a la Dawes), and expect smooth sailing, justice, respect for human rights, economic well-being, and all other good things. *That* would be utopian. This ideology and system have been thoroughly discredited in recent years. Belli's texts clearly opt for an inclusive politics of alliance—more a "free for all," a dictatorship of none in a democratic process of ongoing negotiation.

Having broken with the FSLN hard-liners, Belli has pursued her feminist priorities. In the early 1990s, she still considered herself a Sandinista but preferred to maintain a critical distance from the official "party line" because of what she perceived to be its continuing machismo. At the time of this writing, she and Claribel Alegría supported the candidacy of leftist, social democratic reformer and writer Sergio Ramírez for president of Nicaragua in the 1996 elections. Belli is now working on a third novel, *Waslala. Memorial del futuro*, which will be political and especially feminist in its perspective (interview). The discourse of resistance, liberation, and feminism begun in *La mujer habitada* carries on in a more distilled and focused manner to the feminism of *Sofía de los presagios,* and it promises to influence Belli's future work.

Characteristics of Testimonial Novels
as Practiced in Central America

Conclusions

We can draw several conclusions regarding both the testimonial function in the novels of the four writers studied here and the formulation of a set of characteristics of testimonial novels as written in Central America. First, we have defined testimonial function as primarily the self-representation of the Other in a text. How and to what extent do Arturo Arias, Manlio Argueta, Gioconda Belli, and Claribel Alegría cause the Other to represent him- or herself?

1. All four show an identification with women as Other. Alegría and Belli consistently assume a feminist perspective especially as the liberation of women is linked to the liberation of society as a whole. Following her political novel, *La mujer habitada,* Belli goes on to deal with exclusively feminist issues in *Sofía de los presagios*. Argueta appropriates the feminine first person as he narrates later novels. In *Los caminos de Paxil* Arias chooses the powerful Indian women Ixchel and Ik'Chawa as his symbols of indigenous resistance, conservators of culture, and defenders of the earth.

Women as protagonists in the struggles of their country are as strong as, if not stronger than, their male counterparts. All of the writers place the ideal woman in close connection to nature and in opposition to a male-dominated discourse of rape and despoliation of the earth. In the zeal to treat women's issues justly, there is a tendency to tilt the scales in their behalf, especially in novels by Argueta and Belli. Argueta idealizes some of his characters and women in general for their long-suffering endurance of abuse. Belli presents more complex female characters, but her sympathies clearly lie with heroic and defiant women.

Alegría and Flakoll add a transcultural dimension to the tensions of gender, bringing the North/South dialectic to a personal level.

2. Popular folk traditions among peasants, such as the legends of the Siguanaba, the Cipitío, and the cadejo—handed down through generations orally—find their way into the texts of especially the Salvadorans, Alegría and Argueta. In this regard, they are the heirs of Salarrué. They recreate popular language and culture as opposed to "elite," imported culture.

3. As the writers incorporate oral histories, they move from the city to the countryside where those traditions are strongest. Argueta's shift of setting is the most obvious, although Arias too makes the change as he redirects his interest from the bourgeois urban battlegrounds of *Después de las bombas* to the indigenous highlands in *Los caminos*. Alegría and Flakoll root their characters more firmly in either the provincial towns or the capital itself because they are primarily concerned with the struggles of the middle sectors. When they do highlight the experiences of the dispossessed, they focus more on the rural areas such as the pueblo of Izalco, the mountain hideouts of the guerrilla fighters, and the plots of the poor in Luisa's Realityland. Belli's Lavinia moves back and forth from mountain training ground of the Movimiento to the streets of the capital where she and her comrades wage war. Belli's indigenous heroine Itzá takes the reader to the countryside where the rich, fertile earth and shapely mountains become the metaphor for the creative and nurturing female. For her nature is woman's space.

4. Indigenous myth and magic, inspirations for the ways in which native peoples conceptualize the world, provide the frame for several of Belli's and Arias's novels. Arias also includes passages of the Quiché language in his texts.

5. Wit, humor, and irony have a place in all of the narratives to deconstruct the discourses of power and to engage the readers (who might be so repelled by the documentation of horror after horror that they would simply close the book and read no more). In *Después de las bombas,* Arias—more than the others and in the tradition of Guatemalan novelists—relishes the power of the word, the play of language, and the outrageousness of his insolence. Belli, too, delights

in images that shock and amuse in *Sofía*. The humor of the two Salvadoran writers is more subtle, less overtly mocking. Nevertheless, it is still present despite the atrocious circumstances they describe.

6. Poetry has long been valued as an artistic expression—especially in its oral form—among illiterate communities of Central America. The language of poetry blends with the prose of Alegría, Belli, and Argueta to add a new twist to the journalistic style and referential function often typical of testimonial discourse. They experiment with ways of arriving at both "poetic truth" and documentary proof ("the facts") of the brutal realities of Central America.

7. Liberation theology, a theory and praxis developed by the Third World and specifically Latin America as an authentic expression of the faith of an oppressed people, with its preferential option for the poor, is an important discourse of alterity in the texts of Alegría and Argueta. The Salvadoran testimonial novel seems particularly susceptible to its influence because of the martyrdom of Oscar Romero and many other priests.

8. All four writers have suffered marginalization and testify to being displaced and disenfranchised. To some extent each of them records events he or she has personally experienced as an eyewitness and in which he or she has felt personally and politically persecuted; each has received death threats and has gone into exile either by choice or by imposition. (As Gioconda Belli observed in her interview, all novels are in some respect autobiographical.) Alegría's work offers perhaps the best example of the blending of autobiographical and testimonial discourses with the attendant issues and tensions of authority as opposed to decentered discourse, the monologic and the dialogic, metaphor and metonymy, singularity and the collective, and the exceptional and the ordinary.

Her professional career also plots the trajectory and frames the work of the other three: from poetry to prose to a hybrid expression incorporating both; from bourgeois, apolitical individual to fellow traveler and intellectual in solidarity with the people. At the same time that they speak as Other and on behalf of Others, they ironically serve as educated, middle-class intermediaries—the bridge to the public sphere, the written word, and power. They perform a dual function as agents of society's dispossessed and as recorders of historical struggle.

9. Beyond their own personal experiences, the inclusion of actual

testimony from other eyewitnesses—taken in much the same ways that ethnographers use in their research—strengthens the "effect of the real" in their novels. For many readers it is the closest one can come to "presence," to actually hearing the voice of the Other. Argueta is the best known of the four novelists for his consistent incorporation of verbatim testimony.

Given these thematic and functional similarities and differences, can we arrive at some general definition or theorization of the testimonial novel based on the examples studied here? First of all, the term *testimonio* must be grounded historically. Even though the word itself has a long history from religious narrative to legal evidence, it has been used in the last two decades in Latin America to characterize a particular paradigm of "literature"—a term many writers and givers of testimony would reject immediately as elitist—that is rooted in the margins. A reaction to and a reformulation of the great Boom texts, testimonio signaled several crises: the political up-heavals during the 1970s and 1980s of oppressed people who suffered at the hands of corrupt, dependent, and neocolonial nation states; and the failure in Central America of the great narratives of modernity—in this case, capitalism especially in its imperialistic stage on the outside and its mercantilist stage within—to promote the general well-being and to estab-lish just societies. Testimony appeared as a cultural form through which the voiceless could at least partially find a voice.

Testimonial function injected an explosive political message into the novel at a particular sociohistorical moment. In the novel—which is itself a socially symbolic act, to use Jameson's terminology—this function joined a long project of economic, political, social, and cultural decolonization that started with the Conquest five hundred years ago and continues with the national-popular insurrections in the neocolonial societies of twentieth-century Central America. Especially significant for the writers studied here are pivotal dates in the recent history of their respective countries: in Arias's Guatemala, the revolution of 1944–54 and the "ethnic cleansing" against indigenous peoples during the 1970s and 1980s; in Argueta and Alegría's El Salvador, the Matanza of 1932 and popular uprisings also in the 1970s and 1980s; and in Belli's Nicaragua, the legend of Sandino and the rise of national-popular movements with the extraordinary success of the FSLN in 1974 and its ascent to power in 1979.

If we consider formal aspects, we find that testimonial novels—as Argueta,

Alegría, Arias, and Belli write them—share several features beyond a geographical, historical, and perhaps ideological proximity. Obviously, a testimonial function—the representation of voices of, by, and (in some cases) for the Other—must be present if the novel is to be termed "testimonial." Beyond this function, various means exist by which the novelist can organize, enhance, edit, and generally mediate the material; the result is that, as a form or genre, the novels may resemble each other very little. The following diagram describes the varying features and kinds of testimonial novels based on the manner in which and the degree to which the author mediates his or her material. It is schematic and runs the risk of over-simplification, but I do believe it helps us to understand the range of expressions we find in various testimonial novels. Suggested examples of each type are offered in parentheses:

```
              e
              y
Historical    e        Narrative elaborations
event         w
              i
[Fact]        t        A   B   C   D   E   F        [Fiction]
              n
              e        Degree of mediation by novelist
              s        (a continuum)
              s
```

A. "Pure" testimony (*Me llamo Rigoberta Menchú*). The opposite of "pure" is not "contaminated" but rather "mediated" or "elaborated." Below I clarify this term further.
B. *Testimonio novelado* (novelized testimony; Alegría, interview) (*No me agarran viva*).
C. Testimonial function combined with autobiographical elements (*Cenizas, Luisa, La mujer habitada*).
D. Testimonial function combined with Boom-style narrative techniques (*Después de las bombas, Caperucita*).
E. Testimonial function and narrative combined with poetry, myth, and/or the magically real (*Luisa, La mujer habitada, Los caminos de Paxil*).
F. "Pseudo-testimony" in which the novelist invents an eyewitness account that resembles testimony and incorporates testimonial function (*Después de las bombas, La mujer habitada*).

Whether the eyewitness account is an oral or a written one, it is already mediated by language and perception. Thus, the term "pure" is relative. In this diagram the novelist may or may not be the eyewitness. As we can see, some novels fit more neatly into categories than others. For example, Argueta's novels *Un día* and *Cuzcatlán* incorporate aspects of B through F, just as Arias's *Después de las bombas* and Belli's *La mujer habitada* fall easily into more than one category. Furthermore, there may be more categories than those presented here. This diagram does not pretend to be complete; it is simply descriptive of the major features one can find in some of the better-known testimonial novels of Central America.

One can also look at the diagram and ask at what point a narrative is no longer a testimony but a novel. Such a question is impossible to answer using the proposed diagram based on a continuum. Keeping in mind Sklodowska's suggestion that testimony *sensu stricto* may be the "post-bourgeois" novel since it theoretically uses the same rhetorical devices and narrative strategies as its historical counterpart (that is, the nineteenth-century historical novel or the realist novel), we remember that all of the types listed above are mediated—fictionalized?—or at least tailored in some way to the view of reality of the writer/witness. What unites them under the rubric "testimonial novel" is their testimonial function and their historical situation of enunciation.

Certainly, the traditional dichotomy of fact versus fiction in the diagram is somewhat misleading, as we mentioned previously. I qualify it here and, for this reason, have bracketed these terms. First, I do not offer the continuum as a progression or a hierarchy of values, nor do I want to privilege fact over fiction or vice versa. Neither do I want to equate historical event or fact with "truth" and fiction with "nontruth" or "lie"—a common trap that results in the devaluation of fiction. I should immediately propose another diagram right after the first in order to emphasize that I do not privilege the truth of rationalism. Poetic truth is every bit as valid for many people whose tastes include some appreciation of the subjective, the sentimental, and the aesthetic.

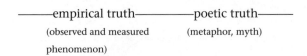

————empirical truth————poetic truth————
(observed and measured   (metaphor, myth)
phenomenon)

The two truths are not poles. There may be other "truths" in other epistemologies. But this line may be helpful in considering the distinction between the traditional categories of "fact" and "fiction." I offer this explanation because the "effect of the real," which critics point to as a consequence of testimony's "illusion of presence" and "veridiction contract," does tend to support the idea that the literal, empirical truth of rationalism is the "best" kind. Indeed, the writers and givers of Central American testimonio have resorted to this strategy of piling up documentary evidence in order to persuade readers elsewhere to believe their accounts and support their cause. Perhaps that tack is to be expected since there is a tendency to favor the empirical in cultures of technologically advanced societies such as the United States.

If we return to our discussion of both the historical and the formal aspects of the testimonial novel, we find that these two aspects meet and overlap. Testimonial function situates its texts within the currents of contemporary resistance literature from the perspective of what Angel Rama calls "contestatarios del poder" (those who contest power). Writers like Alegría, Argueta, Arias, and Belli see history differently from what official sources document and interpret, and they challenge these versions accordingly. They also contest the authority of the arbiters of literary taste and the defenders of the canon.

Testimonial function is a product of a postmodern democratic enterprise with its heterogeneity, multiplicity of voices, and decentering of the authorial figure and its tendency toward fragmentation, dispersal, deconstruction, immanence, and metonymy—to use some ideas from Ihab Hassan's tentative schema for postmodernism. Deconstructing official discourses, testimonial function also questions the traditional valorization of *haute littérature* and the concept of the canon itself. Testimonial function is sometimes expressed in unorthodox forms that are themselves "performative" and that challenge dominant modes of representation. Literature is no longer a locus of privilege. The testimonial function, in its incorporation of oral history and popular idiom, is an attempt to redefine art.

To the extent that testimony has been institutionalized in postrevolutionary societies such as Cuba and Sandinista Nicaragua, it has lost its subversive punch and perhaps its critical objectivity as an outsider looking in—and even, we might suggest, its moral high ground as the discourse of the marginalized. Has it been coopted and neutralized by being admitted to the canon there? In many cases, testimony has become a vehicle for recovering voices of the popular struggle and for glorifying the prerevolutionary ascent to power. At the same time, however, political prisoners of these revolutionary societies continue to write testimony protesting the injustices of the new regimes. Revolutionary or not, power of any kind seems to invite a counterdiscourse. There is still a place for testimony.

Is testimony in danger of the same neutralization if members of the Euro-American academic and literary establishments legitimize it as a "universal" discursive practice or even a "genre"? Or is it indicative of democratic progress made in these societies and institutions? The answer is probably yes to both questions. I am thinking specifically of Rigoberto Menchú's as the best-known example. She has enjoyed success in that she has gained a microphone for her cause and better treatment for her people. In the process, though, she has lost some of her connectedness to the indigenous communities she has represented as they have grown suspicious of her ties to the outside world. The price of democratic inclusion may be the partial relinquishment of autonomy and identity. Testimonies of experiences such as Menchú's are packed with internal tensions and besieged by external ones.

Like testimony and traditional genres in the academy, testimonial function as it is found in novels of Central America coexists with belles lettres sensibilities, with more traditional modes of representation such as nineteenth-century realism, social realism, and magical realism, and with discourses whose features are more closely identified with modernism, such as centering, metaphor, totalization, and transcendence, again recalling Hassan. Novels incorporating testimonial function are, as a result, hybrid texts.

We need also to consider the role of the novelist in this enterprise in these concluding remarks. Novels, including those of the testimonial variety, take time to write and time to read. Not everyone has these luxuries, especially those whose voices normally give the testimony in the first place. The writers of testimonial novels are educated and are accustomed to having people listen to them. They have had to rethink their roles as artists in society and, in the case of Central America, as artists in the struggle for national liberation. In order to fit into the revolutionary project, they have had to discover how to communicate the conscience of the nation to all its citizens. This objective helps us understand why they have often abandoned highly sophisticated new narrative techniques that would alienate or perhaps never even reach a national readership. The process abounds in contradictions, but if one were to take Spivak at her word—that the subaltern cannot speak and that any effort to help him or her do so may be paternalistic and potentially colonizing—one could end up in a state of paralysis that would be irresponsible and, I daresay, unethical.

We might compare the testimonial novelist to a composer of symphonies—a great form of Euro-western musical hegemony—who incorporates popular melodies and folk dances (the oral traditions of music) into a monumental opus. Does it seem contradictory? Yes, superficially. But where else will one find the soul of a nation if not among its people, including the humble and the ordinary as well as the high and the mighty?

No doubt the alliance between artist and testimonial subject smacks of condescension and paternalism. But the relationship can be a two-way street whereby the eyewitness receives or takes something in return for his or her testimony—attention, sympathy, recognition, and political clout. Speaking of the relationship pragmatically, one hopes that it is more than a zero-sum arrangement, that both parties win something. This relationship would serve as one example of various possibilities of alliance in a pluralistic political and cultural arena.

As we conclude, we may ask what is to become of testimony and the testimonial novel now that most of the major emergencies of Central America's recent past have subsided. Rather than writing the epitaph on testimony, we may just see it tabled for a while. Some of the historical crises that precipitated and accompanied testimony have dissipated, others have been resolved, still others fester beneath the surface. Even the "fatigue factor" can partly explain the absence of open warfare. If this is the case in Central America, it is only a matter of time until public rage explodes once again and popular cultural forms such as testimony return to the fore. Meanwhile, testimonial discourse and function will surely continue in novels as writers recover lost histories and novelize reality and their experience of it. Conditions certainly exist in other parts of the world that favor the writing of testimony. We need only look to the north where Mexico's recent uprisings provide fertile ground. Farther north desperate urban wastelands of the United States may soon witness an explosion of the crisis of growing disparities between haves and have nots, giving rise to popular testimony and other letters of emergency.

Testimonial novels written by Alegría, Arias, Argueta, and Belli posit resistance and revolution often at the level of the signifier, always at the level of the signified. They have experimented with the form and function of the novel to capture the perplexing realities of Central America; democratic impulses urge them to adopt the point of view—or "translate" it, as the case may be—of people who have traditionally been silenced and denied access to the public sphere, the corridors of power, or even simply the written word. They envision a literature for and by all, a culture that forms part of a more just, equitable, and ethical society. Sometimes utopian, sometimes quite modest, their dreams point to national sovereignty and autonomy as a good to be claimed and won from oppressive forces within the nation and imperialist interests beyond.

Notes

Chapter 1. Testimony in Theory and Practice: Issues of Postmodernism, Subalternity, Decolonization, and Nationalism

1. Beverley and Zimmerman term this collapse the "loss of aesthetic autonomy" (xii). The binary opposition of "high versus low," for example, is one that Derrida deconstructs by showing the ideological agenda behind such a hierarchy.

2. I would apply Spivak's term of "epistemic violence" to what Gugelberger does as he compares the writings of Neruda ("obviously a Third World writer") to those of Borges, whom he deems canonical: "the fact that he comes from a Third World nation does not suffice to make him a Third World writer" (508). His construct of the Third World imposes his judgment of what ought and ought not constitute "membership" in the Third World and thus runs the risk of inaccurate representation.

3. In his *Orientalism*, Said examines the Orient as a European invention, an Other that European writers have attempted to represent: "The exteriority of the representation is always governed by some version of the truism that if the Orient could represent itself, it would; since it cannot, the representation does the job, for the West, and *faute de mieux*, for the poor Orient" (21). He finds a relationship of domination between the "superior" imperialist power and the "inferior" colonized peoples. See also his more recent *Culture and Imperialism*.

4. See Marge Piercy for a discussion of the role of art (for example, the novel) in validating the experiences of groups farthest from the centers of

power (113). She writes: "The farther you are from the centers of power in this society, the less likely you are to find validation for your experiences, your insights, your ideas, your life. Therefore, the more important it is for you to find in art that validation, that respect for your experiences that no minority except the wealthy can take for granted" (112–13).

5. Achugar maintains that testimony's newly found position of power does not undermine its discourse of otherness since one must indeed consider the historicity of what is being narrated, the situation of enunciation, and the ideological position of the subject of that enunciation. This emphasis distinguishes his position from that of González Echevarría in *Voices of the Masters* (Achugar 1987, 291). Jorge Narváez also emphasizes the historical in arguing that testimony is not limited to one socioeconomic class but rather is capable of expressing the history of any ideological group that is marginalized (238), a position supporting my main thesis of testimonial function as the expression of otherness.

6. This genre shares some "postmodernist territory" with Central American testimony but obviously differs in ideological and historical situations of enunciation. For further discussion of this narrative mode and examples of it, see studies by both Mas'ud Zavarzadeh and Robert Augustin Smart.

7. Testimonial narrative's link to poetry should not be overlooked, although I will only briefly call it to the reader's attention here. It is treated in later chapters as it relates to the work of Alegría, Argueta, and Belli. For further reference, see Chapter 2 of Harlow on resistance poetry and Chapters 1–6 of Beverley and Zimmerman.

8. See JanMohamed for an explanation of how the project of "literacy" subsumed and transformed primarily oral cultures (1983, 283), which then were forced to appropriate the "sign" as their only means of resistance.

Chapter 2. Development of the Novel and Testimony in Guatemala, Nicaragua, and El Salvador

1. This overview is certainly not exhaustive. Only some of the better-known writers and texts will be mentioned. For further examples see Beverley and Zimmerman (1990) and Zimmerman (1995a).

2. The *Popol Vuh* is regarded as the source of the magical realism of Asturias, Monteforte, and Arias of Guatemala and of Escoto and Díaz Solano of Honduras (Acevedo 1982, 26).

3. All translations of Burgos/Menchú are by Ann Wright.

4. These stories are written not for children but from the perspective of children and with their language. Borgeson notes that Salarrué "is one of the few writers anywhere to reproduce the speech of children in highly local language without sounding paternalistic" (523).

5. See Sklodowska's comments regarding the Dalton-Mármol relationship (1992, chapter 1).

6. Ileana Rodríguez thinks that Dalton changed more than he admits—even Mármol himself complained that Dalton edited out parts of his love life. Rodríguez laments the loss: "One understands immediately that this censoring cuts off the possibility of the study of the machista ideology within the militant left"—anecdotes that would be highly interesting to feminist scholars examining the oppression of women and gender relations (1982, 91–92). Manlio Argueta claims that he recorded Mármol's love testimonies, complete with names, dates, and poems; apparently Mármol had asked him to write down these love stories when Roque did not (Z. N. Martínez, 53–54). However, when I asked Argueta about the testimonies, he replied that he had no plans to publish them.

7. At the time of writing (late 1996), Guatemala appeared close to final peace accords and on the verge of a process of demilitarization. The mood at the time was the most hopeful in years.

Chapter 3. Claribel Alegría: Family Ties/Political Lies

1. For a discussion of Frank's role as Other—a marginalized, disaffected North American—see Acevedo 1988 (80–82).

2. All translations of *Cenizas* are by Flakoll. His is not always a word-for-word translation. He has occasionally added text, some of which I will point out as it affects my analysis.

3. "Conformity" is only mentioned in Flakoll's version (1989, 125).

4. I use the word *liberal* in the context of Salvadoran politics of the 1930s, the same way the text uses it. Liberal meant openness to reform but still within a capitalist framework.

5. Hernández Martínez is eventually responsible for the Matanza that takes over thirty thousand lives. A strange man, "he wouldn't kill a mosquito or a cockroach, but people were a different matter" (94) (1989, 76 in English translation).

6. This quote is only in Flakoll's English version. The combination of leftist discourse and Christianity prefigures liberation theology. Although Latin American bishops were formulating their theories throughout the 1960s, the new theology was not formally articulated until the Medellín Conference of 1968, two years after the publication of this novel although well before Flakoll's English version was published in 1989. (Perhaps this is the reason for the addition in Flakoll's translation.) Here Eduardo's observations are also reminiscent of Mariátegui's work and also of Vatican documents from the turn of the century, linking the Church's mission to the social gospel.

7. In a popular joke, Latin Americans laugh at the double meaning of the Spanish term *Alianza Para Progreso,* which can mean either "Alliance for Progress" or "Alliance Stops Progress," depending on whether one translates "para" as the preposition "for" or a form of the verb *parar,* "to stop."

8. The fact that the narrator mentions a *Los Angeles Times* article is significant; nothing was reported about the murders in the heavily censored Salvadoran papers. It took a number of days for the news to filter back to the Salvadoran left through their contacts in the United States. Regarding an actual article in the *Times,* I searched a microfilm copy of the issue and could find no reference to the alleged episode. The episode appears to be fictional. Its reference to a real newspaper adds to the documentary quality of the story.

9. The English and the Spanish versions of *Luisa* are not identical. Alegría's husband Darwin Flakoll translated the Spanish and apparently took liberties, making changes and additions. Both the English and Spanish bear Claribel's name as sole author, and both were published in 1987. It is tempting to consider Flakoll's English version a "second edition" of the Spanish and to treat each as a separate text. The particular passage cited here appears only in the English text. In examples presented in the following pages, I will indicate whether there is a discrepancy in the translation.

Chapter 4. Manlio Argueta: Conscience, Oral Traditions, and the Feminization of the Salvadoran Struggle

1. Pointing to many examples of testimony outside Latin America, Sklodowska criticizes Yúdice for similar claims (1993).

2. *El valle de las hamacas* won first prize in the Certamen Cultural

Centroamericano 1968 under the auspices of the Consejo Superior Universitario Centroamericano. *Caperucita en la zona roja* was awarded the Casa de las Américas prize for best novel in 1977.

3. Published by Children's Book Press, San Francisco.

4. Winner of the Premio Nacional de Novela in 1980 from UCA/Editores (University of Central America).

5. All translations of *Un día en la vida* are by Bill Brow.

6. A reference to FECCAS (Federación de Campesinos Cristianos de El Salvador) and UTC (Unión de Trabajadores del Campo), two of many popular organizations active at the end of the 1970s.

7. Philip Berryman's *The Religious Roots of Rebellion* presents a full discussion of these developments and their impact on Central America.

8. In his study of the Zapatista rebellion in Chiapas, Mexico, George A. Collier, with Elizabeth Lowery Quaratiello, suggests that Protestant and Evangelical churches offered area inhabitants a more grassroots approach to organization and a more democratic experience in their congregations than had the traditional Catholic hierarchical model. In addition, Protestantism was more welcoming toward women and children (1994, 55–56).

9. The united guerrilla forces mounted a sustained attack on government troops in January 1981 that was called at the time the "Final Offensive"—and which is the historical referent for the 1981 episodes of this novel; history has since changed the name of the action to the "General Offensive of 1981."

10. For a related treatment of technological imperialism from the United States, see Honduran writer Julio Escoto's *Rey del albor: Madrugada* (King of the Dawn: Madrugada) (Tegucigalpa: Centro Editorial, 1993).

Chapter 5. The Word According to Arturo Arias

1. All translations of *Después de las bombas* are by Asa Zatz.

2. In his later novel, *Los caminos de Paxil,* Arias's narrator explains that the combination of yellow and white corn formed various drinks from which "came strength and stockiness. With it they created the muscles and vigor of man" (18–19).

3. Most references to the church in *Después de las bombas* are negative; the official church is linked to the abuse of power.

4. Carlos Castillo Armas, who led the coup in 1954; Enrique Peralta

Azurdia (president, 1963–66); Carlos Arana Osorio (president, 1970–74); Kjell Laugerud García (president, 1974–78); Miguel Ydígoras Fuentes (president, 1958–63). Only the dictators' names have been distorted. Heroes of the revolution like Arévalo, Arbenz, and Toriello, and the guerrilla fighters Yon Sosa and César Montes, are not targets of Arias's name-calling.

5. Menton writes that the name of the musical group performing at the masquerade ball, "Los Flamas," evokes the dance of Tohil, Mayan god of fire (1985, 362).

6. Not only a play on the names of two Spanish provinces but also a combination of the names of Guatemalan poets Otto René Castillo (a contemporary resistance poet who was assassinated) and Luis Cardoza y Aragón (see Chapter 2), both of whom Arias admires.

7. Paxil is a legendary mountain associated with Coyote and Pig, the discovery of corn, and the creation of man (Edmonson 87).

8. Arias describes the real-life Guzmán in his essay "Changing Indian Identity" as a "principal of the principals of Nebaj and First Confrere of the Cofradía de Santa María"; in 1973 he sent a letter to General Arana Osorio seeking his intervention in Indian affairs because "there is now among us a bad seed, the communists, who are fighting against us with cooperatives and other idiocies" (247). This was the first time, notes Arias, that the Indian bourgeoisie had leveled the charge of communism against other Indians.

9. Cross-cultural union is also the theme of his essay on Claribel Alegría (1994).

Chapter 6. The Indian Princess and the High-Heeled Warrior: Gioconda Belli's Revolting Women

1. See Doris Tijerino's account of these events to Margaret Randall (176) and Jaime Wheelock Román's *Diciembre victorioso*.

2. The *princesa* is an especially important image in Darío's second collection of poetry, *Prosas profanas*. Aristocratic, fragile, pale, she sits on her golden seat. Her "boca de fresa" (strawberry mouth) and her blue eyes define her classic beauty. Some critics have found her completely frivolous.

3. It is interesting to note how close the name Vela is to the Spanish *vuela*—"he flies"; instead, the name Vela means "he is vigilant, he watches over" (*velar*). Other appropriate definitions of the verb include "to veil, to hide, to cover over."

4. See Lancaster's discussion of the role of gender in the UNO victory and the Sandinista defeat (290–93). He writes: "Chamorro's election was both a triumph and a perversion of feminism in Nicaragua: a triumph in that a majority of the electorate should vote for a woman for president; a perversion in that her entire appeal was couched in the most unfeminist of terms" (293).

Bibliography

Acevedo, Ramón Luis. 1982. *La novela centroamericana* (The Central American novel). Río Piedras, P.R.: Editorial Universitaria.

———. 1986. "La violencia en la novela salvadoreña" (Violence in the Salvadoran novel). *Proyecto: Crisis y alternativas en Centroamérica.* (Project: Crisis and alternatives in Central America). San José: Instituto Centroamericano de Documentación e Investigación Social, 53–78.

———. 1988. *"Cenizas de Izalco* de Claribel Alegría y Darwin Flakoll o la armonización posible" (Claribel Alegría and Darwin Flakoll's *Ashes of Izalco* or possible harmonization). *Studi di litteratura ispano-americana* 21:77–88.

———. 1992. "Claribel Alegría." In *Spanish American Authors: The Twentieth Century,* ed. Angel Flores. New York: Wilson.

Achugar, Hugo. 1987. "Notas sobre el discurso testimonial latinoamericano" (Notes on Latin American testimonial discourse). In *La historia en la literatura iberoamericana: Memorias del XXVI Congreso del Instituto Internacional de Literatura Iberoamericana,* ed. Raquel Chang-Rodríguez and Gabriella de Beer, 279–94. New York: City College of the City University of New York.

———. 1992. "Historias paralelas/historias ejemplares: La historia y la voz del otro" (Parallel histories, exemplary histories: History and the voice of the other). *Revista de crítica literaria latinoamericana* 18, no. 36: 49–71.

Adams, Richard. 1990. "Ethnic Images and Strategies in 1944." In *Guatemalan Indians and the State: 1540 to 1988,* ed. Carol A. Smith, 141–62. Austin: University of Texas Press.

Adorno, Rolena. 1989. *Cronista y príncipe* (Chronicler and prince). Lima: Fondo Editorial de la Pontificia Universidad Católica del Perú.

Ahmad, Aijaz. 1987. "Jameson's Rhetoric of Otherness and the 'National Allegory'." *Social Text* 17 (Fall): 3–25.

Albizures, Miguel Angel. 1987. *Tiempo de sudor y lucha* (Time of sweat and struggle). Mexico City: Praxis.

Albizúrez Palma, Francisco. 1983. *Grandes momentos de la literatura guatemalteca* (Great moments of Guatemalan literature). Guatemala: Editorial José de Pineda Ibarra.

———. 1990. "La narrativa guatemalteca contemporánea" (Contemporary Guatemalan narrative). In *Centroamericana,* ed. Dante Liano, vol. 1 of *Studi di Letteratura Ispanoamericana,* ed. Giuseppe Bellini, 25–39. Rome: Bulzoni Editore.

Alegría, Claribel. 1978. *Sobrevivo* (I survive). Havana: Casa de las Américas.

———. 1981. "Literatura y liberación nacional en El Salvador" (Literature and national liberation in El Salvador). *Casa de las Américas* 21, no. 126 (May–June): 12–16.

———. 1982. *Cenizas de Izalco* (Ashes of Izalco). San José: EDUCA.

———. 1982. *Nicaragua: La revolución sandinista: Una crónica popular/1855–1979* (Nicaragua: The Sandinista revolution: A popular chronicle/1855–1979). Mexico City: Editorial Era.

———. 1983. *No me agarran viva: La mujer salvadoreña en lucha* (They won't take me alive: Salvadoran woman in struggle for national liberation). Mexico City: Editorial Era.

———. 1986. *Despierta mi bien despierta* (Wake up my love wake up). San Salvador: Universidad de Centroamerica.

———. 1986. *Pueblo de dios y de mandinga* (People of God and the Devil). Barcelona: Editorial Lumen.

———. 1987a. *Luisa en el país de la realidad* (Luisa in Realityland). Mexico City: Joan Boldó i Climent, Editores.

———. 1987b. *Luisa in Realityland.* Trans. Darwin J. Flakoll. Willimantic, Conn.: Curbstone.

———. 1987c. *They Won't Take Me Alive: Salvadoran Women in Struggle for National Liberation.* Trans. Amanda Hopkinson. London: The Women's Press.

———. 1991a. *Family Album.* Trans. Amanda Hopkinson. Willimantic, Conn.: Curbstone.

———. 1991b. Personal interview by author. April 5, Washington, D.C.

———. 1995. Telephone interview. October 31.

Alegría, Claribel, and Darwin J. Flakoll. 1989. *Ashes of Izalco.* Trans. Darwin J. Flakoll. Willimantic, Conn.: Curbstone.

Alegría, Fernando. 1986. *Nueva historia de la novela hispanoamericana* (New history of the Hispanic American novel). 4th ed. Hanover, N.H.: Ediciones del Norte.

Allende, Isabel. 1989. "Writing as an Act of Hope." In *Paths of Resistance: The Art and Craft of the Political Novel.* Ed. William Zinsser. Boston: Houghton Mifflin, 39–63.

Anderson, Benedict. 1983. *Imagined Communities: Reflections on the Origin and Spread of Nationalism.* London: Verso.

Apuy, Otto. 1978. "En la zona roja: Manlio Argueta, Caperucita y el lobo" (In the red zone: Manlio Argueta, Red Riding Hood, and the wolf). *Alero* 27: 125–29.

Arellano, Jorge Eduardo. 1982. *Panorama de la literatura nicaragüense* (Panorama of Nicaraguan literature). Managua: Editorial Nueva Nicaragua.

———. 1988. "Introduction to the Poetry of Pablo Antonio Cuadra." In Pablo Antonio Cuadra, *The Birth of the Sun.* Trans. Steven F. White. Greensboro, N.C.: Unicorn Press.

Arenal, Electa. 1981. "Two Poets of the Sandinista Struggle." *Feminist Studies* 7, no. 1 (Spring): 19–37.

Argueta, Manlio. 1970. *El valle de las hamacas* (Valley of hammocks). San José: UCA Editores.

———. 1982. "War and the writer in El Salvador." *Index on Censorship* 11 (April): 3–5.

———. 1986a. *Cuzcatlán donde bate la mar del sur* (Cuzcatlan where the southern sea beats). Tegucigalpa: Editorial Guaymuras.

———. 1986b. "Intervención de Manlio Argueta: Mesa redonda sobre narrativa centroamericana" (Conversation with Manlio Argueta: Roundtable on Central American narrative). *Tragaluz,* December 2, 23–26.

———. 1988. *Un día en la vida* (One day of life). 5th ed. San Salvador: UCA Editores.

———. 1991. *Caperucita en la zona roja* (Little Red Riding Hood in the red zone). 6th ed. San José: UCA Editores.

———. 1992a. *One Day of Life.* Trans. Bill Brow. New York: Vintage.

———. 1992b. Personal interview. September 26, Los Angeles.

———. 1994. "Autovaloración literaria" (Literary self-evaluation). In *Cambios estéticos y nuevos proyectos culturales en Centroamérica: Testimonios, entrevistas y ensayos* (Aesthetic changes and new cultural projects in Central America:

Testimonies, interviews, and essays), ed. Amelia Mondragón. Washington, D.C.: Literal Books, 27–34.

———. 1995a. *Milagro de la paz* (Miracle of peace). 2d ed. San Salvador: Adelina Editores.

———. 1995b. Telephone interview. October 25.

Arias, Arturo. 1979a. *Después de las bombas* (After the bombs). Mexico City: Joaquín Mortiz.

———. 1979b. *Ideologías, literatura y sociedad durante la revolución guatemalteca, 1944–1954* (Ideologies, literature, and society during the Guatemalan revolution, 1944–1954). Havana: Casa de las Américas.

———. 1981. *Itzam Na*. Havana: Casa de las Américas.

———. 1987. "Consideraciones en torno al género y la génesis de Guatemala, las líneas de su mano" (Considerations regarding the gender and genesis of Guatemala, the lines of its hand). *Tragaluz* 15 (May): 24–28.

———. 1989. *Jaguar en llamas* (Jaguar in flames). Guatemala City: Ministerio de Cultura y Deportes.

———. 1990a. *After the Bombs*. Trans. Asa Zatz. Willimantic, Conn.: Curbstone.

———. 1990b. "Changing Indian Identity: Guatemala's Violent Transition to Modernity." In *Guatemalan Indians and the State: 1540 to 1988*, ed. Carol A. Smith, 230–57. Austin: University of Texas Press.

———. 1990c. *Los caminos de Paxil* (The roads of Paxil). Guatemala City: Editorial Cultural.

———. 1990d. "Nueva narrativa centroamericana" (Central American new narrative). *Centroamericana* I. Rome: Bulzoni Editore.

———. 1992a. "Conciencia de la palabra: Algunos rasgos de la nueva narrativa centroamericana" (Awareness of the word: Several characteristics of the Central American new narrative). *Hispamérica* 61 (April): 41–58.

———. 1992b. Personal interview. September 24–25.

———. 1994. "Claribel Alegría's Recollection of Things to Come." In *Claribel Alegría and Central American Literature,* ed. Sandra M. Boschetto-Sandoval and Marcia Phillips McGowan, 22–44. Athens: Ohio University Center for International Studies.

Armijo, Roberto. 1986. "La novela póstuma de Roque Dalton" (The posthumous novel of Roque Dalton). In *Recopilación de textos sobre Roque Dalton* (Collection of texts on Roque Dalton), ed. Magdalena Quijano, 384–88. Havana: Casa de las Américas.

Armstrong, Robert, and Janet Shenk. 1982. *El Salvador: The Face of Revolution*. Boston: South End Press.

Báez Alvarez, Gladys. 1992. Personal interview. April 24, Chicago.

Bakhtin, M. M. (Mikhail Mikhaòilovich). 1984. *Rabelais and His World*. Trans. Helene Iswolsky. Bloomington: Indiana University Press.

Barnet, Miguel. 1968. *Biografía de un cimarrón* (Biography of a runaway slave). Mexico City: Siglo veintiuno.

———. 1983. *La fuente viva* (The live source). Havana: Editorial Letras Cubanas.

Bauer, Dale M., and Susan Jaret McKinstry. 1991. *Feminism, Bakhtin, and the Dialogic*. Albany: State University of New York Press.

Belli, Gioconda. 1978. *Línea de fuego* (Line of fire). Havana: Casa de las Américas.

———. 1988. *La mujer habitada* (The inhabited woman). Managua: Vanguardia.

———. 1989. *From Eve's Rib*. Trans. Steven F. White. Willimantic, Conn.: Curbstone.

———. 1990. *Sofía de los presagios* (Sofia of the omens). Managua: Vanguardia.

———. 1993. Telephone interview. January 12.

Bennington, Geoffrey. 1990. "Postal Politics and the Institution of the Nation." In *Nation and Narration*, ed. Homi K. Bhabha, 121–37. London: Routledge.

Berryman, Philip. 1984. *The Religious Roots of Rebellion: Christians in Central American Revolutions*. Maryknoll, N.Y.: Orbis.

———. 1985. *Inside Central America*. New York: Pantheon.

———. 1994. "The Coming of Age of Evangelical Protestantism." *NACLA Report on the Americas* 27, no. 6: 6–10.

Beverley, John. 1987. *Del Lazarillo al Sandinismo: Estudios sobre la función ideológica de la literatura española e hispanoamericana* (From Lazarillo to Sandinismo: Studies on the ideological function of Spanish and Hispanic American literature). Minneapolis, Minn.: Prisma Institute.

———. 1991. "'Through All Things Modern': Second Thoughts on Testimonio." *boundary* 2, no. 18: 1–21.

———. 1992. Introducción. *Revista de Crítica Literaria Latinoamericana* 18, no. 36: 7–18.

Beverley, John, and Marc Zimmerman. 1990. *Literature and Politics in the Central American Revolutions*. Austin: University of Texas Press.

Bhabha, Homi K., ed. 1990. *Nation and Narration*. London: Routledge.

Boff, Leonardo, O.F.M. 1988. *When Theology Listens to the Poor*. Trans. Robert R. Barr. San Francisco: Harper & Row.

Borge, Tomás. 1982. *Carlos, el amanecer ya no es una tentación* (Carlos, the dawn is no longer beyond our reach). Managua: Editorial Nueva Nicaragua.

Borgeson, Paul W., Jr. 1987. "El Salvador" and "Nicaragua." In *Handbook of Latin American Literature*, comp. David William Foster, 517–28 and 405–14. New York: Garland.

Boschetto-Sandoval, Sandra M., and Marcia Phillips McGowan, eds. 1994. *Claribel Alegría and Central American Literature*. Athens: Ohio University Center for International Studies.

Brennan, Timothy. 1990. "The National Longing for Form." In *Nation and Narration*, ed. Homi K. Bhabha, 44–70. London: Routledge.

Brown, R. McKenna. 1995. "Gaspar Pedro's Portrayal of Guatemalan Ethnic Relations in *La otra cara*." Paper presented at the Latin American Studies Association Congress, Washington, D.C., September.

Cabezas, Omar. 1982. *La montaña es algo más que una inmensa estepa verde* (Fire from the mountain). Managua: Editorial Nueva Nicaragua.

Cardenal, Ernesto. 1982. "Defendiendo la cultura, el hombre, y el planeta" (Defending culture, man, and the planet). *Nicaráuac* 7 (June): 149–52.

Carmack, Robert M., ed. 1988. *Harvest of Violence: The Maya Indians and the Guatemalan Crisis*. Norman: University of Oklahoma Press.

Cavallari, Hector Mario. 1986. "Ficción, testimonio, representación" (Fiction, testimony, representation). In *Testimonio y literatura*, eds. René Jara y Hernán Vidal, 73–84. Edina, Minn.: Society for the Study of Contemporary Hispanic and Lusophone Revolutionary Literatures.

Cayetano Carpio, Salvator. 1982. *Secuestro y capucha* (Kidnapping and the hood). 6th ed. San José: EDUCA.

Chávez Alfaro, Lisandro. 1969. *Trágame tierra* (Swallow me earth). Mexico City: Editorial Diógenes.

———. 1980. "Nación y narrativa nicaraguense" (Nation and Nicaraguan narrative). *Casa de las Américas* (May–June): 69–73.

Cherry, Sharon Young. 1977. "Fantasy and Reality in Salarrué." Ph.D. diss., Northwestern University.

Cifuentes, Edwin. 1979. *El pueblo y los atentados* (The people and outrages). Guatemala City: Serviprensa Centroamericana.

Codina, Iverna. 1977. "La novela en la zona roja" (The novel in the red zone). *Casa de las Américas* 104 (Sept.–Oct.): 134–36.

Collazos, Oscar. 1970. "La encrucijada del lenguaje" (The crossroads of language). In Oscar Collazos, Julio Cortázar, and Mario Vargas Llosa,

Literatura en la revolución y revolución en la literatura, 7–37. Mexico City: Siglo Veintiuno.

Collier, George A., with Elizabeth Lowery Quaratiello. 1994. *Basta! Land and the Zapatista Rebellion in Chiapas*. Oakland, Calif.: Institute for Food and Development Policy.

Cornejo Polar, Antonio. 1980. *Literatura y sociedad en el Perú: La novela indigenista* (Literature and society in Peru: The indigenista novel). Lima: Editorial Lasontay.

Cortázar, Julio. 1970. "Literatura en la revolución y revolución en la literatura: Algunos malentendidos a liquidar" (Literature in the revolution and revolution in literature: Several misunderstandings to clear up). In *Literatura en la revolución y revolución en la literatura*, 38–77. Mexico City: Siglo Veintiuno.

Craft, Linda J. 1996a. "International Adoption as a Fictional Construct: Francisco Goldman's *The Long Night of White Chickens*." In *Romance Languages Annual*, ed. Jeanette Beer, Patricia Hart, Ben Lawton, 430–35. West Lafayette, Ind.: Purdue Research Foundation.

———. 1996b. "Testinovela/Telenovela: Latin American Popular Culture and Women's Narrative." *Indiana Journal of Hispanic Literatures* 8 (Spring): 197–210.

Crosby, Margaret B. 1994. "Claribel Alegría." *Dictionary of Literary Biography*, ed. William Luis and Ann Gonzalez, I: 4525–32. Detroit: Bruccoli Clark Layman.

Cuadra, Pablo Antonio. 1985. "In Defiance of Censorship: Culture and Ideology in Today's Nicaragua." *Journal of Contemporary Studies* 8, no. 3 (Summer/Fall): 117–26.

Dalton, Roque. 1978. *Las historias prohibidas del pulgarcito* (Prohibited stories from the little thumb). 3d ed. Mexico City: Siglo Veintiuno.

———. 1982. *Miguel Mármol: Los sucesos de 1932 en El Salvador* (Miguel Marmol: The events of 1932 in El Salvador). San José: EDUCA.

———. 1989. *Pobrecito poeta que era yo* (Poor poet that I was). 4th ed. San José: EDUCA.

"Darwin Flakoll: Journalist, Translator, 72." 1995. *Union-Tribune* [San Diego], April 30, editions 1, 2, p. B5.

Davis, Lisa, y Sonia Rivera. 1984. "Guatemala: Hacia la victoria: Conversación con Arturo Arias y María Vázquez" (Guatemala: Toward victory: Conversation with Arturo Arias and María Vázquez). *Areito* 37: 32–35.

Dawes, Greg. 1993. *Aesthetics and Revolution: Nicaraguan Poetry 1979–1990*. Minneapolis: University of Minnesota Press.

Donovan, Josephine. 1991. "Style and Power." In *Feminism, Bakhtin, and the Dialogic,* ed. Dale M. Bauer and Susan Jaret McKinstry, 85–94. Albany: State University of New York Press.

D'Souza, Dinesh. 1991. *Illiberal Education: The Politics of Race and Class on Campus.* New York: Free Press.

Edmonson, Munro S. 1965. *Quiché-English Dictionary.* New Orleans: Middle American Research Institute of Tulane University.

Engelbert, Jo Anne. 1988. Introduction. In *And We Sold the Rain: Contemporary Fiction from Central America,* ed. Rosario Santos. New York: Four Walls Eight Windows.

Escobar, F. A. 1980. "El Salvador, una novela sin novelistas" (El Salvador, a novel without novelists). *Estudios centroamericanos* 35 (January–February): 95–96.

Flores, Marco Antonio. 1976. *Los compañeros* (The companions). Mexico City: Joaquín Mortiz.

Foley, Barbara. 1986. *Telling the Truth: Practice of Documentary Fiction.* Ithaca, N.Y.: Cornell University Press.

Forché, Carolyn. 1984. "Interview with Claribel Alegría." *Index on Censorship* 13, no. 2 (April): 11–13.

Foucault, Michel. 1980. "Truth and Power." In *Power/Knowledge: Selected Interviews and Other Writings, 1972–1977,* ed. Colin Gordon, 109–33. New York: Pantheon.

Franco, Jean. 1967. *The Modern Culture of Latin America: Society and the Artist.* London: Pall Mall Press.

———. 1991."¿La historia de quién? La piratería postmoderna" (Whose history? Postmodern pirating). *Revista de crítica literaria latinoamericana* 17, no. 33: 11–20.

Galich, Manuel. 1949. *Del pánico al ataque* (From panic to the attack). Guatemala City: Departamento de Publicidad de la Presidencia de la República.

Gallegos Valdés, Luis. 1981. *Panorama de la literatura salvadoreña* (Panorama of Salvadoran literature). 3d ed. San Salvador: UCA Editores.

Gibson, Charles. 1966. *Spain in America.* New York: Harper & Row.

Goldman, Francisco. 1992. *The Long Night of White Chickens.* New York: Atlantic Monthly Press.

González Echevarría, Roberto. 1985. *The Voices of the Masters: Writing and Authority in Modern Latin American Literature.* Austin: University of Texas Press.

Guadamuz, Carlos José. 1982. *Y . . . "Las casas quedaron llenas de humo"*

(And the houses remained full of smoke). Managua: Editorial Nueva Nicaragua.

Gugelberger, Georg M. 1991. "Decolonizing the Canon: Considerations of Third World Literature." *New Literary History* 22: 505–24.

Gutiérrez, Gustavo. 1973. *A Theology of Liberation.* Trans. and ed. Sister Caridad Inda and John Eagleson. Maryknoll, N.Y.: Orbis.

Harlow, Barbara. 1987. *Resistance Literature.* New York: Methuen.

Hassan, Ihab. 1982. *The Dismemberment of Orpheus: Toward a Postmodern Literature.* 2d ed. Madison: University of Wisconsin Press.

Herndl, Diane Price. 1991. "The Dilemmas of a Feminine Dialogic." In *Feminism, Bakhtin, and the Dialogic,* ed. Dale M. Bauer and Susan Jaret McKinstry, 7–24. Albany: State University of New York Press.

Hodges, Donald C. 1986. *Intellectual Foundations of the Nicaraguan Revolution.* Austin: University of Texas Press.

Jakobson, Roman. 1960. "Closing Statement: Linguistics and Poetics." In *Style in Language,* ed. Thomas A. Sebeok, 350–77. Cambridge, Mass.: MIT Press.

Jameson, Fredric. 1981. *The Political Unconscious: Narrative as a Socially Symbolic Act.* Ithaca, N.Y.: Cornell University Press.

———. 1986. "Third-World Literature in the Era of Multinational Capitalism." *Social Text* 15 (Fall): 65–88.

———. 1989. "The Politics of Theory: Ideological Positions in the Postmodernism Debate." In *Contemporary Literary Criticism,* ed. Robert Con Davis and Ronald Schleifer, 418–27. New York: Longman.

JanMohamed, Abdul R. 1983. *Manichean Aesthetics: The Politics of Literature in Colonial Africa.* Amherst: University of Massachusetts Press.

———. 1985. "The Economy of Manichean Allegory: The Function of Racial Difference in Colonialist Literature." *Critical Inquiry* 12, no. 1 (Autumn): 59–87.

Jara, René. 1986. "Prologo." In *Testimonio y literatura* (Testimony and literature), ed. René Jara and Hernán Vidal. Edina, Minn.: Society for the Study of Contemporary Hispanic and Lusophone Revolutionary Literatures.

Jitrik, Noé. 1975. *Producción literaria y producción social* (Literary and social production). Buenos Aires: Editorial Sudamericana.

Kaminsky, Amy. 1993. "Gioconda Belli." In *Contemporary World Writers,* ed. Tracy Chevalier. Detroit: St. James Press.

Kelly, Kathryn Eileen. 1992. *La nueva novela centroamericana* (The new Central American novel). Ann Arbor, Mich.: UMI.

Khare, R. S. 1992. "The Other's Double—The Anthropologist's Bracketed

Self: Notes on Cultural Representation and Privileged Discourse." *New Literary History* 23, no. 1 (Winter): 1–23.

Kufeld, Adam. 1990. *El Salvador: Photographs.* Poetry by Manlio Argueta. New York: W. W. Norton.

Lancaster, Roger N. 1992. *Life Is Hard.* Berkeley: University of California Press.

Lejeune, Philippe. 1980. *Je est un autre: L'autobiographie de la littérature aux médias* (I is another: The autobiography of literature in the media). Paris: Editeurs du Seuil.

León-Portilla, Miguel, ed. 1985. *Visión de los vencidos: Crónicas indígenas* (Vision of the vanquished: Indigenous chronicles). Madrid: Historia 16.

Liano, Dante. 1994. "La obsesión histórica en Arturo Arias" (Historical obsession in Arturo Arias). In *Cambios estéticos y nuevos proyectos culturales en Centroamérica,* ed. Amelia Mondragón, 67–72. Washington, D.C.: Literal Books.

Lienhard, Martin. 1987. "Los callejones de la etnoficción ladina en el área maya (Yucatán, Guatemala, Chiapas)" (Blind alleys of ladino ethnofiction in Mayan areas). *Nueva revista de filología hispánica* 35, no. 2: 549–70.

Lión, Luis de. 1985. *El tiempo principia en Xibalba* (Time begins in Xibalba). Guatemala City: Serviprensa Centroamericana.

Liss, Sheldon B. 1991. *Radical Thought in Central America.* Boulder, Colo.: Westview Press.

Lorand de Olazagasti, Adelaida. 1968. *El indio en la narrativa guatemalteca* (The Indian in Guatemalan narrative). Universidad de Puerto Rico: Editorial Universitaria.

March, Kathleen. 1990. "Gioconda Belli: The Erotic Politics of the Great Mother." *Monographic Review/Revista Monográfica* 6: 245–57.

Marcos, Juan Manuel. 1987. "El género popular como meta-estructura textual del post-Boom latinoamericano" (The popular genre as a textual meta-structure of the Latin American post-Boom). *Revista monográfica* 3: 268–78.

Mariátegui, José Carlos. 1976. *Siete ensayos de interpretación de la realidad peruana* (Seven interpretive essays on the Peruvian reality). Barcelona: Editorial Crítica.

Martin, Gerald. 1989. *Journeys through the Labyrinth: Latin American Fiction in the Twentieth Century.* London: Verso.

Martínez, Ana Guadalupe. 1978. *Las cárceles clandestinas de El Salvador* (Hidden prisons in El Salvador). Tomado de la publicación "El Salvador en Lucha" del partido de la Revolución Salvadoreña (PRS), Ejército Revolucionario del Pueblo (ERP).

Martínez, Zulma Nelly. 1985. "Entrevista con Manlio Argueta" (Interview with Manlio Argueta). *Hispamérica* 15, no. 42: 41–54.

Maxwell, Judith. 1992. Telephone interview. October 18.

McClintock, Michael. 1985. *The American Connection.* Vol. 1, *State Terror and Popular Resistance in El Salvador.* London: Zed Books.

McGowan, Marcia Phillips. 1994. "Mapping a New Territory: *Luisa in Realityland.*" In *Claribel Alegría and Central American Literature,* ed. Sandra M. Boschetto-Sandoval and Marcia Phillips McGowan, 111–30. Athens: Ohio University Center for International Studies.

Melgar Brizuela, Luis. 1976. "El subarte y la subliteratura en El Salvador" (Subart and subliterature in El Salvador). *Estudios centroamericanos* 33 (June–July): 277–88.

———. 1979. *Literatura hispano-centroamericana y salvadoreña* (Hispanic–Central American and Salvadoran literature). San Salvador: Editorial del Pulgarcito.

Menchú, Rigoberta, with Elisabeth Burgos Debray. 1983. *Me llamo Rigoberta Menchú, y así me nació la conciencia* (My name is Rigoberta Menchú, and thus, my conscience was born). Havana: Casa de las Américas.

———. 1984. *I, Rigoberta Menchú: An Indian Woman in Guatemala.* Trans. Ann Wright. London: Verso.

Menton, Seymour. 1972. "La narrativa centroamericana (1960–1970)" (Central American narrative 1960–1970). *Nueva narrativa hispanoamericana* 2, no. 1 (January): 119–29.

———. 1985. *Historia crítica de la novela guatemalteca* (Critical history of the Guatemalan novel). 2d ed. Guatemala City: Editorial Universitaria.

———. 1993. *Latin America's New Historical Novel.* Austin: University of Texas Press.

Mignolo, Walter. 1991. "Teorizar a través de fronteras culturales" (Theorizing across cultural frontiers). *Revista de crítica literaria latinoamericana* 17, no. 33: 103–12.

———. 1993. "Colonial and Postcolonial Discourse: Cultural Critique or Academic Colonialism?" *Latin American Research Review* 28, no. 3: 120–34.

Mohanty, Chandra Talpade. 1984. "Under Western Eyes: Feminist Scholarship and Colonial Discourses." *Boundary 2* 12, no. 3–13, no. 1 (Spring–Fall): 333–58.

Mondragón, Amelia. 1991. *"La mujer habitada,* el feminismo y la razón patriarcal" (*La mujer habitada,* feminism and patriarchal reason). Paper presented at the Latin American Studies Association Congress, Washington, D.C., April 5.

———. 1994. *Cambios estéticos y nuevos proyectos culturales en Centroamérica: Testimonios, entrevistas y ensayos* (Aesthetic changes and new cultural projects in Central America: Testimonies, interviews, and essays). Washington, D.C.: Literal Books.

Monteforte Toledo, Mario. 1948. *Entre la piedra y la cruz* (Between the rock and the cross). Guatemala City: Editorial "El libro de Guatemala."

Montejo, Víctor. 1987. *Testimony: Death of a Guatemalan Village.* Willimantic, Conn.: Curbstone.

Morales, Mario Roberto. 1978. *Los demonios salvajes* (Savage demons). Guatemala City: Departamento de Actividades de la Dirección General de Cultura y Bellas Artes de Guatemala.

———. 1986a. *El esplendor de la pirámide* (Splendor of the pyramid). San José: EDUCA.

———. 1986b. "La nueva novela guatemalteca y sus funciones de clase: La política y la ideología" (The new Guatemalan novel and its class functions: Politics and ideology). In *Proyecto: Crisis y alternativas en Centroamérica* (Project: Crisis and alternatives in Central America), 81–94. San José: Instituto Centroamericano de Documentación e Investigación Social.

———. 1994a. "Entre la verdad y la alucinación: Novela y testimonio en Centroamérica" (Between truth and hallucination: Novel and testimony in Central America). Paper presented at the Congreso Internacional de Literatura Centroamericana, Tegucigalpa, Honduras, February.

———. 1994b. *Señores bajo los árboles* (Men under the trees). Guatemala City: Librerías Artemis-Edinter.

———. 1995. "Oralitura y testinovela: La cuestión de la representación del subalterno en la literatura" (*Oralitura* and *testinovela:* The question of the representation of the subaltern in literature). Paper presented at the Congreso Internacional de Literatura Centroamericana, Guatemala City, February.

———. "Señores bajo los árboles" (Face of the earth, heart of the sky), trans. Edward Waters Hood, unpublished.

Murphy, Patrick D. 1991. "Prolegomenon for an Ecofeminist Dialogics." In *Feminism, Bakhtin, and the Dialogic,* ed. Dale M. Bauer and Susan Jaret McKinstry, 39–56. Albany: State University of New York Press.

Namer, Claudio. 1976. "Una entrevista a Claribel Alegría" (Interview with Claribel Alegria). *Alero* 19: 39–43.

Narváez, Jorge. 1986. "El testimonio 1972–1982: Transformaciones en el sistema literario" (Testimony 1972–1982: Transformations in the literary system). In *Testimonio y literatura*, ed. René Jara and Hernán Vidal, 235–79. Edina, Minn.: Society for the Study of Contemporary Hispanic and Lusophone Revolutionary Literatures.

O'Connor, Mary. 1991. "Subject, Voice, and Women in Some Contemporary Black American Women's Writing." In *Feminism, Bakhtin, and the Dialogic*, ed. Dale M. Bauer and Susan Jaret McKinstry, 199–217. Albany: State University of New York Press.

Ohmann, Richard. 1980. "Politics and Genre in Nonfiction Prose." *New Literary History* 11 (Winter): 237–44.

Ong, Walter. 1982. *Orality and Literacy.* London: Methuen.

Osses, Esther María. 1986. *La novela del imperialismo en Centroamérica* (The novel of imperialism in Central America). Maracaibo, Ven.: Universidad del Zulia Vicerrectorado Académico.

Perera, Victor. 1985. *Rites: A Guatemalan Boyhood.* San Diego: Harcourt Brace Jovanovich.

———. 1995. *The Cross and the Pear Tree.* New York: Random House.

Piercy, Marge. 1989. "Active in Time and History." In *Paths of Resistance: The Art and Craft of the Political Novel*, ed. William Zinsser, 89–123. Boston: Houghton Mifflin.

Popol Vuh, El: Las antiguas historias del Quiché (The Popol Vuh: Ancient stories of the Quiché). 1989. Trans. and ed. Adrián Recinos. Tegucigalpa: Editorial Guaymuras.

Prada Oropeza, Renato. 1986. "De lo testimonial al testimonio: Notas para un deslinde del discurso-testimonio" (From the testimonial to testimony: Notes to limit testimonial discourse). In *Testimonio y literatura*, ed. René Jara and Hernán Vidal, 7–21. Edina, Minn.: Society for the Study of Contemporary Hispanic and Lusophone Revolutionary Literatures.

Quintana, Emilio. 1985. *Bananos* (Bananas). Rev. ed. Managua: Editorial Nueva Nicaragua.

Rama, Angel. 1982. *La novela en América latina: Panoramas 1920–1980* (The Latin American novel: Panoramas 1920–1980). Montevideo: Fundación Angel Rama.

Ramírez, Sergio. 1977. *¿Te dio miedo la sangre?* (Did blood scare you?) Caracas: Monte Avila Editores.

———. 1983. *Balcanes y volcanes y otros ensayos y trabajos* (Balkans and volcanoes and other essays). Managua: Editorial Nueva Nicaragua.

———. 1984. "El escritor centroamericano" (The Central American writer). *Texto crítico* 10, no. 29 (May–August): 66–74.

———. 1988. *Castigo divino* (Divine punishment). Managua: Editorial Nueva Nicaragua.

———, ed. 1976. Introduction. *El cuento nicaragüense* (The Nicaraguan short story). Managua: Editorial el Pez y la Serpiente.

———, ed. 1984. Introduction. *Antología del cuento centroamericano* (Anthology of the Central American short story). San José: EDUCA.

Randall, Margaret. 1984. *Risking a Somersault in the Air: Conversations with Nicaraguan Writers*. Trans. Christina Mills. San Francisco: Solidarity Publishing.

Randall, Marilyn. 1991. "Appropriate(d) Discourse: Plagiarism and Decolonization." *New Literary History* 22: 525–41.

Rice-Sayre, Laura P. 1986. "Witnessing History: Diplomacy versus Testimony." In *Testimonio y literatura,* ed. René Jara and Hernán Vidal, 48–72. Edina, Minn.: Society for the Study of Contemporary Hispanic and Lusophone Revolutionary Literatures.

Richards, Timothy A. B. 1991. "Resistance and Liberation: The Mythic Voice and Textual Authority in Belli's *La mujer habitada.*" In *Critical Essays on the Literatures of Spain and Spanish America,* ed. Luis T. González-del-Valle and Julio Baena. Boulder, Colo.: Society of Spanish and Spanish-American Studies.

Robleto, Hernán. 1930. *Sangre en el trópico: La novela de la intervención yanqui en Nicaragua* (Blood in the tropics: The novel of Yankee intervention in Nicaragua). Madrid: Editorial Cenit.

Rocha, Luis. 1995. "Yo digo esto: 'Bud y Clari' en mi cámara" (I say this: Bud and Clari in my camera). *Nuevo amanecer cultural,* April 22, 7.

Rodríguez, Ileana. 1981. "El texto literario como expresión mestizo-creole: In memoriam" (The literary text as a mestizo-Creole expression). *Casa de las Américas* 21, no. 126 (May/June): 56–62.

———. 1982. "Organizaciones populares y literatura testimonial: Los años treinta en Nicaragua y El Salvador" (Popular organizations and testimonial: The thirties in Nicaragua and El Salvador). In *Literatures in Transition: The Many Voices of the Caribbean Area: A Symposium,* ed. Rose S. Minc. Gaithersburg, Md.: Hispamérica, 1982; Upper Montclair, N.J.: Montclair State College.

———. 1985. "*Trágame tierra*: una narrativa consistente" (*Trágame tierra*: a consistent narrative). *Casa de las Américas* 25, no. 150 (May/June): 79–89.

———. 1986. "El concepto de cultura nacional durante los años de formación del FSLN" (The concept of national culture during the formative years of the FSLN). In *Proyecto: Crisis y alternativas en Centroamérica* (Project: Crisis and alternatives in Central America), 7–51. San José: Instituto Centroamericano de Documentación e Investigación Social.

———. 1994a. "Dios/Pater–Patria/Libertad" (God/Father–Fatherland/Liberty). In *Cambios estéticos y nuevos proyectos culturales en Centroamerica* (Esthetic changes and new cultural projects in Central America), ed. Amelia Mondragón, 95–105. Washington, D.C.: Literal Books.

———. 1994b. *House, Garden, Nation: Space, Gender and Ethnicity in Post-colonial Latin American Literatures by Women.* Durham, N.C.: Duke University Press.

———. 1994c. "*Testimonio* and Diaries as Narratives of Success or Failure in *They Won't Take Me Alive.*" In *Claribel Alegría and Central American Literature,* ed. Sandra M. Boschetto-Sandoval and Marcia Phillips McGowan, 45–57. Athens: Ohio University Center for International Studies.

Rodríguez Ruíz, Napoleón. 1950. *Jaraguá.* San Salvador: Editorial Universitaria.

Rojas-Trempe, Lady. 1991. "La alteridad indígena y mágica en la narrativa de Elena Garro, Manuel Scorza y Gioconda Belli" (Indigenous alterity and magic in the narrative of Elena Garro, Manuel Scorza, and Gioconda Belli). *Alba de América* 9: 141–52.

Román, José. 1983. *Maldito país* (Damned country). Managua: Editorial el Pez y la Serpiente.

Said, Edward. 1978. *Orientalism.* New York: Pantheon.

———. 1993. *Culture and Imperialism.* New York: Knopf.

Salarrué. 1943. *Cuentos de barro* (Stories of mud). Santiago: Editorial Nascimento.

Salgado, María A. 1987. "Guatemala." In *Handbook of Latin American Literature,* comp. David William Foster, 291–305. New York: Garland.

Schaefer, Claudia. 1987. "La recuperación del realismo: ¿*Te dio miedo la sangre?* de Sergio Ramírez" (The recovery of realism: Sergio Ramirez's ¿*Te dio miedo la sangre?*). *Texto crítico* 13, nos. 36–37: 146–52.

Schlesinger, Stephen, and Stephen Kinzer. 1982. *Bitter Fruit: The Untold Story of the American Coup in Guatemala.* New York: Doubleday.

Schwab, Gail M. 1991. "Irigarayan Dialogism: Play and Powerplay." In

Feminism, Bakhtin, and the Dialogic, ed. Dale M. Bauer and Susan Jaret McKinstry, 57–72. Albany: State University of New York Press.

Schwartz, Kessel. 1971. *A New History of Spanish American Fiction.* Vol. 2, *Social Concern, Universalism, and the New Novel.* Coral Gables, Fla.: University of Miami Press.

Shea, Maureen. 1988. "A Growing Awareness of Sexual Oppression in the Novels of Contemporary Latin American Women Writers." *Confluencia* 4 (Fall): 53–59.

Sklodowska, Elzbieta. 1990–91."Hacia una tipología del testimonio hispanoamericano" (Toward a typology of Spanish American testimony). *Siglo XX–Twentieth Century* 8: 103–20.

———. 1992. *Testimonio hispanoamericano: Historia, teoría, poética* (Hispanic American testimony: History, theory, poetics). New York: Peter Lang.

———. 1993. *"The Autobiography of a Runaway Slave:* How to Recognize a Testimonio When You Want to See One." Lecture, Northwestern University Department of Hispanic Studies. Evanston, February 3.

Smart, Robert Augustin. 1985. *The Nonfiction Novel.* Lanham, Md.: University Press of America.

Smith, Carol A. 1990. Introduction: "Social Relations in Guatemala over Time and Space." In *Guatemalan Indians and the State,* ed. Carol A. Smith, 1–30. Austin: University of Texas Press.

Sobrino, Jon. 1989. *Spirituality of Liberation.* Trans. Robert R. Barr. Maryknoll, N.Y.: Orbis.

Sommer, Doris. 1988. "Not Just a Personal Story: Women's *Testimonios* and the Plural Self." In *Life/Lines: Theorizing Women's Autobiography,* ed. Bella Brodzki and Celeste Schenck, 107–30. Ithaca, N.Y.: Cornell University Press.

———. 1990. "Irresistible Romance: The Foundational Fictions of Latin America." In *Nation and Narration,* ed. Homi K. Bhabha, 71–98. London: Routledge.

Sommer, Doris, and George Yúdice. 1986. "Latin American Literature from the 'Boom' On." In *Postmodern Fiction: A Bio-Bibliographical Guide,* ed. Larry McCaffery, 189–214. New York: Greenwood Press.

Spivak, Gayatri Chakravorty. 1988. "Can the Subaltern Speak?" In *Marxism and the Interpretation of Culture,* ed. Cary Nelson and Lawrence Grossberg, 271–313. Urbana: University of Illinois Press.

———. 1990. *The Post-Colonial Critic: Interviews, Strategies, Dialogues.* Ed. Sarah Harasym. New York: Routledge.

Sternbach, Nancy Saporta. 1990. "Claribel Alegría." In *Spanish American Women Writers*, ed. Diane E. Marting, 9–19. New York: Greenwood.

Tijerino, Doris, with Margaret Randall. 1977. *"Somos millones . . ."* (We are millions). Mexico City: Extemporáneos.

Toruño, Juan Felipe. 1957. *Desarrollo literario de El Salvador* (Literary development of El Salvador). San Salvador: Ministerio de Cultura.

Treacy, Mary Jane. 1994. "Creation of the Woman Warrior: Claribel Alegría's *They Won't Take Me Alive*." In *Claribel Alegría and Central American Literature*, ed. Sandra M. Boschetto-Sandoval and Marcia Phillips McGowan, 75–96. Athens: Ohio University Center for International Studies.

United Nations. Commission on the Truth for El Salvador. 1993. *From Madness to Hope: The 12-Year War in El Salvador*. Report of the Commission on the Truth for El Salvador. New York: United Nations. (In Spanish: *De la locura a la esperanza: la guerra de 12 años en El Salvador*. Informe de la Comisión de la Verdad para El Salvador. San Salvador and New York: Naciones Unidas.

Vargas Llosa, Mario. 1970. "Luzbel, Europa y otras conspiraciones" (Luzbel, Europe, and other conspiracies). In Oscar Collazos, Julio Cortázar, and Mario Vargas Llosa, *Literatura en la revolución y revolución en la literatura* (Literature in the revolution and revolution in literature), 78–93. Mexico City: Siglo Veintiuno.

Vázquez, Miguel Angel. 1989. *Operación Iscariote*. Guatemala City: Impreofset Oscar de León Palacios.

Wheelock Román, Jaime. 1982. *Diciembre victorioso* (Victorious December). Managua: Editorial Nueva Nicaragua.

White, Hayden. 1976. "The Noble Savage Theme as Fetish." In *First Images of America: The Impact of the New World on the Old*, ed. Fredi Chiappelli, 1:121–35. Berkeley: University of California Press.

White, Steven. 1986. *Culture and Politics in Nicaragua*. New York: Lumen.

Wycoff, Adriann Constantine. 1984. "The Life and Works of Claudia Lars." Diss. Northwestern University.

Yanes, Gabriela, et al., eds. 1983. *Arme y desarme: Fragmentos de la actual literatura salvadoreña* (To arm or disarm: Fragments of current Salvadoran literature). Querétaro: Comisión Editorial Universidad Autónoma de Querétaro.

———. 1985. *Mirrors of War: Literature and Revolution in El Salvador*. Trans. Keith Ellis. New York: Monthly Review Press.

Yúdice, George. 1985. "Letras de emergencia: Claribel Alegría" (Emergency letters: Claribel Alegría). *Revista iberoamericana* 51 (July–December): 953–64.

———. 1992. "Testimonio y concientización" (Testimony and conscientization). *Revista de crítica literaria latinoamericana* 18, no. 36: 207–27.

Zavarzadeh, Mas'ud. 1976. *The Mythopoeic Reality: The Postwar American Nonfiction Novel.* Urbana: University of Illinois Press.

Zimmerman, Marc. 1991. "Testimonio in Guatemala: Payeras, Rigoberta, and Beyond." *Latin American Perspectives* 18 (Fall): 22–47.

———. 1992. "Concluding Perspectives and Projections." Unpublished manuscript.

———. 1994. "Afterword." In *Claribel Alegría and Central American Literature,* ed. Sandra M. Boschetto-Sandoval and Marcia Phillips McGowan, 213–27. Athens: Ohio University Center for International Studies.

———. 1995a. *Literature and Resistance in Guatemala.* 2 vols. Athens: Ohio University Press.

———. 1995b. Unpublished review of Klaas S. Wellinga, *Entre la poesía y las pared: Política cultural sandinista, 1979–1990* (Between poetry and the wall: Sandinista cultural politics, 1979–1990). Amsterdam: Thela Publishers; San José, Costa Rica: FLASCO, Foro Hispánico. Review to appear in *Revista hispánica de los países bajas.*

———, ed. 1988. *El Salvador at War: A Collage Epic.* Minneapolis: MEP Publications.

Index

Acevedo, Ramón Luis: on Alegría, 72, 79, 85–87, 89, 197n.1; on the novel in Central America, 36, 37; on the novel in Guatemala, 39, 196n.2; on the novel in Nicaragua, 52; on the Salvadoran novel, 63, 66, 69

Achugar, Hugo, 11, 12, 16, 19, 20, 58, 196n.5

Adams, Richard, 42

Adorno, Rolena, 34

AEA (Association of Antifascist Writers), El Salvador, 66

aesthetics, 23, 190; and ethics, 18, 24, 35, 39, 43, 48, 65 (*see also* Argueta); and immediacy, 69; and political emergency, 122; socialist and communist, 40

Agee, James, 18

Ahmad, Aijaz, 9

Albizures, Miguel Angel, 38, 46

Albizúrez-Palma, Francisco, 39

Alegría, Ciro, 35, 66

Alegría, Claribel, 4, 23, 72–105, 185–91, 193; autobiographical elements in texts of, 73, 80, 81, 97, 99; and bicultural tensions, 74, 84, 86, 89, 97, 105, 200n.9; and the Church, 82, 87, 96, 97, 103; and classism, 80, 86, 89; conscientization of, 73, 88, 95–97; and feminism, 74–75, 94, 96–98, 101, 105; and gender relationships, 75, 76, 82, 83, 86, 94, 102, 105; and gendered discourses, 83–85, 89; influences on, 74, 75, 79; life of, 72–79; *locura* (craziness), theme of, 73, 101; and machismo, 74, 82, 83, 86, 88, 93, 97, 98, 103; and *Matanza*, 73, 80, 81, 103, 105, 197n.5; and orphans, 93, 103; and other Salvadoran writers, 62, 67, 69, 70, 74–75, 106; and poetry, 72–75; 80, 99, 104–5, 196n.7; and political activism, 73, 75; and racism, 86, 89, 103; and Santa Ana, 72, 80, 81, 83, 88, 89, 100–102, 105; *Siguanaba* in, 80; and storytelling as

221

Paxil (Guatemalan mythical
paradise), 155–56, 200n.7
Peralta Azurdia, Enrique, 199–
200n.4
Perera, Víctor, 49, 157
Piercy, Marge, 195n.4
poetry: in El Salvador, 62; and
narrative, 37; in Nicaragua, 50,
55, 57; shift from, to prose, 70;
and testimonial narrative, 187,
189, 196n.7
poetry workshops (*talleres*),
Nicaragua, 60
Poirier, Eduardo, 52
political act, literary text as, 10
political correctness, 7, 17; debate
on, on U.S. college campuses, 1,
2
Poniatowska, Elena, 18
Popol Vuh, 41, 153, 196n.2
popular vs. elite culture, 3, 8, 186.
See also postmodernism
positivism: as narrative of modernity, 7; and conscientization,
118
postcolonialism and de-
colonization, 27–32; postcolonialist intellectual, 15, 17.
See also decolonization;
deconstruction
postmodernism, 4, 6–10; and anti-
elitism and democracy, 2; and
blurring of generic lines, 22;
and erosion of boundaries of art
and documentation, 24; and
fiction (Argueta as example),
130; fragmentation in, 31; and
novel, 6; Other, and representation of, 10; in politics and
ethics, 11, 17, 47; and pop
culture, 148
poststructuralist practices, 7, 8, 9

Prada Oropeza, Renato, 6, 132
PRI (Partido Revolucionario
Institucional–Mexico), 25
Protestant evangelicalism and
fundamentalism: in Central
America, 118–19; in Mexico,
199n.8
PT (Proletarian Tendency),
Nicaragua, 183

Quincentennial, 1, 3
Quintana, Emilio, 52, 55

racism, 31, 54, 66. *See also* Other
Rama, Angel, 35–36, 46–48, 133,
191
Ramírez, Sergio: and Belli, 167;
Castigo divino, 59–61; and
decolonization, 30; *narrativa
social,* 55; on representation of
indigenous people 13, 56; and
Sandinista cultural project, 60;
and testimony, 52, 58–59; on
vernacular literature, 51; on
writer as politician, 10, 184; *¿Te
dio miedo la sangre?* 58-59
Randall, Margaret, 57, 60, 160,
176, 200n.1
Randall, Marilyn, 8, 10, 28
readership and reading public, 3,
29, 37, 192; in El Salvador, 62;
and market, 46, 157; and taste,
23
Recinos, Adrián, 153
Register, Cheri, 158
representation of subject by writer,
14–15; process of mediation,
19–20; problems in, 15. *See also*
Other
resistance literature, 3, 4, 7, 191; as
defined by Harlow, 26–27; and
emergency, 71; and politics and

national consolidation, 25, 162;
on autobiography, 75–76, 80;
on "incompatible codes," 92,
97, 159; on mediation of
testimony, 20; on metonymic
protagonist of testimony, 21,
75–76; on relationship of
woman to earth, 165
Somoza regime and somocismo,
53, 59, 158, 163; Anastasio
Somoza Debayle, 51, 159, 161,
162, 165; Anastasio Somoza
García, 54
Sontag, Susan, 2
Soto-Hall, Máximo, 37
Spivak, Gayatri Chakravorty: and
deconstruction, 7, 8, 25; on
epistemic violence, 13, 149,
195n.2; on ethics and politics,
29; on heterogeneity, 171; on
the subaltern, 13–15, 20, 192
Stone, Merlin, 163
structuralism as narrative of
modernity, 7
subaltern, the: definition of, 38;
issues of, 4, 13, 192; and the
nation, 30; stereotypical or
folklorist/criollista representations of, 35; and study groups,
22; as subject, 14. See also Other
surrealism, 39, 41

telenovela, 158
Terralla y Landa, 34
testimonial discourse, 16, 187; and
autobiography, 189; in Belli,
160; canonization of, 17;
characteristics of, 19–20, 30, 59;
development of, 38; in El
Salvador, 76; and new narrative,
38, 46, 50, 57; in Nicaragua, 54,
58–61; as performative, 16;
popularity of, 17; in translation,

46. See also testimonial function; testimonial novel; testimony
testimonial function, 16, 192;
defined, 185, 188; as expression
of otherness, 4, 5, 196n.5; as
part of postmodern democratic
enterprise, 191
testimonial novel: and art, 23–24;
and autobiography, 187;
characteristics of, 185–94; as
epic, 26; as field of conflict, 5;
historical context of, 5, 36; and
hybrid texts, 3, 23, 34, 46, 48,
49, 80, 89, 98, 158, 192; as
mediation by novelist, 189; and
nationalism, 24–27; and Other,
32; problems of, 3; as resistance
narrative, 3; types of, 23. See
also Alegría; Argueta; Arias;
Belli; novel; testimonial
discourse and function; testi-
novela
testimony (testimonio), 2; antecedents of, 3, 33, 34; and art, 35;
and authenticity, 2; and
autobiography, 21; canonized
by academy, 6; characteristics
of, 16–23, 36–37, 69; conditions
giving rise to, 15, 71, 188;
continued vitality of, 59;
coopted or neutralized, 22;
defined, 16–17, 45; as democratic project, 20; in El Salvador,
62, 67–69, 76; and ethics and
morality, 21, 29; European and
Soviet examples of, 18; future
of, 22, 193; as genre (discursive
status), 22, 37; in Guatemala,
43–46; historical grounding of,
188; history and memory,
recovery of, 30, 193; literary
"worthiness" of, 6, 17;

Vargas Llosa, Mario, 43, 47, 107
Vásquez, Miguel Angel, 38, 48, 50, 69
Viezzer, Moema, 18

Wheelock Román, Jaime, 200n.1
White, Hayden, 11
White, Steven, 60
Wolfe, Tom, 18
women: courage of, 57; exclusion of, 31; exploitation of, 57; liberation of, 17; and nature, 185, 186; totalizing representations of, 13. *See also* Alegría; Argueta; Arias; Belli; feminism; Other
Wright, Ann, 197n.3
writer, role of, 10, 14, 76, 192; and Alegría, 99, 105; and Argueta, 107, 130, 131; in Arias, 134, 142–44; and authority, 20; in El Salvador, 69; in Nicaragua, 52. *See also* testimony, mediation of
Wycoff, Adriann Constantine, 74
Wyld Ospina, Carlos, 37, 39

Ydígoras Fuentes, Miguel, 200n.4
Yon Sosa, Marco Antonio, 200n.4
Yúdice, George, 88, 94, 198n.1

Zago, Angela, 18
Zamora, Daisy, 160
Zapatistas. *See* Chiapas
Zatz, Asa, 199n.1
Zavarzadeh, Mas'ud, 24, 196n.6
Zimmerman, Marc: on Alegría, 72; on Belli and the Sandinistas, 182–83; on deconstruction, 195n.1; on decolonization, 28; on El Salvador, 64, 68, 70; on Guatemala, 40–43, 48, 50, 132, 156; on ideology and the text, 10; on Nicaragua, 54, 58, 59, 61; and the Other, 196.1; on testimony and poetry, 196n.7; testimony, definition of, 6, 17, 26; on types of testimonial novels, 23
Zipes, Jack, 111